# Nurturing Morality

**Issues in Children's and Families' Lives**

*Series Editors*:
**Thomas P. Gullotta,** *Child and Family Agency of Southeastern Connecticut, New London, Connecticut*
**Herbert J. Walberg,** *University of Illinois at Chicago, Chicago, Illinois*
**Roger P. Weissberg,** *University of Illinois at Chicago, Chicago, Illinois*

NURTURING MORALITY
Edited by Theresa A. Thorkildsen and Herbert J. Walberg

A BLUEPRINT FOR THE PROMOTION OF PRO-SOCIAL BEHAVIOR
IN EARLY CHILDHOOD
Edited by Elda Chesebrough, Patricia King, Martin Bloom, and
Thomas P. Gullotta

ASPERGER SYNDROME
A Guide for Professionals and Families
Edited by Raymond W. DuCharme and Thomas P. Gullotta

CHANGING WELFARE
Edited by Rachel A. Gordon and Herbert J. Walberg

PREVENTING YOUTH PROBLEMS
Edited by Anthony Biglan, Margaret C. Wang, and Herbert J. Walberg

# Nurturing Morality

Edited by

## Theresa A. Thorkildsen

*University of Illinois at Chicago*
*Chicago, Illinois*

and

## Herbert J. Walberg

*University of Illinois at Chicago*
*Chicago, Illinois*

 Springer

Library of Congress Cataloging-in-Publication Data

ISBN: 0-306-48499-4

© 2004 by Springer Science+Business Media, Inc.
233 Spring St., New York, New York 10013

springeronline.com

10 9 8 7 6 5 4 3 2

A C.I.P. record for this book is available from the Library of Congress

Permissions for books published in Europe: permissions@wkap.nl
Permissions for books published in the United States of America: permissions@wkap.com

Printed in the United States of America

# Foreword

*Nurturing Morality* is a volume in The University of Illinois at Chicago (UIC) Series on Issues in Children's and Families' Lives. The UIC series began in response to the "Great Cities" initiative taken by our former chancellor and current president of the University of Illinois system, James Stukel. At its inception, Lascelles Anderson helped establish a working group of UIC faculty to design and offer advice on this series. Currently, the series is sponsored by Sylvia Manning, the current UIC chancellor, as well as other senior administrators, trustees, and civic leaders in Chicago. The purpose of this series is to marshal scholarly resources to facilitate understanding and solutions to problems within American cities by including ideas with far-reaching implications.

Books in this series provide an interdisciplinary and "interprofessional" approach to problems facing children and the adults who care for them. The target audience for the series includes policymakers, practitioners, scholars, students, and lay citizens who seek a greater understanding of ideas for social and educational reform. Given the wide spectrum of intended audiences, the volumes in the series are unlike many other academic volumes. Rather than emphasizing norms within a particular discipline, the series draws upon knowledge and guidance from nearly all the social, educational, and health sciences. These fields include psychology, sociology, education, economics, social work, criminal justice, law, public policy, and the allied health fields. The common thread within each book concerns programs and policies for use in solving particular social dilemmas.

Reflecting this broad approach, the first volume in the UIC Series set the stage for later more specialized volumes. Titled *Children and Youth: Interdisciplinary Perspectives*, it reviews diverse ways in which families, schools, and the health care system influence and enhance the social, emotional, cognitive, and physical development of young people (Walberg, Reyes, & Weissberg, 1997). The second volume, *Promoting Positive Outcomes,* focuses on solutions to the problems facing children and youth. It features education and child development programs, policies, and practices (Reynolds, Walberg & Weissberg, 1999). *Long Term Trends in the Well-being of Children and Youth* shows scholars and practitioners how successive cohorts of children and youth have been changing over long time periods with respect to a variety of specialized fields such as education and health (Weissberg, Walberg, O'Brien, & Kuster, 2003).

*Early Childhood Programs for a New Century* highlights trends in preschool education and care, evidence-based programs and practices, and policies that will enhance the quality of wide-scale programming for children (Reynolds, Walberg, & Wang, 2003). *Preventing Youth Problems* discusses policies and practices that prevent smoking, alcohol and drug abuse, sexual risk behaviors, and antisocial behavior (Biglan, Wang, & Walberg, 2003). The title of *Changing Welfare* is intended to reflect both how welfare policy and practice has been changing in recent years and how it should be changed (Gordon & Walberg, 2003). The current volume, *Nurturing Morality,* addresses personal and environmental supports as well as impediments to moral functioning in a wide variety of societal institutions.

We greatly appreciate the many people who helped make both this volume and the UIC Series on Children and Youth a reality. We thank the distinguished members of our UIC Advisory Board and our National Advisory Board. They provided helpful comments and recommendations on the proposed structure and topic for this volume.

The initial drafts of these chapters were reviewed by participants in a conference cosponsored by The Johnson Foundation and The Laboratory for Student Success (LSS), through a contract with The Institute of Education Sciences (IES) of the U. S. Department of Education. We are grateful for the thoughtful conversations sustained by everyone who came to Wingspread for this event.

We thank Theresa (Terri) Thorkildsen for her intellectual leadership in organizing this volume and recruiting a highly talented group of scholars to share their ample wisdom. We also are very appreciative of the professionals at Kluwer Academic/Plenum Publishers who produce these volumes so efficiently and effectively.

We gratefully acknowledge the Laboratory for Student Success, the Mid-Atlantic Regional Educational Laboratory at Temple University, Center for Research in Human Development and Education for providing intellectual and financial support for the preparation of manuscripts for this volume. We especially thank Danielle Shaw, Stephen Page, and

Marilyn Murphy from LSS for their outstanding work in copy editing chapter manuscripts, promoting developmental conversations between scholars and practitioners, and disseminating the ideas in this book to interested constituencies.

This book was supported in part by the Institute of Education Sciences of the U.S. Department of Education through a contract with the Laboratory for Student Success, the Mid-Atlantic Regional Educational Laboratory, at Temple University Center for Research in Human Development and Education. The opinions expressed do not necessarily reflect the position of the supporting agencies, and no official endorsement should be inferred.

HERBERT J. WALBERG
ROGER P. WEISSBERG
THOMAS P. GULLOTTA

## References

Biglan, A., Wang, M. C., & Walberg, H. J. (Eds.). (2003). *Preventing youth problems.* New York: Kluwer Academic/Plenum Publishers.

Gordon, R., & Walberg, H. J. (2003). (Eds.). *Changing welfare.* New York: Kluwer Academic/Plenum Publishers.

Reynolds, A. J., Walberg, H. J., & Wang, M. C. (Eds.). (2003). *Early childhood programs for a new century.* Washington, D.C.: Child Welfare League of America Press.

Reynolds, A. J., Walberg, H. J., & Weissberg, R. P. (Eds.). (1999). *Promoting positive outcomes.* Washington, D.C.: Child Welfare League of America Press.

Walberg, H. J., Reyes, O., & Weissberg, R. P. (Eds.). (1997). *Children and youth: Interdisciplinary perspectives.* Thousand Oaks, CA: Sage.

Weissberg, R. P., Walberg, H. J., O'Brien, M. U., & Kuster, C. B. (Eds.). (2003). *Long-term trends in the well-being of children and youth.* Washington, D.C.: Child Welfare League of America Press.

# Introduction

The title of this book, *Nurturing Morality*, raises a controversial topic that many investigators would prefer to avoid or obfuscate than to explore in an open and direct manner. The contributors to this volume recognize that with or without adult guidance, young people learn to define and respond to moral dilemmas from many sources. Unfortunately, it has become more common to hear about moral transgressions than moral virtue in this global society, and young people may not notice opportunities for moral action. Relying only on media representations of the world, for example, young people could easily invent distorted views of societal norms and values. In putting together these chapters, we sought to bring balance to public representations of morality and embrace rather than avoid the challenges of stimulating moral functioning.

The title of this book is controversial, partly because individuals disagree on the meaning of *morality*, who is responsible for moral action, what impediments inhibit moral functioning, and how societal institutions offer support for the development and maintenance of moral ideals. Although we do not always agree with one another, contributors to this volume accept that all forms of human interaction are laden with moral content. Aware of the banality of evil, we find it problematic to ignore moral themes in daily life. We see moral questions as thorny and complex and reject deterministic theories of moral functioning. Nurturing morality, in this view, involves more than the indoctrination and policing of rules because morality is not inherent in rules. We challenge attempts to dismiss the moral implications of everyday events and overly simplistic excuses for individuals who fail to live up to moral ideals. Our assumption is that individuals make decisions by looking at the murky details of each situation, weighing the implications of those details, and determining how to coordinate personal and collective agendas. To nurture morality requires an awareness of individual differences in the understanding of morality. In acquiring this awareness, we inevitably learn how people determine a course of action, which problems to avoid, and what kinds of communities to build.

Another controversial feature of the title concerns the term *nurturing*. Our goal in selecting this term over those such as *growth* or *development* is to distinguish moral functioning from moral development. We call attention to the fact that most people can define morality and even label moral ideals but may not live in communities that support optimal levels of moral functioning. Communal pressures to harm or overlook harm are often placed in conflict with pressures to do and support good; conversations about morality may fall on deaf ears. Contributors to *Nurturing Morality* were selected because of their acute awareness of these tensions and their strong research-based approaches to exploring some of the resulting moral dilemmas.

It was surprising to find that the preference for terms such as *nurture* and *support* over terms such as *growth* and *development* coincided with a controversy among investigators interested in policy and practice. Some practitioners work within a promotion model in which adults and experienced community leaders look for opportunities to encourage individuals who are implementing self-designed agendas. These practitioners see the moral vices of monopoly and dominance as highly salient when agendas are imposed on community members. Other practitioners work within a prevention model in which adults or experienced community leaders identify common social problems and generate local programs for addressing those problems. These investigators see that social problems can reproduce themselves without direct attempts to alter their causes, cycles, or consequences.

Research invariably involves a combination of promotion and prevention agendas, but the practical implications of these two systems of thought are quite different. Choosing to nurture morality without considering the value of personal growth would be as foolish as designing programs to teach values that are already commonly accepted among participants or are simply impractical for use in local communities. In this book, we avoid prevention models, not because such models lack value but because strong prevention programs are ideally embedded in local communities and would be contingent on agendas established by the programs' participants. Sharing stories from practical experiences would take a very different form from the general conversations that emerge while learning how to support moral functioning.

Relying on a promotion model, the contributors to this volume illuminate a variety of important themes that are worthy of careful consideration. The title is intended to call attention to moral questions rather than to people because morality is seen as a complex means of organizing thoughts and actions. Individuals may identify the characteristics of people who are highly committed to moral ideas, but morality is not a feature of personality. It is also possible to imagine the moral implications of decisions, but decisions are not inherently moral or immoral. Instead, individuals' moral questions, values, and commitments offer structural guides for living that are challenged or reinforced in the context of a community. Personal choices about whether to construct and rely on moral guides are likely to be influenced by social supports for maintaining moral functioning. The chapter authors seek to understand the nature and availability of such supports.

The chapters are presented in four sections, emphasizing different levels of organization associated with nurturing morality. The first section, *Definitions of Moral Functioning*, raises questions of how individuals are likely to think and act when noticing moral dilemmas. The chapters link past and current debates about definitions of morality, raise a host of moral themes, and illustrate how investigators have begun to explore those themes. This section makes the case that definitions of morality have long been debated and will probably continue to remain controversial among scholars. Lawrence J. Walker, Sandra Graham, and Albert Bandura show how attempts to nurture morality are likely to fail if individuals do not take responsibility for their behavior or if caregivers are unable to agree on desirable outcomes. They challenge the idea that morality is a set of rules to be obeyed and offer three approaches for thinking about moral functioning. These authors show how researchers generally highlight different facets of moral functioning and multiple means for nurturing growth.

The second set of chapters, *Impediments to Moral Functioning*, offers more detail on personal responsibility and constraints on moral functioning. As an illustrative example, Karl H. Hennig shows several ways that caring for others can go awry. Jennifer Steele and her collaborators elaborate on how prejudice, stereotypes, and discrimination become impediments to moral functioning and perpetuate forms of social inequality that can encourage antisocial behavior. Susan Opotow looks at how conflict resolution techniques highlight the importance of resilience in the face of challenging life events. These are only some of the common personal and societal impediments that inhibit moral functioning. Difficulties in forming and maintaining relationships differ from intrapsychic concerns. Impediments reinforced by societal structures pose a third level of organization. Nevertheless, all these levels may be so fused in an individual's ontogeny that it becomes difficult to distinguish them. Attempts at conflict resolution invariably call forth some, if not all, of the impediments in ways that permit closer scrutiny and can sometimes foster resilient responses to moral dilemmas.

A third set of chapters, *Institutional Supports for Moral Functioning*, concerns the means by which institutions can nurture young people's moral growth or encourage them to maintain high levels of moral functioning. Although many institutions affect the lives of young people, selected chapters represent institutions that appear to have the strongest influence. Many young people are in direct contact with families, schools, churches, and neighborhood organizations. In these contexts, they learn and test the viability of their beliefs. Nancy Eisenberg looks at how moral behavior is socialized within the family context. Theresa Thorkildsen illustrates how individuals are encouraged to imagine the expectations of strangers as well as their own needs in educational settings. Daniel Hart and his collaborators explore how religion facilitates the examination of moral commitments and the degree to which churches facilitate such forms of inquiry. Constance Flanagan highlights how community-based or neighborhood organizations can offer helpful structures for encouraging individual reflection and group solidarity. These chapters illustrate the importance of establishing a sufficient balance among personal and collective agendas and some of the age-specific concerns associated with such goals.

The book ends with *Considering the Common Good*, offering direct advice on nurturing morality and an elaboration of our agenda. Using examples of personal responsibility in academic settings, Robert Sternberg and Steven Stemler describe how adults might integrate wisdom and morality. They emphasize how thoughtful consideration of the common good is essential to generating wise policies. Because the book was conceived with a liberal arts agenda, we also include an afterward commenting on our approach to nurturing morality. Martin Marty identifies the themes—pluralism, responsibility, complexity, affectivity, and practicality—that are embedded in the chapters and justifies their importance.

Taken together, these chapters offer a diverse array of perspectives on how moral functioning is defined as well as some impediments and supports for moral functioning. Despite the reductionistic trends that have begun to dominate the fields of moral development and character education, these authors make compelling cases for how matters of achievement motivation, wisdom, stereotyping, and the structure of institutional practices are central to nurturing morality. The promotion approach adopted here hinges on looking carefully at how individuals define morality, use the resulting mental structures to negotiate daily events, and act on their beliefs. Our hope is that by starting this conversation, others will be inspired to challenge the views presented here, offer other concerns and impediments that we have failed to consider, and imagine new mechanisms for supporting individuals who seek to be and do good.

# Contents

## INSTITUTIONAL SUPPORTS FOR MORAL FUNCTIONING

## CONSIDERING THE COMMON GOOD

# Definitions of Moral Functioning

Morality is a fundamental and pervasive aspect of human functioning with both interpersonal and intrapsychic components; more specifically, it refers to voluntary actions that have, at least potentially, some social and interpersonal implications and that are governed by internal psychological mechanisms fused in ontogeny.

—*Lawrence J. Walker*

Social misbehavior as illustrated by aggression toward others and achievement misconduct are both part of the same moral system and can be understood within the same overarching framework. That framework involves the moral construct of perceived responsibility, in both other people and the self.

—*Sandra Graham*

The exercise of moral agency has dual aspects—inhibitive and proactive. The inhibitive form is manifested in the power to refrain from behaving inhumanely. The proactive form of morality is expressed in the power to behave humanely.

—*Albert Bandura*

# Chapter 1

# What Does Moral Functioning Entail?

## Lawrence J. Walker

The past several years have been marked by renewed interest and vigorous debate regarding character formation and moral development. This situation has been provoked partly by the clash of moral values apparent in stridently competing worldviews; by recurrent observations regarding the claimed deterioration in moral standards and behavior in our society; and by frequently voiced concerns regarding the adequacy of the moral socialization that typically occurs in many contexts, including families, schools, peers, and the media. This chapter sets out the scope of the moral domain to keep us mindful of its breadth and complexity and to help guide our attempts to nurture moral maturity in children and adolescents. The enormity of the enterprise is often overwhelming. The recurring risk we face as we attempt to make sense of morality and the factors that foster its functioning is a loss of perspective that occurs as we focus on and become invested in a particular theory, aspect of development, or intervention program.

## Scope of the Moral Domain

This chapter argues that the field currently suffers from a conceptual skew that yields an inadequate and incomplete depiction of moral functioning and that thus provides ineffectual means for fostering moral maturity. Two centuries of modernity have bequeathed to the fields of moral psychology and moral education a legacy that is rich in understandings of moral rationality but impoverished in terms of its appreciation of other aspects of moral functioning. Moral psychology and education, similar to many other disciplines within the social sciences and beyond, have been pervasively influenced by the philosophies of the Enlightenment Era. These philosophies were concerned with establishing a rational basis for moral understandings and convictions in order to avoid the perils of ethical relativism.

Two primary concerns exist regarding the effects of this philosophical tradition. The first is that it regarded moral issues primarily as those pertaining to interpersonal conflicts and relationships and, hence, it has framed modern ethical thinking with an emphasis on individualism, justice, rights, duties, and welfare. The consequence of this preoccupation with the interpersonal aspects of moral functioning is that it has marginalized the intrapsychic aspects that involve the characteristics of the good person and the aim of the good life (i.e., basic values, lifestyle, identity, and character). Notably, this preoccupation supplanted ethical thinking's centuries-old concern with moral virtues and character (i.e., the Aristotelian tradition), the concern that perhaps better fits with commonsense notions of moral life.

The second concern regarding the effects of this philosophical tradition is that its understanding of human nature is unremittingly dualistic—reason versus passion, with rationality forming the core of moral functioning and with the "passions" (e.g., personality, emotions, desires, personal projects) regarded with suspicion (and even blatant hostility) as corrupting biases that must be surmounted in order to attain to the pure standard of autonomous moral rationality. Moral psychology's dominant models have implicitly assumed these emphases with their focus on moral judgments regarding interpersonal dilemmas. Psychology, in general, has been subjected to a veritable cognitive revolution over the past half century. Behavioral and psychoanalytic theories have gradually been eclipsed by cognitive and information-processing approaches, reflecting the liberal optimism that marked the decades after World War II. The widespread interest in Kohlberg's (1984) cognitive-developmental model clearly exemplifies these trends.

Kohlberg's theory illustrates some of the dangers of a philosophically bound model of moral functioning. Clearly, Kohlberg's conceptual, empirical, and applied contributions to the field have been monumental. By overcoming the philosophical naïveté of much of the early research on morality, he can be credited with legitimizing moral development as a field of psychological inquiry. However, his allegiance to the formalist tradition in moral philosophy and to the structuralist tradition in developmental psychology led him to explicate an account of moral functioning that was defined by reason and revealed through the developmental process. He argued that moral conflicts are optimally resolved through principles of justice and that such reasoning is automotivating, or sufficient to impel moral action. Kohlberg's depiction of moral maturity features principled moral judgment, an ideal ethical stance that requires abstracted impartiality as we divorce ourselves from our own personalities and interests to adhere to the dictates of universalizable moral principles. The philosophical constraints and psychological emphases inherent in this model of moral functioning impart a vision of moral maturity that is seemingly barren, limited, and suspect. Kohlberg's theory is not alone in its restricted perspective on moral functioning; most theories in contemporary moral psychology have inadvertently assumed these philosophical perspectives and, as a result, have focused on moral reasoning as applied to interpersonal relationships while ignoring the intrapsychic aspects of moral personality that reflect our basic values, lifestyle, and character.

The inevitable consequence of programmatic research within a specific philosophical tradition is restriction of perspective, a conceptual skew that results in a particular view of moral functioning that is likely to be limited. This is not to deny the essential role that moral philosophy plays in informing and undergirding psychological research in moral development. Rather, it is simply a reminder that any philosophical or psychological theory is inherently perspectival and that it is important to take a step back from time to time and attempt to regain a broader and perhaps more veridical perspective. This chapter argues that moral psychology and moral education need to be more closely aligned with how people understand and experience morality in their daily lives than with the tight constraints of philosophical conceptualizations.

I am hoping to engender a more balanced and comprehensive account of the moral domain and the scope of moral functioning along with a more realistically attainable depiction of moral maturity. A shared understanding of what is meant by "morality" is basic to this enterprise; therefore, I propose a working definition of morality. The recurrent controversies in moral philosophy regarding any such definition and the historically changing and individually variable boundaries of the moral domain strongly imply that any agreed-upon definition is not in the immediate offing. By proposing a definition, I am attempting to make explicit my starting-point assumptions and understandings and to provide a framework for this discussion. The definition is purposively broad, erring on the side of being overly inclusive rather than narrow.

In my view, morality is a fundamental and pervasive aspect of human functioning that consists of interpersonal and intrapsychic components.

More specifically, morality refers to voluntary actions that have, at least potentially, some social and interpersonal implications and that are governed
by internal psychological (i.e., both cognitive and emotive) mechanisms.

Several things should be noted about this working definition. First,
morality entails interpersonal aspects of life because it regulates people's
interactions and adjudicates their conflicts. It clearly involves the impact
of people's actions on others' rights and welfare. But morality involves
more than resolving conflicts and ordering relationships with others; it
also refers to people's fundamental values, lifestyles, and identities. Such
intrapsychic aspects of life reference people's basic goals and reflect their
responses to the existential question, "How shall we then live?" When we
do not having pressing interpersonal conflicts to arbitrate, what should
we be doing? These intrapsychic aspects of moral functioning have obvious implications for interpersonal interactions because values, goals, and
character get directly played out in interactions with others. As already
discussed, the interpersonal aspects of moral functioning have been well
incorporated into contemporary moral psychology and education, as reflected by their focus on interpersonal rights and welfare; however, that has
not been the case for the intrapsychic aspects. Dominant theories in moral
psychology have defined the domain rather selectively and have largely
ignored issues such as the development of values and the acquisition of
moral character. (It should be noted that this working definition of morality
does not address the important issue of whether the purview of the moral
domain should include the potential implications of humans' actions for
animals and the environment, beyond any instrumental consequences for
humans.)

The second thing to note about this working definition of morality is that it claims that moral functioning is necessarily multifaceted,
involving the dynamic interplay of thought, emotion, and behavior.
Unhelpfully, moral psychology's major theoretical models have obfuscated
the interactive—indeed, interdependent—nature of thought, emotion, and
behavior in moral functioning in that each model has regarded a different component of psychological functioning as the essence of morality. These different emphases have created a destructive trichotomy (i.e.,
thought, emotion, behavior) that implies that these are separable aspects of
moral functioning. However, these aspects are necessarily interdependent.
Single-variable theories of moral psychology are untenable in the face of
the complexity of moral functioning. For example, moral emotions such
as guilt and empathy always occur with some accompanying cognitions.
Thoughts about one's personal values or relationships with others always
have some emotional tone, whether they are hot or cold. Voluntary behaviors always have some intentional basis that determines their moral

quality (only reflexive ones do not). Thoughts impact behavior either directly in overt action or indirectly through behavioral dispositions. ("Pure" thought, such as a daydream, if it has no consequent or attendant behaviors and if it does not preclude meeting some other moral obligation, is not morally relevant, just as unintentional, reflexive action is not morally relevant, regardless of its consequences.) Thus, any theoretical model that focuses exclusively on one particular component of moral functioning trivializes the domain. A comprehensive understanding of how these different components holistically relate to each other is a pressing mandate for moral psychology.

One notable exception to the single-variable depiction of models in contemporary moral psychology is Rest's four-component model (Rest, Narvaez, Bebeau, & Thoma, 1999), which provides a comprehensive explication of the various psychological processes that, in complex interaction, contribute to observable moral behavior. The components of this model include (a) moral sensitivity (interpretation, awareness of relevant moral factors, empathy), (b) moral judgment (deliberation and judgments regarding right action and moral ideals), (c) moral motivation (commitment to the moral course of action, self-identity), and (d) moral character (implementation skills and character dispositions that foster moral action). To date, research within the framework of the componential model has focused on the two components of moral sensitivity and judgment but not on moral motivation and character and not on the relationships among these components.

A third thing to note about this working definition is that it holds that morality is a pervasive feature of human functioning. Over the past few decades, proponents of domain theory (Nucci, 2001; Turiel, 1983) have argued that social understandings can be parsed into separate domains, notably, the moral, social–conventional, and personal–prudential domains. In this theory, the moral domain refers to justice, rights, and welfare concerns; the conventional domain refers to arbitrary but shared uniformities in social norms; and the personal domain refers to actions that pertain primarily to oneself and that preclude justifiable social regulation. A prototypic example of a moral violation is striking someone else; an example of a violation of conventional norms is eating with your hands in a culture that prescribes the use of utensils; and an example of a behavior that is frequently judged to be in the personal domain is alcohol and drug use. Although many people do make such distinctions, domain theory unhelpfully defines the moral domain too narrowly. The moral domain should be considered as much more pervasive in daily life. The mode of eating food is, indeed, a convention; however, after these norms are established, violation of them can provide moral offense. For example, if you are attending a dinner party honoring a distinguished visitor and you eat with your hands, it will embarrass and hurt your host and fail to show respect for the other guests. Similarly, the judgment that substance use (and abuse) is simply a matter of personal jurisdiction fails to recognize that its health and behavioral consequences can negatively impact others. It is difficult to limit the moral domain if people believe that injustice or harm will follow from an action (regardless of how seemingly trivial it may be). Furthermore, such a circumscribed definition of morality does not adequately acknowledge that the domain includes the development of our basic values, lifestyle, and character. To reiterate, morality pervades life and it is unconstructive (both conceptually and practically) to define it too narrowly.

The prevailing emphasis on moral rationality, noted earlier, has eclipsed attention to other aspects of moral functioning and has belied the complexity of the moral life. The danger of this reification of moral rationality is that it separates people from their own personalities and character and risks negating their motivation to be moral. The philosopher Owen Flanagan (1991) has similarly critiqued the marginalization of moral character in moral philosophy and faulted current ethical frameworks for failing to adequately guide moral action because these frameworks presuppose psychological functioning that is difficult, if not impossible, for people to ordinarily attain. In other words, models of moral functioning have become isolated from everyday experience and from psychological possibility. Instead, Flanagan argued for the development of a more realistic conception of moral functioning and moral ideals, one that is psychologically possible and that acknowledges the things that give meaning to each person's life (i.e., the principle of minimal psychological realism).

## Conceptions and Experiences of Morality

In response to this conceptual skew that characterizes the field and the perceived need to provide a broader and perhaps more veridical perspective on morality, a recent series of empirical studies (Walker & Pitts, 1998; Walker, Pitts, Hennig, & Matsuba, 1995) has examined people's conceptions and experiences of morality. It is hoped that this research will lead to a more balanced account of moral functioning that meaningfully integrates moral cognition with moral personality and action and that addresses both the interpersonal and intrapsychic aspects of the domain. This research reflects a two-pronged approach to developing such an integrated account of moral functioning. The first approach examines people's ordinary conceptions of moral functioning; the second approach examines the psychological functioning of actual moral exemplars (i.e., people who have been identified as leading lives of moral virtue, integrity, and commitment). By examining people's conceptions—notions that are embedded in everyday language and common understandings—the intention is to reveal the breadth of the domain and aspects of morality that have been ignored by dominant models. This should show what people regard as important about morality. People's notions about morality are important to study because they are operative and influential in everyday life and can serve as needed complements to philosophically derived theories. Examining the psychological functioning of moral exemplars should reveal the aspects of psychological development that contribute to extraordinary moral action. These different empirical strategies are mutually informative and should provide convergent evidence regarding aspects of moral functioning that are significant in everyday life and that should be incorporated into theories of moral development and approaches to character education.

One study (Walker et al., 1995) included extensive open-ended interviews with participants regarding their conceptions of morality and their handling of actual moral problems from their personal experiences. Several findings from this project apply to the current discussion. First, an examination of the content of participants' actual moral problems revealed that people frequently deal with issues in everyday life that are not well tapped by dominant models and measures of moral development. For example, intrapsychic moral issues, which pertain more to the pursuit of ideals and the maintenance of one's sense of integrity, were common in people's experiences. Such intrapsychic, characterologic issues are not reflected in models of moral psychology that focus on the interpersonal aspects of morality (e.g., rights, responsibilities, welfare). Other commonly confronted moral issues were relational ones that involved obligations to friends, spouses, parents, and children; again, such issues are not well reflected in models of moral psychology that emphasize justice and universal principles. Among the wide range of moral problems reported, particularly common among children and adolescents, were ones revolving around honesty, cheating, and substance use. Character education programs should deal with moral issues that children typically confront and find difficult rather than ones that would stymie moral philosophers.

A second pertinent finding from Walker et al.'s (1995) research is that, in their handling of moral problems, many people reported aspects of moral functioning to which our models have paid minimal attention. For example, people frequently relied on intuition in resolving moral issues and evaluating their actions. Understandably, notions of intuition and habitual responding are alien to the rationalistic models that have dominated the field; however, because they are persistent themes in people's self-awareness, they require some attention. Haidt (2001) recently proposed that intuition is actually the default process in moral functioning and that the process of moral deliberation, if and when it is activated at all, is actually an ex post facto process intended more for impression management and social persuasion than for decision making. Intuition, of course, reflects the internalization of a range of moral virtues and, in Confucian thought, at least, connotes mature moral character.

Concerns regarding practical considerations and outcomes were another aspect of moral functioning evident in people's handling of various moral issues. These were concerns that people held to be valid factors within a moral framework, but most models of moral development dismiss these concerns as immature. However, when dealing with difficult moral problems in everyday life, people assert the moral relevance of psychological reality, reminiscent of Flanagan's argument that ethical theories must recognize that people are legitimately partial to their own projects and interests. Models of moral functioning need to account for the role of practical realities in everyday functioning.

Notions of faith, religion, and spirituality comprised another aspect of moral functioning that people referenced in their handling of actual moral problems. Moral psychology and education have shied away from consideration of the role of religion in moral functioning in deference to an academic climate that is predominantly humanistic and the perceived American requirement that moral education programs be uncontaminated by religious influence. However, for many people, morality and spirituality are not separate domains; rather, moral values and actions are firmly embedded in their religious and faith commitments. It is important that models of moral functioning and approaches to character education take account of the fact that the moral and spiritual domains are inextricably intertwined for many people.

A third pertinent finding to note from this research was the apparent individual variability in moral sensitivity. When prompted to recall a recent moral issue in their personal experience, some people responded easily by noting several they had encountered that day; however, others sincerely claimed that they had not encountered a moral problem for many years, sometimes decades. This suggests that there is considerable variability in people's conceptualization of the moral domain and their interpretation of everyday issues and problems. Different aspects of morality may characterize individuals' identities and may have differing degrees of centrality in their lives.

Another research project that has helped to inform an account of moral functioning examined people's conceptions of moral excellence

(Walker & Pitts, 1998). Many theories of moral development accord insufficient attention to definitions of moral exemplarity, but such definitions provide the telos for our intervention efforts. Kohlberg's vision of moral maturity, for example, entails dilemma-busting principles of justice, but a more compelling and full-bodied conception is needed. Walker and Pitts' research project entailed a sequence of three studies (using free-listing, prototypicality-rating, and similarity-sorting procedures) that allowed them, through various statistical techniques, to derive a taxonomic description of moral functioning that is implicit in people's understandings.

Analyses identified two dimensions that underlie people's conceptions of moral functioning. These dimensions explain how the moral domain is ordinarily understood and represented. The dimensions were labeled a self–other dimension and an external–internal dimension. The opposite ends of each dimension have contrasting emphases. One end of the self–other dimension consists of traits that emphasize personal agency and commitment; the other end contains traits that focus more on care for others. This dimension incorporates some of the dynamics of the notions of dominance and nurturance (or agency and communion) as fundamental in the understanding of personality and behavior. Of course, the range of these moral virtues means that they are sometimes in tension, which is important to recognize. For example, the importance of strongly held moral values and principles needs to be balanced by an openness to new perspectives and a sensitivity to the circumstances of others (incidentally, achieving this balance was one observation arising from Colby & Damon's [1992] case-study analysis of a small sample of moral exemplars). Similarly, the external–internal dimension reflects the occasional tension between external moral standards and a personal conscience, and it implies that moral maturity requires a sensitivity both to shared moral norms and to autonomous moral values and standards.

Given the significance of faith and spirituality in many people's actual moral decision-making processes, Walker and Pitts (1998) also examined the relationships among people's understanding of the moral, religious, and spiritual domains, relationships that can be explored when some of the ascribed attributes are unique to each domain and others are shared across domains. Analyses indicated that these domains are, indeed, related in people's understandings, but in an asymmetrical pattern. Moral virtues were found to be somewhat independent of religious and spiritual ones; in other words, to be a moral person, one does not need to manifest characteristics that are central to religion and spirituality. On the other hand, notions of religion and spirituality were found to be somewhat embedded in notions of morality. That is, central to what it means to be a religious or spiritual person is the embodiment of moral virtues, consistent with the observation that moral guidelines have always been a central component of religious imperatives.

In summary, this research identified aspects of moral functioning that figure prominently in people's understandings but that have been inadequately represented in moral psychology and character education and that now warrant more careful consideration. However, one questionable implication from this research should be flagged: whether there is a single prototype for moral maturity. This listing of moral virtues may represent an amalgamation of traits that would be impossible—indeed, incoherent—for any one person to embody. At present, we have little understanding of how these aspects of moral character interact in psychological functioning.

The suggestion pursued in a subsequent research project (Walker & Hennig, in press) is that moral exemplarity can be evidenced in quite divergent ways. In other words, there may be no single viable prototype for moral maturity or ideal of moral character; indeed, there may be many different types of moral excellence and moral exemplars. Think of various moral heroes that are sometimes held up for emulation (e.g., Martin Luther King, Jr., Oskar Schindler, Mother Teresa). These exemplars are recognized for quite different collections of virtues (i.e., social justice, bravery, and self-sacrificial care, respectively). So the critical questions here are: What moral traits cluster for each type of moral exemplar and are unique to each, and what traits are common across different types of moral exemplarity, suggestive of the virtues that are foundational to moral functioning in general? Walker and Hennig (in press) explored conceptions of three types of moral exemplarity—just, brave, and caring—because they are salient in both philosophical thought and everyday experiences. But, of course, other important types could be considered as well. As in the previous project, this research entailed a sequence of three studies that allowed identification of typologies in people's understanding.

The analyses revealed rather dissimilar personality profiles for these different moral exemplars. The brave exemplars were associated with traits of agency, extraversion, self-confidence, and self-sacrifice; the caring exemplars were associated with traits of agreeableness, nurturance, and altruism; and the just exemplars were typified by objectivity, conscientiousness, level-headedness, and wisdom. However, many traits were found to be common to these three types of moral exemplars; these common traits could be considered the core of moral functioning. Among these core traits were honesty, dependability, and self-control as well as many traits of an interpersonal nature that reflect a positive communal emotionality and sociability, clearly an other-oriented perspective. Other themes included personal agency, positivity, emotional stability, and openness. These common denominators across types of moral exemplarity are clearly foundational for moral functioning in general and warrant further conceptual and empirical scrutiny.

Other analyses identified the dimensions underlying people's understandings of the different types of moral exemplarity that illustrate the range of virtues frequently in tension. For just exemplars, the character dimension highlighted the tension between the characterologic and cognitive aspects of exemplarity in terms of justice, and the particularity dimension illustrated the recurrent tension between strict objectivity and partiality to those with whom one is in relation. For brave exemplars, the selfless dimension was anchored at one end by attributes that reflect a lack of concern for oneself and at the other end by attributes that are more self-focused; the agentic dimension tapped traits of personal agency and initiative. For care exemplars, the genuine dimension reflected traits of interpersonal sincerity at one end and traits of self-denial and perhaps (though not necessarily) a lack of authenticity at the other end; the emotive dimension was indicative of traits of positive emotionality in contrast to ones that were more behavioral.

Despite the evidence that people identify a set of core virtues across disparate types of moral exemplarity, it was also evident that the personality trait attributions regarding just, brave, and caring exemplars were quite different. Each typified a relatively distinct moral personality. It is important to note that it is quite possible—indeed, probable—that all moral traits are not necessarily compatible and may sometimes be antithetical. On a related theme, most virtues have maladaptive, or at least morally questionable, aspects to their expression in some circumstances or when taken to excess. Virtues can take on less-than-authentic manifestations, and moral psychology would be well served by careful conceptual and empirical analyses of the maladaptive aspects of some central moral traits.

The major limitation to the study of conceptions of moral functioning is that it simply describes people's understandings rather than the actual psychological functioning of real moral exemplars. It is unclear whether real moral paragons evidence the range of moral virtues that are extant in people's conceptions. Colby and Damon's (1992) analysis of people who evidenced extraordinary commitment to moral ideals and causes revealed some valuable insights, but more systematic data are required for a full-bodied account of moral functioning. Thus, the other prong of Walker's (2003) current program of research focuses on comprehensive analyses of the psychological functioning of moral exemplars. The research is using the template of the most valid models and measures of human development. However, it should be noted that the identification of actual moral exemplars is sometimes controversial. The individual moral heroes mentioned earlier (i.e., Martin Luther King, Jr., Mother Teresa, Oskar Schindler), for example, have all been somewhat contentious in their designation as moral exemplars. Nevertheless, many types of moral exemplars are less controversial.

One study (Matsuba & Walker, 2004) compared the psychological functioning of a young adult group of exemplars (identified for their extraordinary moral commitment as volunteers in social service agencies) with a matched comparison group. Variables indicative of all levels of personality assessment distinguished the moral exemplars from comparison individuals (despite matching on demographic variables). At the level of dispositional personality traits, the exemplar group was found to be higher on the factor of agreeableness than the comparison group. At the level of contextualized concerns in understanding personality functioning, the exemplar group was found to be more mature in their identities, reflecting a stronger commitment to values and having greater stability; they evidenced more mature faith development, reflecting the process by which they make meaning in life; and they used more advanced moral reasoning, confirming its critical role in moral functioning. At the level of personality assessment that examines integrative narratives of the self, themes in participants' life stories were coded, with the expectation that exemplars' narratives would be characterized by more themes of both agency and communion than would be evident for the comparison individuals. This hypothesis was partly supported in the finding of a greater frequency of agentic themes in exemplars' accounts. This research indicates several psychological processes that contribute to exceptional moral character and action. However, it should be remembered that moral maturity can be exemplified in different ways (beyond volunteer activity), and it is important for our understanding of moral functioning to determine what is distinctive about different types of moral exemplars as well as what the common core may be. It should be more obvious now how this research on individuals' conceptions of the moral domain dovetails with the research on the psychological functioning of moral exemplars.

To address this issue, a research project (Walker, 2003) is examining the character and personalities of two contrasting types of moral exemplars: exceptionally brave versus caring people. The sample is composed of Canadians who have received national awards (from the Governor-General) in recognition of either their acts of bravery in risking their lives to save others (the Medal of Bravery) or for their extraordinary care to individuals, groups, or communities or their support for humanitarian causes (the Caring Canadian Award). It is anticipated that the eventual findings of this research will yield a more comprehensive understanding of moral functioning that integrates cognition, personality, and action.

## Applications and Conclusions

This chapter is meant to foster a more holistic and balanced account of what moral functioning entails and thereby prompt more effective means by which to nurture children's moral and character development. Some practical applications and recommendations for scholars and practitioners include:

- Models of moral functioning and approaches to moral education must address both the interpersonal and the intrapsychic aspects of the domain; both are essential. It is important for children to learn not only how to regulate their relationships with others and to resolve conflicts but also how to acquire the fundamental values and goals that should characterize their identities and ways of living.

- Similarly, models and methods of moral education should address the multifaceted complexity of moral functioning and include meaningful attention to moral reasoning, moral emotions, and moral action.

- It is essential to sensitize children to the breadth of the moral domain and the moral implications of their values, decisions, and actions. Making children more aware of the moral domain helps foster the development of a moral identity so that moral concerns become relevant to most activities in life. It is important that children recognize the pervasive nature of morality and do not compartmentalize it as a circumscribed and largely irrelevant facet of life.

- Intervention efforts should address moral issues that are developmentally appropriate and that children frequently encounter and find difficult and troubling.

- Models of moral functioning and approaches to character education must take account of the finding that, for many people, the moral and religious domains are intertwined in significant ways.

- Moral education should entail a critical discussion of moral virtues, particularly ones that form the core of the moral domain. Simply extolling the worth of virtues does little to engender good moral character; rather, children need to come to appreciate the complexities and the maladaptive aspects of many virtues such as honesty and care and to struggle with how to exemplify these traits daily. For example, the virtue of honesty needs to be sensitively tempered by considerations of avoiding hurt to others. Similarly, the virtue of care needs to be based on an authentic sense of oneself and not be manipulative.

- Children need to struggle with some of the underlying tensions in moral functioning and to recognize the complexity of issues they deal with frequently. The dimensions identified in people's understanding of the moral domain illustrate some of these tensions (a) between the importance of commitments to moral values and principles and the need to be sensitive to new ideas and to the circumstances and needs of others; (b) between the importance of respect for the moral standards of one's community and the value of the carefully considered moral ideals and principles of one's conscience; (c) between the need for objective fairness and the importance of nurturing particular relationships; (d) between the importance of a meaningful orientation to others and the need for authentic self-fulfillment; and (e) among the various aspects of moral functioning (e.g., character, cognition, emotion, and behavior).

- Moral heroes are worthy of some emulation, and children should explore the lives of well-known, visible exemplars as well as local, personal ones. However, exemplars' lives should not be examined superficially; rather, they should be looked at in all their fullness, including the complexity of their personalities, the formative aspects of their experiences, and their weaknesses and struggles. Children should not only study moral exemplars and moral issues, but their involvement in meaningful moral action should also be encouraged and facilitated.

- It is important for children to recognize the diversity in types of moral excellence and to find personal moral exemplars with whom they can identify. A single model of moral maturity should not necessarily be promulgated; rather, children should be encouraged to foster different areas of moral excellence.

These will hardly be the last words on what is entailed in moral functioning, but it is hoped that this contribution will further the discussion on what nurtures children's moral development.

# References

Colby, A., & Damon, W. (1992). *Some do care: Contemporary lives of moral commitment.* New York: Free Press.

Flanagan, O. (1991). *Varieties of moral personality: Ethics and psychological realism.* Cambridge, MA: Harvard University Press.

Haidt, J. (2001). The emotional dog and its rational tail: A social intuitionist approach to moral judgment. *Psychological Review, 108,* 814–834.

Kohlberg, L. (1984). *Essays on moral development: Vol. 2. The psychology of moral development.* San Francisco: Harper & Row.

Matsuba, M. K., & Walker, L. J. (2004). Extraordinary moral commitment: Young adults working for social organizations. *Journal of Personality, 72,* 413–436.

Nucci, L. P. (2001). *Education in the moral domain.* Cambridge, UK: Cambridge University Press.

Rest, J. R., Narvaez, D., Bebeau, M. J., & Thoma, S. J. (1999). *Postconventional moral thinking: A neo-Kohlbergian approach.* Mahwah, NJ: Erlbaum.

Turiel, E. (1983). *The development of social knowledge: Morality and convention.* Cambridge, UK: Cambridge University Press.

Walker, L. J. (2003). *In search of moral excellence: Brave and caring Canadians.* Research in progress.

Walker, L. J., & Hennig, K. H. (in press). *Differing conceptions of moral exemplarity: Just, brave, and caring.* Manuscript submitted for publication.

Walker, L. J., & Pitts, R. C. (1998). Naturalistic conceptions of moral maturity. *Developmental Psychology, 34,* 403–419.

Walker, L. J., Pitts, R. C., Hennig, K. H., & Matsuba, M. K. (1995). Reasoning about morality and real-life moral problems. In M. Killen & D. Hart (Eds.), *Morality in everyday life: Developmental perspectives* (pp. 371–407). Cambridge, UK: Cambridge University Press.

# Chapter 2

# The Role of Perceived Responsibility in Nurturing Morality

## Sandra Graham

Most definitions of morality emphasize social behavior: It is considered morally right to treat other people fairly and morally wrong to intentionally harm others for personal gain. Thus, for example, when children at school are observed to aggress against others, as when the strong bully the weak or older youths harass younger targets, their behavior elicits anger from teachers because it so clearly violates society's shared beliefs about moral conduct.

Yet moral misconduct can also be observed in behaviors that do not involve harm to others. Take achievement, for example. A century ago, the philosopher Max Weber called attention to the close ties between individual achievement strivings and morality, and many contemporary theorists argue that achievement is a moral system (Weiner, 1995). Teachers tend to reward high effort in their students and punish low effort because there is a shared belief in American culture that students should feel morally obligated to try hard in school.

This chapter makes the case that social misbehavior, as illustrated by aggression toward others, and achievement misconduct, as illustrated by students who do not try, are both part of the same moral system and can be understood within the same overarching framework. This framework involves the moral construct of perceived responsibility, in both other people and the self. Children who aggress against others do so partly because they make inaccurate inferences about whether other people are responsible for negative events. Similarly, children who perform poorly in school do so partly because they do not take personal responsibility for their own achievement. One approach to nurturing morality in the social and academic domains is, therefore, to focus on ways to increase social skills related to accurately inferring responsibility in others and to build academic skills related self-responsibility for school learning.

The chapter begins with a discussion of the conceptual framework that guides my thinking about responsibility as a moral construct that is applicable to both social behavior and achievement strivings. Then it illustrates some principles from that theoretical framework in my research with high-risk ethnic minority children and adolescents, youths whose life experiences often limit their opportunities to display moral virtues (e.g., good social skills, academic motivation). The chapter also presents some early findings of an intervention designed to nurture morality in at-risk youths by decreasing their motivation to aggress against others and increasing their motivation to try hard in school. We do this by changing perceptions of responsibility in other people and ourselves. The chapter concludes with a discussion of guidelines for school-based interventions that can nurture morality.

## An Attributional Analysis of Perceived Responsibility

I am a developmental psychologist who studies responsibility. Responsibility can be examined from the perspective of attribution theory. Causal attributions are answers to "why" questions, such as "Why did I fail the examination?" or "Why doesn't anyone like me?" Individuals make causal attributions about other people as well as themselves. "Why" questions are also asked about world events. For example, most of the immediate commentary associated with terrorist attacks of September 11, 2001 implicitly or explicitly asked "why": Were the hijackers religious fanatics? Was airport security too lax? Should U.S. intelligence have known? People especially seek answers to "why" questions about themselves and others after unexpected, unusual, or negative outcomes.

Causal search can lead to an infinite number of attributions. In the achievement domain, which has served as a model for the study of causality in other contexts, the main perceived causes of success and failure are aptitude or ability, effort, task difficulty or ease, luck, mood, and help or hindrance from others. The dominant perceived causes of crime tend to be such factors as the mental instability of the offender, poor parenting, and poverty. The most salient causes of poverty include laziness or poor management skills plus social causes such as unemployment, poor schooling, and discrimination.

Because specific attributions vary greatly across domains and between individuals, attribution theorists have focused on the underlying dimensions or properties of causes in addition to specific causes. Three such dimensions have been identified; they are *locus*, or whether a cause is internal or external to a person; *stability*, which designates a cause as constant or varying over time; and *controllability*, or whether a cause is subject to volitional influence. For example, aptitude is typically perceived as internal, stable, and uncontrollable. Low aptitude as a cause for failure resides within the individual, is constant over time, and is not subject to volitional control. This is in contrast to lack of effort, which is also internal but is more often perceived as unstable and under an individual's control.

Each of these causal dimensions has both psychological and behavioral consequences. This chapter focuses on the consequences of perceived controllability, both in oneself and in others. Controllability connotes responsibility and intentionality, hence the link to moral evaluation. Failure attributed to controllable causes (e.g., lack of effort) leads to the inference that the person is responsible and the behavior was intended. On the other hand, failure attributed to an uncontrollable cause (e.g., low aptitude) leads to an inference of nonresponsibility and unintended behavior. A large body of attribution research documents that when others are perceived as being responsible for negative events (i.e., their behaviors are controllable), the attribution elicits anger and the desire to neglect, inflict harm, or punish (Weiner, 1995). These principles can partly explain, for example, the behavior of abusive parents toward their misbehaving children, violent spouses in distressed marriages, and teachers' reactions to gifted but lazy students. Attribution theorists further propose that causal thoughts, feelings, and actions are interrelated in a particular way. Causal thoughts tell people how to feel; in turn, their feelings guide behavior.

Individuals constantly use attribution principles in their efforts to understand their environment. Yet even the most competent lay attribution theorists are not immune to biases or errors in the way they perceive their causal world. For example, people tend to take credit for their successes and blame their failures on external causes, a phenomenon known as *hedonic bias*. They also tend to make trait attributions about others (e.g., "He's a dishonest person") and situational attributions about themselves (e.g., "Everyone else was cheating"), which has been called the *actor–observer bias*. Attributional biases become dysfunctional when they lead to poor interpersonal relationships, ineffective problem solving, or undue hostility toward others. The next section discusses a kind of attributional bias that has these characteristics and that may be prevalent in aggressive youths.

## Aggression and Biased Beliefs About Others' Responsibility

A great deal of research on peer aggression has shown that aggressive youths (primarily boys) display a *hostile attributional bias* (see review in Coie & Dodge, 1998). That is, aggressive boys overattribute negative intent to others, particularly in situations of ambiguously caused provocation. For example, imagine a situation in which a youngster experiences a social transgression, such as being pushed by a peer while waiting in line, and it is unclear whether the peer's behavior was intended as aggressive or not. Aggressive boys are more likely than their nonaggressive classmates to report that the push occurred intentionally. Attributions to hostile intent then lead to anger and the desire to retaliate. Even among socially competent children, individuals who believe that another person acted with hostile intent can feel justified in endorsing aggressive behavior. This justification goes back to basic attribution principles about responsibility inferences, feelings of anger, and their relationships to punitive behavior. Aggressive children often inappropriately or prematurely assume hostile peer intent in ambiguous situations.

A large amount of research literature reveals that hostile attributional bias is correlated with a number of maladaptive outcomes for aggressive children, including conduct disorder, externalizing behavior, and peer rejection (Coie & Dodge, 1998). A common theme underlying those findings is that having a tendency to adopt a blameful stance toward others interferes with the processing of social information (an encoding and attentional deficit), anger management (an emotion-regulation deficit), and effective problem solving (a social skills deficit). My colleagues and I know from our own research that attribution retraining can help aggressive boys learn to infer nonhostile intent in ambiguous situations; however, this retraining has short-term effects in reducing anger intensity and antisocial behavior (Hudley & Graham, 1993). (That intervention, the Best Foot Forward intervention, is discussed later in this chapter.) But on the less positive side, we also know from our research that hostile attributional biases emerge early in aggressive children's lives, that these biases are partly a product of socialization experiences, and that the biases take on a traitlike quality as they become the preferred mode for handling ambiguous provocation (Graham, 1997).

Because childhood aggression is a risk factor for juvenile delinquency, a growing amount of literature examines hostile attributional bias in adolescent offenders. Research has shown that hostile biases are correlated with violent interpersonal crimes (e.g., attempted murder, aggravated assault) but not with property crimes (e.g., burglary, theft) or with status offenses (Lochman & Dodge, 1994). Biases are also displayed more by reactively aggressive offenders—hot-tempered, easily angered, impulsive youths—than by proactively aggressive offenders, who are more motivated by personal gain than by reacting to the perceived threat of others (Dodge, Lochman, Harnish, Bates, & Pettit, 1997).

Research on adolescent offenders from an attributional perspective has identified other correlates of bias (Graham & Halliday, 2000). First, when offenders report high family conflict, they also report more attributional biases about other people's behavior. This finding corresponds with other research that shows that mothers who make negative attributions about their children and other people tend to have children who are more aggressive. Second, offenders who are hypervigilant also display more bias. Hypervigilance is anxiety about being attacked, a belief in a foreshortened future, and the need to be prepared for imminent danger. Vigilance is certainly compatible with an interpersonal style of preemptive reactions to others' provocations. Third, youths who report more neighborhood disorder and violence also display more extreme biases, suggesting that one's tendency to view the world as a hostile place can be predicted by exposure to violence and deviance.

In summary, because of a bias to perceive other people as responsible for negative outcomes, at-risk youths may have difficulty endorsing the attitudes and displaying the behaviors that are associated with moral virtue. Attributional bias is part of a general syndrome of social-cognitive deficits that describe the way aggressive and delinquent youths organize their causal world. Among these deficits are inattention to relevant cues, poor recall of the cues, weak perspective taking, impulsive decision-making behaviors, and a limited ability to generate effective solutions to social dilemmas. This syndrome can put youths at greater risk for immoral behavior. It is not difficult to imagine, for example, a potential offender contemplating assault who is skeptical of his adversary's intentions, adopts a blameful stance at the slightest provocation, misinterprets benign gestures as hostile, is easily angered and therefore unable to attend to relevant information, and has difficulty generating alternative (i.e., prosocial) strategies for dealing with conflict.

The public discourse about juvenile crime and presumed immorality often centers around the perceived causes of immoral behavior such as the kinds of families adolescent offenders come from or the types of neighborhoods where they are reared. The effects of these background factors on moral functioning are probably at least partly explained by attributional biases concerning perceived responsibility in others. If one's goal is to nurture morality through intervention, altering biased attributions might be a reasonable starting point. Social cognitions are far more amenable to change than are family and neighborhood contexts.

## *Achievement Strivings and Self-responsibility*

The same conceptual analysis used for holding others responsible for negative events (which increases aggression) can also be applied to holding oneself responsible for academic outcomes (which increases achievement strivings). The basic assumption is that within an achievement context, as in many social contexts, an individual is faced with the option (i.e., decision) to ascribe responsibility for outcomes to the self (e.g., to lack of effort after failure) or to factors for which the individual cannot be held responsible (e.g., low aptitude, poor teaching). That decision influences the individual's expectancy for success, affective reactions to task performance, and subsequent achievement strivings. It is further assumed that self-responsibility is a particularly adaptive motivational state because it is more likely to result in high expectancy, positive affect, sustained effort, and praise from one's teachers (Graham & Weiner, 1996).

Principles from motivation theory support the argument that self-responsibility promotes achievement strivings. These principles address core issues in the study of motivation, including *choice*, or whether a student prefers easy, moderate, or difficult achievement tasks; *intensity*, or how hard someone actually works at an achievement activity; and *persistence* in the face of academic challenge. Concerning choice, for example, evidence suggests that motivation can be enhanced when students select tasks of intermediate difficulty rather than tasks that are very difficult or very easy. Preference for intermediate difficulty is evident when risk taking and level of aspiration increase after success and decrease after failure. Such "typical shifts" indicate that a person is altering his or her aspirations and expectations to be compatible with likely outcomes. These behaviors also foster self-responsibility, inasmuch as failure at a very difficult task (i.e., taking too high a risk) and success at a very easy task (i.e., taking little or no risk) can be attributed to factors outside of oneself.

The motivational skill of goal setting is related to intermediate risk taking. Recent research from a social-cognitive perspective has documented the motivation-enhancing qualities of setting short-term or proximal goals in contrast to long-term or distal goals (Bandura, 1997). Proximal goals involve mentally decomposing a task into component parts so that it becomes more manageable. As these goals are attained, individuals have a basis for judging how well they are doing and for making the necessary adjustments to their behavior in order to achieve desired outcomes. Therefore, the activity of proximal goal setting increases effort and self-responsibility by providing immediate incentives for performance. Distal goals, in contrast, are often too far removed in time to effectively mobilize effort.

Intermediate risk taking and proximal goal setting are more likely to take place when students are task focused rather than ego focused. In task-focused situations, the goal is to master the task or to acquire new skills. That state is contrasted with ego-focused situations in which the primary goal is to demonstrate high ability relative to others or to conceal low ability (Nicholls, 1984). A similar distinction has been made by some goal theorists, who contrast mastery goals with performance goals. A great deal of research with children documents that task focus and a mastery orientation have positive effects on students' self-perceptions and willingness to engage in achievement activities (Ames, 1992). Furthermore, a task focus promotes self-responsibility because the students determine success and failure by comparison with self-standards rather than the normative standards created by comparison with others. Hence, outcomes tend to be ascribed more to effort and less to external factors such as the good or poor performance of peers.

Finally, students are more likely to persist in the face of academic difficulty if they attribute failure to controllable factors for which they are responsible (e.g., lack of effort or poor choice of strategy) instead of uncontrollable causes such as low ability or task difficulty (Graham & Weiner, 1996). Persistence is not affected because failure ascribed to a factor that is controllable and for which one is responsible implies that the same outcome need not occur again. It is as if the student thinks, "I failed because I did not put forth enough effort, but I can try harder next time" as opposed to "I failed because the work is too hard, and there is really nothing I can do to change that." Consistent with this principle, a large amount of literature on attribution retraining in achievement contexts documents that students perform better and persist longer when they are taught to attribute failure to controllable causes.

In summary, self-responsibility can affect students' choice of academic activities, how much effort they expend, and how long they persist in the face of failure. The research literature on motivation indicates that students at risk for failure have better outcomes if they choose tasks of intermediate difficulty, set proximal as opposed to distal goals, are task focused rather than ego focused, and attribute failure to controllable causes.

## Self-Responsibility and Achievement Effort in Ethnic Minority Youths

The previous section indicated that some children have difficulty behaving in a morally appropriate way because they make biased attributions about others' responsibility. Many youths, particularly ethnic minority youths with histories of school failure, have difficulty engaging in morally appropriate achievement behavior because they are reluctant to take responsibility for their learning. Some researchers and practitioners take the moral stance and argue that many African American youths do poorly in school because they deny the importance of academic success or because their own life experiences are discrepant with the notion that they should feel morally obligated to exert effort in school. My work with urban teachers has shown how often an implicit focus on values and the morality of achievement emerges in their lay theories about why so many African American adolescents underachieve in school. For example, I hear comments such as: "They can do the work, but they just don't seem to *care*."; "The kids have not come to terms with the reality that you have to work hard in school to guarantee success in life."; and "In their peer culture, they risk rejection if they exert effort in school."

As a researcher, I can say little to either support or refute these teachers' laments because very little research has directly examined the achievement values of ethnic minority youths. However, recent thinking from the disciplines of sociology and anthropology does provide some insight into the question of whether African American youths devalue achievement and trying hard in school. For example, sociologists point to the opportunity structure in American society and argue that economic and social disadvantage have led many African American students to believe that their efforts in school will have relatively little payoff in terms of economic and social mobility (Mickelson, 1990). That is, the perceived barriers imposed by a society that perpetuates inequality along race and class lines communicate to minority youngsters that there is little relationship between their efforts and eventual outcomes.

Anthropologists who focus on the historical circumstances and cultural forces that have shaped the experiences of African Americans provide a related analysis. They argue that for many African Americans who live with the legacy of slavery, acceptance of mainstream values about working hard and school success may be perceived as threatening to their social identity (Fordham & Ogbu, 1986). Particularly during adolescence, African American youngsters may adopt oppositional identities whereby they show relative indifference—or even disdain—toward achievement behaviors that are valued by the larger society. Fordham and Ogbu (1986) coined the term "acting white" to describe African American high school students' perceptions of their same-race peers who work hard to do well in school.

My colleagues and I have been tackling this complex question of race and the valuing of effort has been examined in a series of studies with African American and Latino youths in elementary and middle school (Graham & Taylor, 2001). The studies used a very simple methodology of asking students to write down the names of their classmates whom they most admired, respected, and wanted to be like. The rationale for these questions was that when a student identifies the characteristics of a classmate he or she admires, respects, and wants to resemble, the student reveals something about what he or she values.

The results were illuminating. Because ethnic minority girls in elementary and middle school wanted to be similar to classmates (mainly other girls) who do well in school and are perceived to try very hard, it was clear that they valued effort. The same pattern was true for ethnic minority boys in elementary school (second and fourth graders), who valued other high-achieving boys. For African American and Latino middle school boys, however, the data were quite different. Across three studies, which have now been replicated, middle school African American and Latino boys reported that they valued (i.e., admire, respect, want to be like) other boys who were *low* achievers and were perceived as *not* trying hard. Perceived barriers to opportunity were related to devaluing effort among these boys. In other words, the adolescent boys who reported that societal barriers (i.e., external, uncontrollable causes) would keep them from getting the education or job that they wanted were also the boys who reported valuing low achievers. The sociologists who write about achievement values, the opportunity structure, and the morality of aspiration are probably correct. Ethnic minority adolescents who perceive barriers to success on the basis of race and social class (i.e., factors outside their control) may find it difficult to sustain effort and otherwise assume self-responsibility for achievement.

## Nurturing Morality: An Intervention Approach to Changing Perceived Responsibility

The previous sections of this chapter have laid out the theoretical framework that guides my thinking about perceived responsibility as one feature of moral functioning in both the social and academic domains. The discussion has focused on my research with at-risk ethnic minority youths, who encounter many challenges in their efforts to develop the attitudes and behaviors that are valued by the larger society and that are associated with moral virtue. The next section examines intervention with at-risk African American youths. It describes some early results of a curriculum that my colleagues and I have developed and that focuses on nurturing morality as defined here. In particular, the intervention is organized around the causal construct of perceived responsibility in both other people and the self. The intervention considers whether peers are perceived as responsible for negative events, which has implications for reducing the motivation to aggress against those peers. It also examines the degree to which individuals perceive themselves as responsible for their academic outcomes, which has implications for increasing their own motivation to achieve.

## Overview of the Intervention

The intervention, titled Best Foot Forward, was designed for elementary school children who have been labeled as aggressive by their teachers and peers. It consists of a 32-lesson curriculum with two separate but interrelated components. The *social skills* component focuses on teaching participants how to make accurate judgments about the causes of other people's behavior, particularly the degree to which others are perceived as responsible for negative outcomes. Accurate beliefs about others' responsibility should then lead to better anger management and aggression control. The *academic motivation* component focuses on training participants to assume self-responsibility for school learning. Participants learn strategies that encourage them to choose tasks of intermediate difficulty, be realistic goal setters, be task focused, and attribute academic failure to lack of effort rather than to factors that are out of their control. All of these strategies derive from principles of motivation that are known to work (i.e., to increase academic motivation).

## Social Skills Training

The social skills component of the curriculum is divided into two sections. The first component addresses *attributional bias*, or inferring hostile intent in others. Adapted from Hudley and Graham (1993), the lessons in this section focus on identifying how and why biased attributions occur. Participants learn how to distinguish accidental from hostile acts and to accurately infer the intentions (responsibility) of others. For example, hypothetical stories are used to demonstrate different intentions, after which students look for examples of such situations in their own lives. Students practice discerning another person's intention by reading nonverbal cues (e.g., tone of voice, facial expression, body language) in videotapes created for the intervention and through matching faces to appropriate feeling labels, pantomiming in small groups, and doing roleplay exercises (e.g., *Think Before You Swing*, Lesson 11).

The second social skills section addresses *account giving*. Accounts are explanations or reasons for social transgressions; they include apology (confession), excuses, justifications, and denials. Effective account giving is an important social skill because accounts help people manage the impressions that others have of them; they influence receivers' judgments about responsibility as well as their emotional reactions to account givers. For example, when late for a play date, a skilled account giver is not likely to say, "I did not feel like showing up." Rather, the transgressor is more likely to offer an excuse that implies nonresponsibility, such as: "I got sick and could not come" (Weiner, 1995). By shifting causal responsibility away from the self, accounts can reduce anger and hostility from others. Even when guilt and self-blame for a transgression are evident, strategic accounts may still serve impression management functions. For example, transgressors who acknowledge responsibility and apologize for their misdeeds are more likely to evoke forgiveness (rather than anger) on the part of the offended person than are individuals who deny or minimize their wrongdoing.

Aggressive boys show less understanding of the consequences of some accounts (i.e., excuses), and they may be less willing to extend forgiveness to peers who offer other accounts. This phase of the intervention teaches participants to understand the characteristics of different kinds of accounts and what they imply about personal responsibility. Participants learn how to use strategic account giving—in other words, the adaptiveness of accepting responsibility for their own misdeeds, as when they apologize (e.g., *The 4 A's: Admit, Apologize, Amend, Assure*, Lesson 8). They also learn to honor the accounts of others by displaying greater forgiveness when others apologize for their misdeeds.

## *Academic Motivation Training*

The academic motivation component of the curriculum is divided into four sections that focus on risk taking, goal setting, task focus, and attribution retraining. The section on risk taking teaches students how to determine what makes a problem easy, medium, or difficult and to recognize the benefits of intermediate difficulty. For example, boys participate in a weekly spelling game in which they can choose words that are easy, medium, or difficult. Although more points (exchangeable for prizes) could be earned by correctly spelling more difficult words, participants learn that the best strategy (more points) over the long run is to concentrate on words of intermediate difficulty. These principles are also incorporated into a number of engaging nonacademic tasks. For example, while playing a competitive game of ring toss, intervention boys are taught to adjust their goals (risk taking) upward after success and downward after failure (e.g., *Take Smart Risks*, Lesson 4). In that way, they learn about the motivational advantages of continuously revising their goals and level of aspiration in the direction of intermediate difficulty.

The section on goal setting teaches participants about the importance of setting proximal or short-term goals rather than (or in addition to) distal or long-term goals. Using concrete everyday examples in which goal setting is likely to be instrumental to success, intervention boys learn how to set their sights on more immediate attainments that lead to longer term successes. Over the course of the intervention, they keep a weekly log in which they enter their daily, weekly, and monthly goals, both academic and nonacademic. They also learn strategies for monitoring their behavior directed toward achieving the goals and for revising their goals in response to success or failure (e.g., *The Best Way from Here to There*, Lesson 24).

Several activities are designed to promote a task orientation to achievement as opposed to an ego focus. First, participants work on a number of achievement tasks (e.g., digit symbol substitution, anagrams) in which success or failure can be manipulated. Intervention boys learn to focus on improvement rather than absolute performance and to reward themselves accordingly. They also practice monitoring their effort (and therefore being more task focused) in the context of becoming more strategic help seekers. Participants learn that the most successful help seekers are those who can show that they have already exerted effort and that they have genuinely reached an impasse (e.g., *The Help Seeking Formula*, Lesson 21).

Finally, the attribution retraining section is designed to promote adaptive explanations for achievement failure. Participants read hypothetical failure scenarios and generate possible causes for the outcomes. This is used as a context for discussing the characteristics of different causes and for examining why some explanations might be more adaptive than others. The boys then work on several achievement tasks that require persistence (e.g., origami puzzles). Here they learn to attribute academic setbacks to factors within their control, such as lack of effort, and to avoid the endorsement of factors outside of their control, such as low ability and bad luck (e.g., *To Blame or Not to Blame*, Lesson 30).

## Curriculum Intervention

Because of the breadth of the curriculum and number of lessons (32 sessions plus pretesting and posttesting), the intervention was implemented as an after-school program. Participants attended the intervention 3 days a week for 12 weeks in sessions that lasted approximately 1 hour each (approximately 3:30 to 4:30 p.m.). One strength of the intervention was that it provided a structured activity for at-risk youngsters during a portion of the after-school hours. A considerable amount of recent research has documented that the hours between 3 and 7 p.m. are critical because they are the times when most delinquent activity is likely to take place (i.e., the prime hours when adult supervision is minimal) (Flannery, Williams, & Vazonyi, 1999).

Participants were selected from a K–5 elementary school located in an economically depressed community in Los Angeles, California. Using well-established methods in the peer aggression literature, a combination of both teacher ratings and peer nominations was used to select eligible participants. The intervention included African American boys in third to fifth grade who were identified by their peers and teachers as most aggressive and by their teachers as having serious motivational problems. The participants included 66 third, fourth, and fifth grade boys who met the eligibility criteria and whose custodial parents or guardians provided informed consent. Thirty-one boys were randomly assigned to the intervention, and 35 were assigned to a no-treatment control group (a few parents agreed to allow their sons to participate only if they were control subjects).

As one might imagine, subject attrition can be a problem in studies such as this. Participation was voluntary and required sustained after-school attendance, which meant that the program did not have the "captive" audience that would have been available had the intervention been run during regular school hours. Over the course of the intervention, nine of the 31 intervention boys left the study: One had an extended hospital stay, one was asked to leave the program because of his continued disruptive behavior, and seven were dropped because of irregular attendance. Among the control subjects, 10 of the initial 35 did not complete both pretesting and posttesting: One boy moved away, two were expelled from school, three voluntarily dropped out of the project, and four were chronically absent from school during the posttesting. Thus, the final sample consisted of 47 third to fifth grade African American boys, including 22 boys in the intervention group and 25 control subjects.

## Outcome Measures

A variety of outcome measures, both attitudinal and behavioral, were included that relied on multiple informants (i.e., self-report, behavioral observations, teacher report, and searches of school records). This is a strength of the intervention approach. The outcome measures assessed improvements in both social skills and academic motivation. For social outcomes, the examiners assessed changes in children's reactions to ambiguous peer provocation and their understanding of accounts. Teacher ratings of children's social behavior before and after the intervention were also examined. Among the academic outcomes, the researchers examined changes in students' goal setting and attributions for achievement failure. They also examined students' cumulative folders for their semester grade equivalents and teachers' comments about academic progress. Finally, both intervention and control group boys participated in a laboratory maze task that both simulated ambiguous peer provocation and measured intermediate risk taking.

## Results of the Intervention

Space limitations do not allow descriptions all of the intervention effects (see Graham, Taylor, & Hudley, in press), but a summary is provided here. Although the sample was small and, therefore, the effects were modest, the results were encouraging. First, boys in the intervention learned the social skills of strategic account giving and assuming nonhostile peer intent in ambiguous situations. Second, they learned the academic motivation skills of intermediate risk taking, realistic goal setting, task focus, and attributions for failure to factors within their control. Third, intervention boys used these social and academic motivation skills in the laboratory maze task that simulated ambiguous provocation and provided opportunities for intermediate risk taking and realistic goal setting. Fourth, boys in the intervention were rated by their teachers as showing more cooperation and persistence than control group boys. They were also judged as having improved more in the social and academic domains on the basis of end-of-semester written comments by their teachers. To my knowledge, this is the first successful intervention with aggressive youths that blended social skills training with motivation skills training under one unifying theoretical framework.

As currently implemented, Best Foot Forward was a pilot intervention, so it could use some improvements. About 25% of the intervention boys did not complete all phases of the program; therefore, it is important to develop more effective and creative strategies for reducing participant attrition in an after-school program. The intervention included a number of incentives, such as a warm and supportive atmosphere, nutritious snacks at each session, small prizes (e.g., UCLA pencils, movie tickets) for regular attendance and good behavior, and the promise of a chance to win a larger prize (e.g., a CD player) for successful completion of the intervention. However, the program still faced the competition of other after-school activities, including free time for play. To help sustain children's commitment to the intervention, closer work with their parents may be needed.

Related to attrition, the intervention was not successful for all participating boys, but the sample was too small to investigate the heterogeneity of participants. With the conservative selection criteria, high-risk boys in this study were aggregated together in treatment groups. The social reinforcement that group members receive from each other for acting out and "talking trash" in discussions of risky behavior sometimes functions as a kind of deviancy training that results in increased problem behavior (Dishion, McCord, & Poulin, 1999). At times, the investigators were struck with how quickly the intervention boys' behavior could deteriorate when such deviancy training escalated. One solution is to have mixed intervention groups that include a balance of high- and low-risk boys.

Inclusion of a follow-up component also is a task for the future. The investigators do not know whether the intervention had any lasting effects beyond the end of the school semester after implementation. Finding out about the intervention's lasting effects is particularly important given the interest in the effect of the intervention on more general outcomes such as academic performance and attitudes about school. These outcomes may be part of more cumulative intervention effects that unfold gradually over time.

Finally, strategies for monitoring intervention fidelity need to be developed. In this situation, fidelity is how thoroughly and consistently the curriculum was carried out. Some lessons worked better than others, just as some outcomes proved more amenable to change. A system is needed for documenting both the extent to which teacher–trainers remained faithful to the intervention and the variations in implementation (e.g., number of activities and lessons taught).

## Implications for Intervention Design

School-based programs are a natural context for nurturing morality and improving social and motivation skills because children spend the bulk of their weekdays at school. Not surprisingly, school-based prevention programs have proliferated in the past two decades at an enormous rate and astronomical cost (Gottfredson, 2001). However, programs supported by these tax dollars remain largely unevaluated, and they are often created by professional curriculum developers rather than experts in the science of prevention and intervention research.

The Best Foot Forward intervention approach (including its strengths and limitations) can serve as a springboard for discussion about how school-based programs for nurturing morality can better conform to the guidelines of good intervention science. Several principles for the effective design and implementation of school-based interventions follow.

*First, interventions should be theory guided.* Unless an interventionist has a clear theory about what causes aggression, school disengagement, or other problem behaviors, it is difficult to avoid what has come to be called a "laundry list" approach (in other words, a curriculum that includes a little bit of everything and not much of anything specific to the targeted behavior). The Best Foot Forward intervention was informed by a particular theoretical perspective on the cognitions, emotions, and behaviors that are precursors to moral virtue, defined here as social competence and academic motivation. That perspective guided the choice of both curriculum activities and outcome measures. Thus, the investigators were able to systematically map specific behaviors targeted for change onto particular outcome measures. When the intervention "worked," the investigators achieved a good understanding of *why* it was successful.

*Second, interventions should have multiple components and multiple informants.* Findings in prevention science over the past decade reveal that the comprehensive intervention programs are the ones that are most successful in reducing antisocial behavior and promoting children's healthy development (Greenberg, 2001). The Best Foot Forward intervention focused on social skills and academic motivation as two important pathways to reducing aggression and improving school engagement. The intervention would have been less novel—and probably less effective—if it had concentrated on only one of these components. Furthermore, multiple sources of data from multiple informants are essential for rigorous evaluation. Relying solely on participants' self-reports is vulnerable to memory distortions, social desirability, and self-presentation concerns. Additionally, relying solely on teachers' reports is susceptible to the subtle biases or unconscious stereotypes that teachers may have about some of their students (particularly students with problem behaviors). And relying solely on archival data such as school grades or cumulative folders is constrained by the accuracy and completeness of school records, as well as the fact that achievement is determined by many factors outside of the range of most interventions (e.g., economic advantage, parental values).

*Third, interventions should build in a longitudinal component so that cumulative effects across critical periods of transition can be examined.* Many of the intervention boys would be entering the major transition to middle school within 6 months or 1 year after the treatment. Because at-risk children are particularly vulnerable to delinquency and school disengagement during the middle school transition, it is important to know whether the intervention served any protective or buffering function. Other successful interventions with children and adolescents have been guided by this transition (or milestone) approach. The underlying assumption is that transitions can result in negative outcomes if they are not successfully negotiated or mastered by those about to experience them. An intervention such as Best Foot Forward, which is aimed at aggression reduction and motivation enhancement for fourth and fifth grade at-risk youths, is ideal for testing this transition approach.

*Fourth, interventions need boosters.* Many successful interventions adhere to a public health model in which the goals are prevention, intervention, and control. Part of prevention involves immunization, as in the prevention of smallpox or polio, and booster shots at critical periods. As part of a longitudinal design, brief "doses" of Best Foot Forward (key lessons with new activities) should be implemented at regular intervals, especially during developmental transitions.

*Fifth, interventions need to be developmentally and culturally sensitive.* Children undergo major cognitive, emotional, social, and biological changes during their school years, and interventions targeted for particular age groups must be sensitive to these developmental shifts. The Best Foot Forward intervention drew on the investigators' expertise as former teachers to create materials that were matched to the cognitive and social maturity of children in middle elementary school. Furthermore, in urban areas, most school-based interventions that address problem behaviors are targeted for ethnic minority children, yet one rarely sees any discussion of the cultural relevance of curriculum materials to which participants are exposed. Cultures differ, for example, in their routines for greeting friends, methods of acknowledging gender and age divides, and a vast array of other strategies for social interaction. Again, the Best Foot Forward investigators made special efforts to develop stories and roleplay activities that reflected the life experience and cultural heritage of ethnic minority boys.

It is sometimes difficult to reconcile the costs of intervention research in relation to perceived benefits. In the case of Best Foot Forward, if we think about reducing the risk that intervention boys will become delinquent as adolescents, then projected savings in terms of the costs of incarcerating even one juvenile (about $35,000 a year) are substantial. Add to this the savings in terms of *human capital*—increased opportunities among at-risk youth for education, personal growth, responsible citizenship, and moral virtue—and then the potential benefits to society of effective school-based interventions are enormous. The time seems ripe for serious attempts to nurture morality in school settings.

# References

Ames, C. (1992). Classrooms: Goals, structures, and student motivation. *Journal of Educational Psychology, 84*, 261–271.

Bandura, A. (1997). *Self-efficacy: The exercise of control.* New York: W. H. Freeman & Company.

Coie, J., & Dodge, K. (1998). Aggression and antisocial behavior. In N. Eisenberg (Ed.), *Handbook of child psychology: Volume 3. Social, emotional, and personality development* (pp. 779–862). New York: John Wiley.

Dishion, T. J., McCord, J., & Poulin, F. (1999). When interventions harm: Peer groups and problem behavior. *American Psychologist, 54,* 755–764.

Dodge, K., Lochman, J., Harnish, J., Bates, J., & Pettit, G. (1997). Reactive and proactive aggression in school children and psychiatrically impaired chronically assaultive youth. *Journal of Abnormal Psychology, 106,* 37–51.

Flannery, D., Williams, L., & Vazonyi, A. (1999). Who are they with and what are they doing? Delinquent behavior, substance abuse, and early adolescents' after school time. *American Journal of Orthopsychiatry, 69,* 247–253.

Fordham, S., & Ogbu. J. (1986). Black students' school success: Coping with the burden of acting white. *Urban Review, 18,* 176–206.

Gottfredson, D. (2001). *Schools and delinquency.* New York: Cambridge University Press.

Graham, S. (1997). Using attribution theory to understand social and academic motivation in African American youth. *Educational Psychologist, 32,* 21–34.

Graham, S., & Halliday, C. (2000). A social cognitive (attributional) perspective on culpability in adolescent offenders. In T. Grisso & R. Schwartz (Eds.), *Youth on trial: A developmental perspective on juvenile justice* (pp. 345–369). Chicago: University of Chicago Press.

Graham, S., & Taylor, A. Z. (2001). Ethnicity, gender, and the development of achievement values. In A. Wigfield & J. Eccles (Eds.), *Development of achievement motivation* (pp. 123–147). New York: Academic Press.

Graham, S., Taylor, A. Z., & Hudley, C. (in press). *Best Foot Forward: A motivational intervention for aggressive youth.* Manuscript submitted for publication.

Graham, S., & Weiner, B. (1996). Theories and principles of motivation. In D. Berliner & R. Calfee (Eds.), *Handbook of Educational Psychology* (pp. 63–84). New York: Macmillan.

Greenberg, M. (2001). The prevention of mental disorders in school-aged children: Current state of the field. *Prevention & Treatment, 4,* 1–61.

Hudley, C., & Graham, S. (1993). An atrributional intervention to reduce peer-directed aggression among African American boys. *Child Development, 64,* 124–138.

Lochman, J., & Dodge, K. (1994). Social-cognitive processes of severely violent, moderately aggressive, and non aggressive boys. *Journal of Consulting and Clinical Psychology, 62,* 366–374.

Mickelson, R. (1990). The attitude-achievement paradox among black adolescents. *Sociology of Education, 63,* 44–61.

Nicholls, J. (1984). Achievement motivation: Conceptions of ability, subjective experience, task choice, and performance. *Psychological Review, 91,* 328–346.

Weiner, B. (1995). *Judgments of responsibility: A foundation for a theory of social conduct.* New York: Guilford Press.

# Chapter 3

# Selective Exercise of Moral Agency

## Albert Bandura

In a recent book titled *Everybody Does It!*, Gabor (1995) documents the pervasiveness of disengagement of moral self-sanctions from harmful conduct by people of all statuses in all walks of life. A full understanding of human morality must explain not only how people come to behave morally but also how they selectively disengage moral self-sanctions in the transactions of their everyday lives.

In the development of a moral self, individuals adopt standards of right and wrong that serve as guides and deterrents for conduct. In this self-regulatory process, people monitor their conduct and the conditions under which it occurs, judge it in relation to their moral standards and perceived circumstances, and regulate their actions by the consequences they apply to themselves. They do things that give them satisfaction and a sense of self-worth, and they refrain from behaving in ways that violate their moral standards because such conduct will bring self-condemnation. Thus, moral agency is exercised through the constraint of negative self-sanctions for conduct that violates one's moral standards and the support of positive self-sanctions for conduct faithful to personal moral standards. In the face of situational inducements to behave in inhumane ways, people can choose to behave otherwise by exerting self-influence. Self-sanctions keep conduct in line with internal standards. Moral conduct is motivated and regulated through the ongoing exercise of evaluative self-influence.

## Dual Nature of Moral Agency

The exercise of moral agency has dual aspects, *inhibitive* and *proactive* (Bandura, 1999). The inhibitive form is manifested in the power to refrain from behaving inhumanely, and the proactive form is expressed in the power to behave humanely. In the latter form of morality, people do good things as well as refrain from doing bad things. This chapter examines how an individual can shift rapidly from a moral disengager to a moral engager through the transformative power of humanization.

Social psychology emphasizes the power of environmental forces over individuals. In the case of proactive moral courage, individuals triumph as moral agents over compelling environmental pressures to behave otherwise. Such moral heroism is most tellingly documented in Holocaust rescuers who saved persecuted Jews from the death camps at great risks to themselves and their families with a heavy burden of extended protective care. The rescuers had no prior acquaintance with those they sheltered and had nothing material or social to gain by doing so. Such moral commitments involve courageous humanness amid overwhelming evil.

Humanization can rouse empathic sentiments and a strong sense of social obligation. This enlists self-evaluative reactions that motivate humane actions on others' behalf at sacrifice of one's self-interest or even at one's own peril (Oliner & Oliner, 1988). The rescuers viewed their behavior as a human duty rather than as extraordinary acts of heroism. After the protective relationship was established, the development of social bonds heightened the force of empathic concern and moral obligation.

Researchers extensively analyze the inhibitive form of morality. Adults are studied for their power to refrain from behaving injuriously under conditions highly conducive to inhumane conduct, and children are studied for the power to resist instigation to transgressive conduct. But the proactive form of morality, in which people behave humanely, often at personal costs, receives relatively little attention.

## Mechanisms of Moral Disengagement

The acquisition of moral standards is only half the story in the exercise of moral agency. Moral standards, whether characterized as conscience or moral principles, do not function as unceasing internal regulators of conduct. Self-regulatory mechanisms do not operate unless they are activated. Many psychosocial maneuvers can be used to disengage moral self-sanctions from inhumane conduct. Selective activation and disengagement of self-sanctions permits different types of conduct by persons

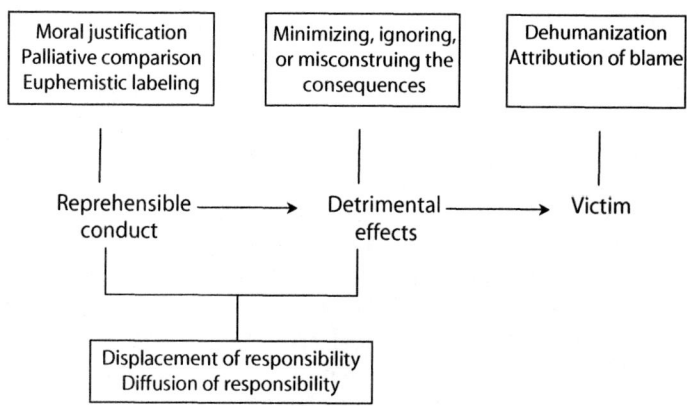

**Figure 3.1.** Mechanisms through which moral self-sanctions are selectively disengaged from detrimental conduct at different points in the self-regulatory process (Bandura, 1986).

with the same moral standards. Indeed, large-scale inhumanities are typically perpetrated by people who, in other areas of their lives, can be quite considerate and compassionate. They can even be ruthless and humane simultaneously toward different individuals. This selectivity of moral engagement is strikingly illustrated by Amon Goeth, a Nazi labor commandant. While dictating a letter replete with empathy and compassion for his ailing father, he sees a captive on the grounds who he thinks in not working hard enough. He takes out his revolver and callously shoots the captive. The commandant is both overcome with compassion and is savagely cruel at the same time.

Figure 3.1 shows the points in the process of moral control at which moral self-censure can be disengaged from reprehensible conduct. The disengagement may center on sanctifying harmful conduct by moral justification, exonerating social comparison, and sanitizing language. It may focus on obscuring personal agency by diffusion and displacement of responsibility so that perpetrators do not hold themselves accountable for the harm they cause. It may involve minimizing, distorting, or even disputing the harm that flows from detrimental actions. And the disengagement may include dehumanizing, demonizing, and blaming the victims of the maltreatment.

Selective engagement and disengagement of moral self-sanctions is central to a full understanding of moral conduct. The present analysis addresses this focal aspect of the moral self within the conceptual framework of social cognitive theory (Bandura, 1991). The sections that follow analyze how each of these types of moral disengagement function in the perpetration of inhumanities, how the mechanisms of moral disengagement operate developmentally, and how knowledge of the selective exercise of moral agency provides guides on nurturing morality.

## Moral Justification

One set of disengagement practices operates by changing the meaning of injurious behavior. People do not usually engage in harmful conduct until they have justified, to themselves, the morality of their actions. In this process of moral justification, worthy ends are used to sanctify pernicious means. People can then act on a moral imperative and preserve a favorable view of themselves as moral agents while inflicting harm on others.

Rapid radical shifts in destructive behavior through moral justification are most strikingly revealed in military pursuits. The conversion of socialized people into dedicated fighters is achieved not by altering their personality structures, aggressive drives, or moral standards. Rather, it is accomplished by cognitively redefining the morality of killing so that it can be done free from self-censure. Through moral justification of violent means, people see themselves as fighting ruthless oppressors, protecting their cherished values, preserving world peace, saving humanity from subjugation, or honoring their country's commitments. Moral justifications sanctify the violent means. Killing becomes an act of heroism. Voltaire put it well when he said, "Those who can make you believe absurdities, can make you commit atrocities."

Over the centuries, much destructive conduct has been perpetrated by ordinary, decent people in the name of righteous ideologies, religious principles, and nationalistic imperatives. The politicization of religion has produced a long bloody history of holy terror. Pope Urban (who launched the Crusades), Osama bin Laden (who mounted a jihad), Rabin's assassin, and the Presbyterian minister who shot a doctor and his assistant at an abortion clinic all saw themselves as serving a holy imperative. In holy terror, perpetrators twist theology and see themselves as courageously doing God's will. Adversaries sanctify their militant actions but condemn those of their antagonists as barbarity masquerading under a mask of outrageous moral reasoning. Each side feels morally superior to the other.

## Euphemistic Labeling

Language shapes thought patterns on which people base their behavior. Activities can take on different appearances, depending on what they are called. Euphemistic language is widely used to make harmful conduct respectable and to reduce personal responsibility for it. Euphemizing is an injurious weapon. People behave much more cruelly when assaultive actions are given sanitized labels than when they are called aggression.

Different varieties of language of nonresponsibility exist. One form relies on sanitizing language. Through the power of sanitized language, even killing a human being loses much of its repugnancy. Soldiers "waste" people rather than kill them. Bombing missions are described as "servicing the target," in the likeness of a public utility. The attacks become "clean, surgical strikes," arousing imagery of curative activities. The civilians the bombs kill are linguistically converted to "collateral damage."

Sanitizing euphemisms are also used extensively in unpleasant activities that people do from time to time. In the language of some government agencies, people are not fired; rather, they are given a "career alternative enhancement" as though they were receiving a promotion. Proposals are not rejected; they are "selected down." In the Watergate hearings, lies became "a different version of the facts." An "involuntary conversion of a 727" is a plain old airplane crash. The television industry produces and markets some of the most brutal forms of human cruelty under the sanitized labels of "action and adventure" programming. The nuclear power industry has created its own specialized set of euphemisms for the injurious effects of nuclear mishaps. An explosion is an "energetic disassembly," and a reactor accident is a "normal aberration."

The agentless passive voice serves as another self-exonerative tool. It creates the appearance that reprehensible acts are the work of nameless forces rather than people. It is as though people are moved mechanically but are not really the agents of their own acts. Even inanimate objects are sometimes turned into agents. Here is a driver explaining to police how he managed to demolish a telephone pole: "The telephone pole was approaching. I was attempting to swerve out of its way, when it struck my front end."

The specialized jargon of a legitimate enterprise is also misused to lend respectability to illegitimate enterprises. In the vocabulary of the Watergate transgressions, criminal conspiracy became a "game plan," and the conspirators were "team players," like the best of sportsmen. The conspirators elevated word corruption to new heights in the service of criminal conduct.

## Advantageous Comparison

How behavior is viewed is colored by what it is compared against. By exploiting the contrast principle, reprehensible acts can be made righteous. Terrorists see their behavior as acts of selfless martyrdom by comparing them with widespread cruelties inflicted on the people with whom they identify (Bandura, 2003). The more flagrant the contrasting inhumanities, the more likely it is that one's own destructive conduct will appear benevolent. Expedient historical comparison also serves self-exonerating purposes. Apologists for the lawlessness of political figures they support point to transgressions by rival administrations as vindications. Adapters of violent means for social change are quick to point out that democracies, such as those of France and the United States, were gained through violence against oppressive rule.

Exonerating comparison relies heavily on moral justification by utilitarian standards. The task of making violence morally acceptable from a utilitarian perspective is facilitated by two sets of judgments. First, nonviolent options are judged to be ineffective to achieve desired changes. This removes them from consideration. Second, utilitarian analyses affirm that injurious actions will prevent more human suffering than they cause.

The utilitarian calculus is quite slippery in specific applications, however. The future contains many uncertainties, and human judgment is subject to a lot of biases. As a result, calculations of long-term human costs and benefits are often suspect. There is much subjectivity in estimating the gravity of potential threats. Judgment of gravity justifies choice of aggressive options, but preference for aggressive options often biases judgment of gravity.

Sanctifying pernicious conduct through moral justifications, sanitizing language, and favorable comparisons is the most effective set of psychological mechanisms for disengaging moral self-sanctions. Investing harmful conduct with high moral purpose not only eliminates self-censure but also engages self-approval in the service of destructive exploits. What was once morally condemnable becomes a source of self-valuation. Functionaries work hard to become proficient in the destructive means and take pride in their accomplishments.

## Displacement of Responsibility

Moral control operates most strongly when people acknowledge that they are contributors to harmful outcomes. The second set of disengagement practices operates by obscuring or minimizing the agentive role in the harm one causes. People behave in ways they normally repudiate if a legitimate authority accepts responsibility for the effects of their injurious conduct (Milgram, 1974). Under displaced responsibility, they view their actions as stemming from the dictates of authorities rather than being personally responsible for them. Because they are not the actual agents of their actions, they are spared self-condemning reactions.

Self-exemption from gross inhumanities by displacement of responsibility is most gruesomely revealed in socially sanctioned mass executions. Nazi prison commandants and their staffs divested themselves of personal responsibility for their unprecedented inhumanities. They claimed they were simply carrying out orders.

In the sanctioning of pernicious conduct in contemporary life, responsibility is rarely assumed openly. Only obtuse authorities would leave themselves accusable of authorizing destructive acts. They usually invite and support harmful conduct in insidious ways by surreptitious sanctioning systems for personal and social protection. Sanctioning by indirection shields them from social condemnation in case things go awry. It also enables them to protect against loss of self-respect for authorizing human cruelty that leaves blood on their hands.

Authorities often act in ways that keep them intentionally uninformed. They do not search for evidence of wrongdoing. Obvious questions that would reveal incriminating information remain unasked, so that officials do not find out what they do not want to know. Implicit agreements and insulating social arrangements are created that leave the higher echelons free from blame.

When harmful practices are publicized, they are officially dismissed as merely isolated incidents arising from misunderstanding of what had been authorized. Efforts are made to limit any blame to subordinates, who are portrayed as misguided or overzealous. Investigators who look for incriminating records of authorization display naiveté about the insidious ways that pernicious practices are sanctioned and carried out. One finds arrangements of nonresponsibility rather than traces of smoking guns.

But obedient functionaries do not cast off all responsibility for their behavior as if they were mindless extensions of others. If they disowned all responsibility, they would be quite unreliable, performing their duties only when commanded to do so. It requires a strong sense of responsibility to be a good functionary. One must, therefore, distinguish between two levels of responsibility—a strong sense of duty to one's superiors and accountability for the effects of one's actions. The best functionaries are those who honor their obligations to authorities but feel no personal responsibility for the harm they cause.

## Diffusion of Responsibility

The exercise of moral control is also weakened when personal agency is obscured by diffusing responsibility for detrimental behavior. Kelman and Hamilton (1989) document the different ways that personal agency gets obscured by social diffusion of responsibility. Responsibility can be diffused by division of labor in which the subdivided tasks seem harmless in themselves. People shift their attention from the meaning of what they are doing to the details of their specific jobs.

Group decision making is another common practice that enables otherwise considerate people to behave inhumanely. Napoleon noted that "collective crimes incriminate no one." When everyone is responsible, no one really feels responsible. Collective action, which provides anonymity, is yet another expedient for weakening moral control. Any harm done by a group can always be attributed largely to the behavior of others. People act more cruelly under group responsibility than when they hold themselves personally accountable for their actions.

## Disregard or Distortion of Consequences

To be able to perpetrate inhumanities requires more than absolving personal responsibility. Other ways of weakening moral control operate by minimizing, disregarding, or even disputing the harmful effects of one's action. When people pursue activities that harm others, they avoid facing the harm they cause, or they minimize it. If minimization does not work, the evidence of harm can be discredited. As long as the harmful results of one's conduct are ignored, minimized, or disbelieved, there is little reason for self-censure to be activated.

It is easier to harm others when their suffering is not visible and when destructive actions are physically and temporally remote from their injurious effects. Death technologies have become highly lethal and depersonalized. We are now in the era of faceless electronic warfare, in which mass destruction is delivered remotely with deadly accuracy by computer- and laser-controlled systems.

When people can see and hear the suffering they cause, vicariously aroused distress and self-censure serve as self-restrainers. In studies of obedient aggression, people are less compliant to the injurious commands of authorities as the victims' pain becomes more evident and personalized. Even a high sense of personal responsibility for the effects of one's actions is a weak restrainer of injurious conduct when aggressors do not see the harm they inflict on their victims.

Most social systems involve hierarchical chains of command in which superiors formulate plans and intermediaries transmit them to functionaries, who then carry them out. The further removed individuals are from the destructive end results, the weaker the restraining power of injurious effects. Disengagement of moral control is easiest for the intermediaries in a hierarchical system—they neither bear responsibility for the decisions nor do they carry them out and face the harm being inflicted.

## Attribution of Blame

Blaming one's adversaries or circumstances is another expedient that serves self-exonerating purposes. People view themselves as faultless victims driven to injurious conduct by forcible provocation. Violent conduct becomes a justifiable defensive reaction to belligerent provocations. Victims get blamed for bringing suffering on themselves. Self-exoneration is also achievable by viewing one's harmful conduct as forced by compelling circumstances rather than as a personal decision. By fixing the blame on others or on compelling circumstances, not only are one's injurious actions excusable, but one can even feel self-righteous in the process.

Justified abuse can have more devastating human consequences than acknowledged cruelty. Mistreatment that is not clothed in righteousness makes the perpetrator rather than the victim blameworthy. But when victims are convincingly blamed for their plight, they may eventually come to believe the degrading characterizations of themselves. Exonerated inhumanity is, thus, more likely to instill self-contempt in victims than inhumanity that does not attempt to justify itself. Seeing victims suffer maltreatment for which they are held partially responsible leads observers to derogate them. The devaluation and indignation aroused by ascribed culpability provide further moral justification for even greater maltreatment.

## Dehumanization

The final set of disengagement practices operates on the recipients of detrimental acts. The strength of moral self-censure depends on how the perpetrators regard the people they mistreat. To perceive another as human activates empathetic reactions through a sense of common humanity. The joys and suffering of those with whom one identifies are more vicariously arousing than are those of strangers or those divested of human qualities. It is difficult to mistreat humanized persons without risking personal distress and self-condemnation.

Self-censure for cruel conduct can be disengaged or blunted by stripping people of human qualities. After they are dehumanized, they are no longer viewed as persons with feelings, hopes, and concerns but as subhuman objects. They are portrayed as mindless "savages," "gooks," and other despicable wretches. If dispossessing one's foes of humanness does not weaken self-censure, it can be eliminated by attributing demonic or bestial qualities to them. They become "satanic fiends," "degenerates," and other bestial creatures. It is easier to brutalize people when they are viewed as low animal forms. During wartime, nations often cast their enemies in the most dehumanized, demonic, and bestial images to make it easier to kill them.

In studies of the perniciousness of dehumanization, people who are given punitive power treat dehumanized individuals more ruthlessly than those who have been invested with human qualities. Combining diffused responsibility with dehumanization greatly escalates the level of punitiveness. By contrast, personalizing responsibility and humanizing others together has a powerful self-restraining effect.

The findings from research on moral disengagement are in accord with the historical chronicle of human atrocities: It requires conducive social conditions rather than monstrous people to produce atrocious deeds. Given appropriate social conditions, decent, ordinary people can do extraordinarily cruel things.

It should be noted that moral disengagement involves social machinations, not just personal, intrapsychic ones. In moral justification, for example, people may be misled by those they trust into believing that injurious means will prevent more harm than they cause. The perils and benefits that are socially declared may be exaggerated or simply pious rhetoric masking less honorable purposes. Cultural prejudices shape which human beings get grouped and dehumanized as well as the types of depraved attributes ascribed to them. Social systems are structured in ways that make it easy for functionaries to absolve themselves of responsibility for the effects of their actions. Media modes and content can be institutionally managed in ways that keep people uninformed or misinformed about the harm caused by the collective action. In short, moral disengagement is a product of the interplay of both personal and social maneuvers.

Many conditions of contemporary life are conducive to impersonalization and dehumanization. Bureaucratization, automation, urbanization, and high mobility lead people to relate to each other in anonymous, impersonal ways. Strangers can be more easily dehumanized than can acquaintances. In addition, social and political practices that divide people into ingroup and outgroup members create human estrangement that fosters dehumanization. Perpetrators group, divide, devalue, and dehumanize those they disfavor.

Conjoint experiences play a central role in creating not only empathetic responsiveness but counter-empathy as well (Bandura, 1992). Past congruent experiences in which a model's pleasure signals reward for oneself and a model's distress signals personal pain heighten observers' empathetic reactions to the model's emotional expression alone. Observers who have undergone discordant experiences (e.g., the model's joy brings suffering to oneself) respond indifferently or counter-empathetically to the model's joy and suffering. Vicarious activation relies heavily on a cognitive conveyance. Thus, when observers are merely led to expect cooperative interactions, the joy and distress of a cooperative model elicit corresponding reactions from observers. By contrast, displays of joy by an alleged competitive model distress observers, and displays of distress calm them.

Similarly, observers respond empathically to the emotional experiences of models simply depicted as in-group members and counterempathetically to those portrayed as outgroup members, in the absence of having shared any experiences with them. If a sense of mutuality has been created, so that the joys and distresses of an outgroup member foretell similar experiences for the observers, correlative outcomes transform disempathy to empathy. The findings of these experimental studies underscore the centrality of a sense of common humanity in human empathy.

Human transactions are increasingly conducted in the cyberworld. The electronic technologies that subserve these functions provide a ready vehicle for moral disengagement. Online behavior differs from face-to-face behavior. Anonymity and pseudonymity in interchanges in the cyberworld remove communication restraints and beget freer expressions of personal views. The cyberworld self is clearly less restrained. Concealment and depersonalization can bring out the worst in people by removing personal and social sanctions for pernicious conduct.

Certain characteristics of electronic technologies increase enlistment of the various forms of moral disengagement. Transgressive acts can be performed in privacy and anonymity toward depersonalized or faceless victims located thousands of miles away. Unlike breaking into offices to steal files, which is difficult to execute and escape detection, one can steal files electronically with little effort without apparent tracks, and the theft leaves the owner's property still in place. The moral disconnect makes it easy to behave transgressively.

The Internet is a highly decentralized system that defies regulation. Because anyone can get into the act and nobody is in charge, Internet users can use this unfettered vehicle for destructive purposes. Several unique features of electronic information technologies make them perilous if used for harmful purposes: They are readily accessible, portable, easily implementable remotely by pushbutton, connected worldwide for far-reaching consequence, and exceedingly difficult to control. Societal vulnerabilities are enormously magnified because virtually all of the systems on which people depend in their everyday lives are interdependently run by computer network systems. These can be easily knocked out, as shown by the computer student in the Philippines who wreaked havoc worldwide by crippling e-mail systems, costing billions of dollars. Smart hackers can do much more serious damage. Cybercrime and cyberterrorism, enacted through the Internet, is a dark side of the cyberworld that will increasingly command societal attention.

## Power of Humanization

Psychological research tends to emphasize how easy it is to bring out the worst in people through dehumanization and other self-exonerating means. The sensational negative findings receive the greatest attention. For example, Milgram's (1974) research on obedient aggression is widely cited as evidence that good people can be talked into performing cruel deeds. What is rarely noted, however, is the equally striking evidence that most people refuse to behave cruelly, even with strong authoritarian commands, toward humanized others, and when they have to inflict pain directly rather than remotely (Bandura, 1999).

The emphasis on obedient aggression is understandable considering the prevalence of people's inhumanities toward one another. But the power of humanization to counteract cruel conduct also has important social implications. The affirmation of common humanity can bring out the best in others. The paramount role of humanization in the nurturing of morality is analyzed later in this chapter in greater detail.

## Developmental Changes in Moral Disengagement

We are beginning to gain some understanding into children's development of moral disengagement and the processes through which it shapes their life courses. In studying moral disengagement developmentally, the various mechanisms are assessed in terms of the concrete forms they take in childhood. Thus, for example, children's moral justifications absolve fighting and lying as a social obligation to protect their friends and to preserve the respect of their peer group or family. In displacement of responsibility, children should not be blamed for transgressions if they were pressured by others or bad circumstances. In diffusion of responsibility, a given child should not be faulted for the trouble a group causes if decisions are made and carried out collectively. In minimization and distortion of consequences, physical provocation, lies, insults, and teasing among children do not really do any harm or are just ways of joking and showing interest in them. Advantageous comparisons absolve thefts, assaults, and property destruction through contrast with much worse offenses in the society at large. Maltreatments are sanitized euphemistically as simply providing "a lesson." In attribution of blame, victims bring maltreatment on themselves by their carelessness and untoward behavior. In dehumanization, some people must be treated roughly because they lack the usual sensitivities or deserve to be treated like animals.

Children learn at an early age how to disengage self-censure from transgressive conduct. Although the various disengagement mechanisms operate in concert in the self-regulatory process, they vary somewhat in the degree to which children enlist them. Construing injurious behavior as serving a worthy purpose, disowning responsibility for harmful effects by fixing the blame on others, and devaluing those who are maltreated are the most widely used modes of self-exoneration. Masquerading censurable activities in palliative language or rendering them benign by favorable comparison with worse conduct, both of which require dexterous cognitive skills, are used less often. Gender differences in moral disengagement do not exist in the earlier years, but before long, boys become more facile moral disengagers than do girls.

Moral development has typically been studied in terms of abstract principles of morality. Adolescents who differ in delinquent conduct do not differ in abstract moral values; almost everyone is virtuous in the abstract. However, the differences lie in the ease of moral disengagement under the conditionals of life. Facile moral disengagers display higher levels of violence than those who bring moral self-reactions to bear on their conduct. This is true regardless of age, gender, race, ethnicity, socioeconomic level, or religious affiliation.

Moral disengagement contributes to social discordance in ways likely to lead down dissocial paths. High moral disengagers experience low guilt over injurious conduct and are less prosocial. They dwell on vengeful rumination and are quick to resort to aggression and transgressive conduct.

## Promotion of Humaneness Through Moral Engagement

The preceding analyses document how disengagement of moral self-sanctions from conduct enables otherwise considerate people to do cruel things. The investment of common humanity at each locus of moral self-regulation tends to foster humaneness. In the exercise of proactive morality, people act in the name of humane principles when social circumstances dictate expedient, transgressive, and detrimental conduct. They disavow use of worthy social ends to justify destructive means, are willing to sacrifice their well-being rather than accede to unjust social practices, take personal responsibility for the consequences of their actions, remain sensitive to the suffering of others, and see human commonalities rather than distance themselves from others or divest others of human qualities.

The transformative power of humanization is graphically illustrated in the midst of a military massacre (Zganjar, 1998). An American platoon, led by Lt. William Calley, had massacred 500 Vietnamese women, children, and elderly men. Detailed analyses of this massacre have documented how moral self-sanctions were disengaged from the brutal collective conduct (Kelman & Hamilton, 1989). A ceremony, 30 years later, was held at the Vietnam Veteran's Memorial honoring the extraordinary heroism of prosocial morality. Hugh Thompson, a young helicopter pilot, had swooped down over the village of My Lai on a search-and-destroy mission as the massacre was occurring. He spotted an injured girl, marked the spot with a smoke signal, and radioed for help. Much to his horror, he saw a soldier flip her over and spray her with a round of fire. Upon seeing the human carnage in an irrigation ditch and soldiers firing into the bodies, he realized that he was in the midst of a massacre.

He was moved to moral action by the sight of a terrified woman with a baby in her arms and a frightened child clinging to her leg. He explained his sense of common humanity: "These people were looking at me for help and there is no way I could turn my back on them." He told a platoon officer to help him remove the remaining villagers. The officer replied, "The only help they'll get, is a hand grenade." Thompson moved his helicopter in the line of fire and commanded his gunner to fire on his approaching countrymen if they tried to harm the family. He radioed the accompanying gunships for help, and together they airlifted the remaining dozen villagers to safety. He flew back to the irrigation ditch, where they found and rescued a 2-year-old boy still clinging to his dead mother. Thompson described his empathetic human linkage: "I had a son at home about the same age."

The transforming effect of perceiving common humanity is further illustrated in a daughter's mission of vengeance (Blumenfeld, 2002). Her father, a New York rabbi, was shot and wounded in Jerusalem by Omar Khatib, a Palestinian militant. Twelve years later, the daughter set out to gain revenge by forcing Khatib to confront his victim's humanity. In the course of exchanging letters under a concealed identity with the jailed gunman, the parental victim, militant gunman, and filial avenger were humanized in the process. In a dramatic courtroom parole hearing, the daughter identified herself to Khatib as she pleaded for his release from prison, vowing he would never hurt anyone again. He wrote to her father, likening his daughter to "the mirror that made me see your face as a human person deserved to be admired and respected." In this case, hatred that breeds escalative cycles of violence instead turned into mutual compassion. At the national level, Nelson Mandela singularly displaced hatred of apartheid with reconciliation by affirming people's common humanity.

Research comparing the early familial management practices of adjudicated delinquents with those of prosocial adolescents in the same milieu sheds some light on the development of empathy and its role as a restrainer of aggression (Bandura & Walters, 1959). In their early socialization practices, parents of sons who adopted aggressive styles of behavior relied heavily on fear-based control. They sought to discourage their sons' aggressive conduct by emphasizing the external punishment it would bring upon them. In contrast, the parents of prosocial sons cultivated empathic-based control, portraying the consequences of aggressive conduct in terms of the injury and suffering it brings to others. In handling problems of misconduct, parental socialization practices that direct attention to the suffering inflicted on others foster development of empathic perspective taking and prosocial behavior (Bandura & Walters, 1959; Hoffman, 2001; Mussen & Eisenberg, 2001). A sense of empathic self-efficacy to involve oneself in the plight of others both promotes prosocialness in the form of helpfulness, sharing, consoling, and supportiveness and curbs socially injurious forms of conduct (Bandura, Caprara, Barbaranelli, Gerbino, & Pastorelli, 2003).

Moral disengagement nullifies behavioral control by self-sanctions. Morality can be nurtured by restoring humanity to conduct so that people live in accordance with their moral standards. McAlister and his colleagues fostered moral reengagement against resort to violent means by peer modeling of prosocial solutions to conflicts and exposure to communications that unmasked the various self-exonerative maneuvers (McAlister, 2001; McAlister, Ama, Barroso, Peters, & Kelder, 2000). Whereas moral engagement reduced support of violent means, boosting self-exonerative vindications raised endorsement of violent means.

## Interplay of Personal and Social Influences

The self-regulation of morality is not entirely an intrapsychic matter. People do not operate as autonomous moral agents, impervious to the social realities in which they are enmeshed. Morality is socially grounded. Social cognitive theory adopts an interactionist perspective to morality. In this view, moral actions are the product of the reciprocal interplay of cognitive, affective, and social influences.

After self-regulatory capabilities are developed, behavior usually produces two sets of consequences: self-evaluative reactions and external outcomes. These effects may operate as complementary or opposing influences on behavior (Bandura, 1986). Self-regulation of moral conduct creates the fewest strains when social influences are compatible with self-evaluative ones. This condition exists when socially rewardable conduct is a source of self-satisfaction and self-pride and socially punishable conduct brings self-censure. Behavior is also highly susceptible to external influences in the absence of countervailing internal standards. People with a weak commitment to personal standards tailor their behavior to fit whatever the situation seems to call for or is most expedient.

People commonly experience conflicts of outcomes when they are rewarded socially or materially for behavior they personally devalue. When self-devaluative consequences outweigh the force of external rewards, the rewards have little sway. There is no more devastating consequence than self-contempt. But if the allure of rewards outweighs self-censure, the result can be cheerless compliance. However, as already noted, people are skilled at reconciling perturbing disparities between personal standards and conduct by selectively disengaging their moral standards.

Another type of conflict of outcomes arises when individuals are punished for activities they value highly. Principled dissenters and nonconformists often find themselves in such predicaments. The relative strength of self-approval and external censure determine whether the courses of action will be pursued or abandoned. However, some individuals' sense of self-worth is so strongly invested in certain convictions that they submit to prolonged maltreatment rather than accede to what they regard as unjust or immoral. It is common for people to endure hardships for unyielding adherence to ideological and moral principles.

## Collective Moral Disengagement at the Social Systems Level

Selective moral disengagement operates at a social systems level, not just individually (Bandura, 1973; 1999). For example, it requires a lot of collective disengagement of moral concerns to operate a tobacco industry whose products kill about 450,000 people annually and requires continuous recruitment of youngsters to pick up the smoking habit. Those who trade in merchandising deadly wares depend heavily on the moral disengagement of a large network of otherwise considerate people. For years, the tobacco industry disputed the view that nicotine is addictive and that smoking is a major contributor to lung cancer.

The vast supporting cast contributing to the promotion of this deadly product includes talented chemists who discovered ammonia as a means to increase the nicotine "kick" by speeding the body's absorption of nicotine; inventive biotech researchers who genetically engineered a tobacco seed that doubles the addictive nicotine content of tobacco plants; creative advertisers who target young people with merchandising and advertising schemes depicting smoking as a sign of youthful hipness, modernity, freedom, and women's liberation; ingenious officials in a subsidiary of a major tobacco company who engage in an elaborate international cigarette smuggling operation to evade excise taxes; popular movie actors who agree to smoke in their movies for a hefty fee; legislators with bountiful tobacco campaign contributions who have exempted nicotine from drug legislation even though it is the most addictive substance and who have passed preemption laws that block states from regulating tobacco products and their advertising; U.S. trade representatives who have threatened sanctions against countries that erect barriers against the importation of U.S. cigarettes; and even a U.S. president who fired his head of the Department of Health, Education and Welfare for refusing to back off on the regulation of tobacco products.

The gun industry provides another example of moral disengagement in the business arena. With the shrinkage of rural populations, guns are used mainly by urban people to hunt people rather than deer. As sales for low-caliber guns stagnated, the gun industry shifted its production to weapons of increasing lethality (Diaz, 1999). The new generation of pistols is faster firing semiautomatic weapons with larger magazines to hold more bullets of higher caliber that magnify their killing power. To protect themselves against being outgunned, the police, in turn, are switching from revolvers to semiautomatic pistols using more lethal ammunition in a deadly escalation.

An executive of a shooting trade organization justifies the production change through advantageous comparison with normal business practices that trivialize the lethality of the product: "Just like the fashion industry, the firearms industry likes to encourage new products to get people to buy its products." Through social justification, he invests the more deadly weapons with worthy self-protective purposes: "If the gun has more stopping power, it is a more effective weapon." Another exonerative device absolves the gun industry of responsibility for the criminal use of the lethal semiautomatic pistols they design and market: "We design weapons, not for the bad guys, but for the good guys. If criminals happen to get their hands on a gun, it is not the manufacturer's fault. The problem is, you can't design a product and ensure who is going to get it." A lawsuit for negligent marketing and distribution practices won by New York City against gun manufacturers charged that they oversupply stores in Southern states with lax gun laws, knowing that the weapons will be bought and resold to juveniles and criminals in cities with tough gun laws.

The television industry markets some of the most brutal forms of human cruelty under the sanitized labels of "action and adventure" programming. Heavy exposure to televised violence has at least four different effects on viewers: It teaches aggressive styles of conduct; weakens restraints over aggressive behavior because the productions legitimize, glamorize, and trivialize human violence; desensitizes and habituates viewers to human cruelty; and shapes viewers' images of reality, making them more distrustful of others and more fearful of being victims of crime. Network memos presented at congressional hearings and interviews with media personnel document the heavy use of moral disengagement in the commercialization of violence (Baldwin & Lewis, 1972).

High moral purposes are assigned to the taking of human life, in the likeness of a national character-building service. "The government wants kids to think that there are values worth fighting for, and that's basically what the leads on our show are doing." "If people who break the society's code resist the law, we have to use violence to suppress them. In doing so, we are in the mainstream of American morality." Modeling violent solutions to problems allegedly builds character and affirms society's legal imperative.

Producers often excuse commercialization of violence by contrasting it with outrageous inhumanities, as though one form of human cruelty exonerates other forms. Why pick on television, the scapegoat disclaimer goes, when societies fight wars? "To examine violence where the end result is a dead body on television glosses over the point. This evades the culpability of a whole society that permits wars."

Another variant in the comparative exoneration is to sanctify brutalizing excesses on television by pointing to revered masterpieces containing some violent episodes. "There is violence in *Oedipus, Hamlet*, and it permeates the Bible." But gratuitous televised violence ain't Shakespeare. Here are some examples of television practices masquerading behind Hamlet's cloak: "I wish we could come up with a different device than running the man down with the car as we have done this now in three different shows. I like the idea of the sadism, but I hope we can come up with another approach for it." "Last week you killed three men; what are you going to do this week?" When the television programs are exported to other countries, much of the gratuitous violence is deleted. But we overdose our own children on it.

Producers of violent fare are quick to displace responsibility for violent events to other sources. "Television and motion pictures are fall guys for a sick society." "Are kids from unstable environments triggered by television violence? Their not having parents is a more serious problem." Producers disclaim using gratuitous violence by attributing evident excesses to the characters they create. Ruthless individuals, or even peaceful folks, confronted with mortal jeopardy demand acts of violence. One of the more candid scriptwriters discounted the asserted dramatic requirement for violence as analogous to saying, "I never put cotton in a wagon that's not prepared for cotton—but I never use anything but a cotton wagon."

Personal responsibility for gratuitous violence is also obscured by diffusing responsibilities for the product. Rewriters alter writers' scripts, directors fill in the details of the scenarios, and editors shape how the filmed events are depicted by what they select from the lengthy footage. Diffusion of the production process reduces a sense of personal responsibility for the final product.

Another way of escaping self-censure is to misrepresent, deny, or ignore harmful effects. Modeling violent solutions is purported to serve a public therapeutic function of draining viewers' aggressive drives (e.g., "Violence is a catharsis for kids." "Exposure to properly presented conflict that results in violence acts as a therapeutic release for anger and self-hatred"). The claimed catharsis effect has long been discredited empirically. Although producers tout the refuted therapeutic effects, they contend that adverse effects of televised violence can never be clearly demonstrated. "Nobody has been able to make a definitive statement about the effects of televised violence."

Viewers are divested of human sensitivities or invested with base qualities that justify serving them gory offerings (e.g., "Man's mind is connected to his stomach, his groin, and his fists. It doesn't float five feet above his body. Violence, therefore, cannot be eradicated." "Not as much action as some, but sufficient to keep the average bloodthirsty viewer fairly happy"). The prevalence of violent content is attributed to the aggressive nature and desire of its viewers.

In fact, there is no relationship between the level of program violence and the Nielson index of program popularity. Situational comedies and variety shows are the big draws. The answer to the prevalence of violent scenarios on TV lies in production costs and other structural factors, not in a human craving for cruelty.

Whenever a violent event occurs that stirs the public, the television networks run a predictable scenario: They assemble the cast of spokespersons for the major suspected sources of violence. The spokespersons promptly divert attention from their possible contributory influence by invoking and repudiating a single-cause theory of violent conduct that no one really propounds. They portray themselves as convenient scapegoats and shift the blame to other contributors. They proclaim that it is not the easy access to automatic weapons that is at fault, but lax enforcement of existing gun laws. It is not television or interactive media that promote assaultive styles of conduct, but detached or deficient parenting that is to blame. It is not parental failings, but a cultural moral decay spawned by secular humanists and an entertainment industry that glamorizes, trains, and rewards proficient assaultiveness.

These self-exonerative sermonettes also provide opportunities for political operatives and social advocates to lobby for their pet remedies—prayer in the schools, school vouchers, boosting self-esteem, and enlarging law enforcement and prison systems. Because no one is singularly at fault, they are all absolved of blame with diversionary damage control.

The television networks would do well to stop restaging the blame game. Instead, they should confront the various contributors to violence as to what they are willing to do in the enterprises they run to reduce violence in our society.

I have analyzed elsewhere the moral disengagement of international weapons merchants who merchandize deathly wares and the latest in terrorist technology (Bandura, 1999). The merchandising of terrorism is not accomplished by a few unsavory individuals. Rather, it requires a worldwide network of reputable, high-level members of society who contribute to the deathly enterprise by insulating fractionation of the operations and displacement and diffusion of responsibility. One group manufactures the tools of destruction. Others amass the arsenals for legitimate sale. Others operate storage centers for them. Others procure export and import licenses to move the deathly wares among different countries. Others obtain spurious end-user certificates that get the weaponry to embargoed nations through circuitous routes. And still others ship the lethal wares. Intermediaries and banks handle the money. The cogs in this worldwide network include weapons manufacturers; former government officials with political ties; ex-diplomatic, -military and -intelligence officers who provide valuable diplomatic skills and contacts; weapons merchants; and shippers and bankers operating legitimate businesses. By fragmenting and dispersing subfunctions of the enterprise, the various contributors see themselves as decent, legitimate practitioners of their trades rather than as parties to deathly operations.

Edmund Burke's aphorism that "the only thing necessary for the triumph of evil is for good men to do nothing," needs a companion adage: The triumph of evil requires a lot of good people doing a bit of it in a morally disengaged way with indifference to the human suffering they collectively cause. Given the many psychological devices for disengaging moral self-sanctions, societies cannot rely solely on individuals, however righteous their standards. Humane life requires, in addition to ethical personal standards, effective safeguards built into social systems that uphold compassionate behavior and curb human cruelty. Regardless of whether inhumane practices are executed institutionally, organizationally, or individually, it should be made difficult for people to remove humanity from their conduct.

## References

Baldwin, T. F., & Lewis, C. (1972). Violence in television: The industry looks at itself. In G. A. Comstock & E. A. Rubinstein (Eds.), *Television and social behavior: Vol. 1. Media content and control* (pp. 290–373). Washington, D.C.: U.S. Government Printing Office.

Bandura, A. (1973). *Aggression: A social learning analysis*. Englewood Cliffs, NJ: Prentice Hall.

Bandura, A. (1986). *Social foundations of thought and action*. Englewood Cliffs, NJ: Prentice Hall.

Bandura, A. (1991). Social cognitive theory of moral thought and action. In W. M. Kurtines & J. L. Gewirtz (Eds.), *Handbook of moral behavior and development: Vol. 1. Theory, research and applications* (Vol. 1, pp. 45–103). Hillsdale, NJ: Erlbaum.

Bandura, A. (1992). Social cognitive theory of social referencing. In S. Feinman (Ed.), *Social referencing and the social construction of reality in infancy* (pp. 175–208). New York: Plenum.

Bandura, A. (1999). Moral disengagement in the perpetration of inhumanities. *Personality and Social Psychology Review* [Special Issue on Evil and Violence], 3, 193–209.

Bandura, A. (2003). The role of mechanisms of selective moral disengagement in terrorism and counter terrorism. In F. M. Mogahaddam & A. J. Marsella (Eds.), *understanding terrorism* (pp. 121–150). Washington, D. C.: American Psychological Association.

Bandura, A., Caprara, G. V., Barbaranelli, C., Gerbino, M. G., & Pastorelli, C. (2003). Impact of affective self-regulatory efficacy on diverse spheres of functioning. *Child Development, 74*, 269–782.

Bandura, A., & Walters, R. H., (1959). *Adolescent aggression*. New York: Ronald Press.

Blumenfeld, L. (2002). *Revenge: A story of hope*. New York: Simon & Schuster.

Diaz, T. (1999). *Making a killing: The business of guns in America*. New York: New Press.

Gabor, T. (1995). *Everybody does it!: Crime by the public*. Toronto: University of Toronto Press.

Hoffman, M. L. (2001). Toward a comprehensive empathy-based theory of prosocial moral development. In A. C. Bohart & D. J. Stipek (Eds.), *Constructive & destructive behavior* (pp. 61–86). Washington, D.C.: American Psychological Association.

Kelman, H. C., & Hamilton, V. L. (1989). *Crimes of obedience: Toward a social psychology of authority and responsibility*. New Haven, CT: Yale University Press.

McAlister, A. (2001). Moral disengagement: Measurement and modification. *Journal of Peace Research, 38*, 87–99.

McAlister, A., Ama, E., Barroso, C., Peters, R., & Kelder, S. (2000). Promoting tolerance and moral engagement through peer modeling. *Cultural Diversity and Ethnic Minority Psychology, 6*, 363–373.

Milgram S. (1974). *Obedience to authority: An experimental view*. New York: Harper & Row.

Mussen, P., & Eisenberg, N. (2001). Prosocial development in context. In A. C. Bohart & D. J. Stipek (Eds.), *Constructive & destructive behavior* (pp. 103–126). Washington, D.C.: American Psychological Association.

Oliner, S. P., & Oliner, P. M. (1988). *The altruistic personality*. New York: Free Press.

Zganjar, L. (1998, March 5). Forgotten hero of Mai Lai to be honored after 30 years. *San Francisco Chronicle*, p. A9.

# Impediments to Moral Functioning

If caring is to be accurate, our understanding of persons must be rich. If caring is to be genuine, we must understand ourselves more deeply. Intervention should aim at social intelligence and the nurture of moral selves-in-relationship. Adult partnerships and healthy peer relationships can foster positive changes.

*—Karl H. Hennig*

Stereotypes, prejudice, and discrimination all serve to undermine the moral functioning of our meritocracy because individual efforts are often overshadowed by inaccurate perceptions and unfair expectations. In our effort to stay true to the ideals of our system, it is of paramount importance that we work to overcome the obstacles that group-based biases impose.

*—Jennifer Steele, Y. Susan Choi, and Nalini Ambady*

Conflict and morals have the potential to be constructive or destructive; are based on particularly situated perceptions that may not be shared by others; and offer opportunities to rethink the status quo of relationships, groups, and institutions.

*—Susan Opotow*

# Chapter 4

# Care Gone Awry
## *The Role of Attachment and Reflective Functioning*

## Karl H. Hennig

From the purview of his book *Humanity: A Moral History*, Jonathan Glover (2000) sees the twentieth century as the most brutal in human history. Consider the Holocaust, Hiroshima, the Stalinist era, Cambodia, Yugoslavia, and Rwanda. These were parts of ideological wars that appealed to an array of hopes and fears, prejudices and envy, even hatred. Glover's contribution to ethical discussion is in portraying these as wars whose main appeal was to a kind of morality. Many wars are fundamentally about ideas regarding how to establish a better world. Hitler appealed to social Darwinism, and Stalin appealed to socialism to justify their utopian social projects. Lenin spoke of breaking eggs to make an omelet, in which the omelet represents the utopian vision and the eggs the millions who died as the necessary means to its realization. Moral enthusiasm goes awry for reasons that moral principles, which tend to oversimplification, are often difficult to apply to complex personal and political situations.

Similar to Glover's approach, my approach to questions of morality has both a negative and a positive thrust. Glover's *negative* (or critical) move is to remind readers of humanity's inhumanity and invite a critical evaluation of the role that abstract "moral" ideals have played in some of the most immoral of human atrocities. Whereas Glover offers instance upon historical instance of *sociopolitical* ideals that have gone awry, this chapter's negative move is to illustrate instances in which *personal* ideals can be seen to go awry. Problems particularly arise when "moral" standards are excessively punitive, are vague and perfectionistic, or are rigidly enjoined irrespective of contexts and persons. The moral ideals of benevolence and care are used in this chapter to illustrate morality gone awry.

Glover's *positive* move is to support the importance of two human resources believed capable of counteracting this propensity to inhumanity: (1) the caring emotions (e.g., empathy, sympathy, and respect) and (2) moral identity, in which one sorts oneself out as to the kind of person one has become and values becoming. This chapter's positive move similarly highlights the authentic role of care within a contextually and psychologically sensitive model of character development.

Following Aristotle, I define morality with respect to concrete situations: doing the right thing, at the right time, toward the right people, for the right ends, in the right way, and with the right motives. Morality is also concerned with a correct fit between a motivated choice of action and particular people within concrete situations. Similar to Glover's (2000) positive thrust, evidence for the importance of the caring emotions and interpersonal understanding is presented, largely from within the paradigm of parent–child attachment. Attachment theory may also be highly informative in distinguishing genuine care from "care gone awry." Evidence from my own research is examined to highlight this important distinction. Two interlocking propositions will be discussed: (1) *if caring is to be accurate, our understanding of persons must be rich* and (2) *if caring is to be genuine, we must understand ourselves more deeply.* Nurturing our understanding of ourselves and others relies less on the explicit education of moral principles or behavioral traits than it does the quality of day-by-day interactions that make up parent–child and teacher–child relationships.

## Giving and Receiving Help

Aristotle's context-sensitive definition of acting rightly directs us away from any simple definition of what makes a moral action praiseworthy or a moral situation complex. It is informative to consider the contrast between moral exemplarity and character disorders in this regard. Whereas moral exemplarity is marked by situational sensitivity and behavioral flexibility, abnormality involves a rigid reliance upon a constricted range of interpersonal behaviors irrespective of situational determinants or norms. Moral development involves a progressive and mutually informative relationship between one's current moral and interpersonal understanding and the idiosyncratic features of each concrete situation.

Accurately interpreting a situation and determining the right action may be difficult, requiring some anticipation of the recipient's response. What is intended as a helpful suggestion on the part of one person may be perceived by another person as a punitive communication of mistrust and criticism. Consider an example witnessed at a fitness facility wherein a young man offered some unsolicited advice to a woman on how to correctly use a piece of exercise equipment. This situation may have seemed like a harmless enough moment to give some objectively needed advice, but the woman's response was immediate, furious, and highly invective. She asked the young man whether he was an employee of the exercise facility and, without waiting for a reply, clearly and humiliatingly made it understood to him—and everyone else within earshot—that she was capable of seeking her own assistance.

Toward nurturing the development of a rich understanding of persons within situations, I use the notion of "reflective functioning." Reflective functioning is a developmental process that permits individuals to respond not only to people's outward behavior but also to their understanding of the other's beliefs, feelings, hopes, wishes, plans, and so forth. Reflective functioning makes possible our capacity to "read" other's minds (as well as our own because we are often opaque to ourselves) and to understand what other people need, why they did what they did, what situational constraints pertain, and so forth. Reflective functioning is a developmental a process that culminates in practical wisdom and is regarded here as an integral component of moral identity. The failure of reflective functioning in individuals is revealed in a body of literature that highlights the many factors donors frequently *fail* to understand when offering aid. Although recipients may be genuinely appreciative and evaluate the donor positively, recipients may also spurn offers of assistance.

Research on people's reactions to receiving aid has been undertaken primarily from four theoretical perspectives: equity theory, reactance theory, attribution theories, and threat-to-self-esteem models. Each one highlights a particular facet of the caring or helping situation, along with corresponding ways in which caring can go awry (for a review, see Fisher, Nadler, & Whitcher-Alagna, 1982). The goal of presenting these perspectives is to highlight a few of the complexities and interpersonal dynamics that pertain to caring situations, thereby advocating the need for developing a reflective understanding of persons and situations.

## Equity Theories

Most people do not long forebear receiving less from others than what they think they deserve. A relationship is in trouble when one of its members perceives him- or herself to be doing the majority of the work or enjoying the least of its benefits. Equity theories assume that people aspire to maintain equitable or fair relationships with one another and that equity's opposite, inequality, gives rise to discomfort, motivating individuals to reduce the imbalance. The demands of individuals for their rights and fair share are only half of the equation. Research shows that people also experience distress in receiving "more than they deserve." The explanation partly comes from the burden of inequity and feelings of indebtedness that arise within imbalanced situations; people do not want to be overly "beholden" of others.

In situations in which recipients have no opportunity to reciprocate and thus restore equity, people refrain from asking for assistance or are slower to do so. Similarly, when opportunity has not been present to repay a past donor, less future help is sought. Social interactions in which opportunities for reciprocity are absent contradict deeply held norms because they can lower the self-esteem of the recipients of care. Efforts to redress the balance of equity may involve attempts at reciprocity as well as changes in the recipient's perception of the donor. When assistance is not acknowledged or welcome, donors can feel unappreciated. Similarly, when donors are overbearing, recipients may be justified in their rejection of care. Several studies have confirmed that in situations in which repayment is not possible, recipients may redefine the aid rendered as the donor's "rightful obligation." From an early age, children insist on their own capability. For example, a child may say, "I wanna do it mine self" in response to an adult who is trying to help tie the child's shoes.

Even less favorably, recipients may blame donors for creating a situation of inequity that leaves them experiencing discomfort. Actions undertaken on behalf of others who perceive themselves as capable are frequently experienced as self-threatening. Recipients typically report feeling dependent, indebted, weak, and incapable as persons.

## Reactance Theory

Reactance theory concerns the motivational importance of personal freedom and the perception of threat associated with anything that would constrain that freedom. When restrictions of freedom are perceived as unreasonable, motivational attention becomes focused on removing the restriction. The ambivalence of parents to alert their children to the dangers in sticking anything in electrical wall outlets tacitly reflects this understanding. Limits may evoke a desire that was not present before the warning. Placing limits may evoke an emergent desire and incite subsequent parent–child conflict.

These findings have implications for the manner in which parents and teachers establish limits. Too much intervention and overcontrol can increase rather than alleviate problems. For example, when recipients are not included in decisions about how intervention aid programs (either national or community programs) are to be run, the programs are less actively implemented, and reciprocity is withheld. As was the case with assisting disabled veterans, when the recipients' goals and freedoms of choice were not amply considered, programs went unimplemented, donors were perceived as incompetent, and aid was resented (Ladieu, Hanfman, & Dembo, 1947).

## Attribution Theories

Attribution theories focus on the understanding recipients make of the helping situation, including the attributions or meanings they make of donors' intentions, themselves, and the situation. An individual's understanding of a helping situation includes at least two questions: "Why did the donor help me?" and "Why did I need help?" To the first question, offers of aid that are perceived as well intentioned are better received than are those that are accompanied by ulterior or malevolent motives. In situations that involve strangers, readily available stereotypes may figure strongly in determining the motivations of the donor. For example, an offer of assistance from a sloppily dressed teenager may evoke suspiciousness. Situations in which assistance is prescribed by a role may not guarantee altruistic motives, but they likely allay concern over a donor's possible malevolent intentions. In the example of unsolicited advice offered to a woman at a fitness center, the young man's failure to conform to his role as a patron was relevant to her perception of the situation. She charged him with not being an employee. Perhaps she would have been more receptive if the advice had come from one of the hired fitness trainers.

The second question (i.e., "Why did I need help?") identifies another potential source of self-threat. When task difficulty is emphasized, offers of assistance are perceived as less of a threat to self-competence (e.g., "It's not that I'm incapable; it's that the task is difficult. Most people would welcome assistance"). On the other hand, an offer of assistance may be construed as a comment on the recipient's (self-perceived) lack of competence (e.g., "Did he think I wasn't sufficiently competent to do this simple task?"). In situations that emphasize the recipient's inadequacy, support seeking decreases and offers of help frequently evoke negative feelings toward both the self and the helper. A study of bereavement, for example, found that survivors' acceptance of professional aid was more likely when the situation was defined as calling for "uncustomary" sources of social support (Gerber, 1969). In general, individuals' reactions are likely to be affected by their perceptions of the donors' motives and the degree to which offers of assistance reflect poorly on their competence. When individuals associate offers of assistance with their self-concept, numerous perceptions are possible, only some of which are readily identifiable.

## Threat to Self-esteem Model

Although attribution theories are concerned with competence that may threaten self-esteem, the model fails to give the self and the maintenance of self-worth a central place. The threat to self-esteem model states explicitly that self-related concerns are central in determining the recipient's response. Situations in which assistance is offered contain a mixture of self-threatening and supportive elements. Accepting the submissive or inferior role is at odds with the developmental drive for mastery, particularly with Western cultural norms that emphasize independence and autonomy. Even a 2-year-old child may flatly refuse assistance. Situations that emphasize differential status or ability or that place the helper in a superior position evoke greater threat to self-esteem.

Even apparently minor details of a situation such as donor–recipient similarity can predict rejection of assistance and negative evaluation of the donor—a likely artifact of the human tendency to compare oneself with others. Assistance from someone who is similar evokes feelings of failure that do not emerge when assistance is obtained from a dissimilar donor. For example, female welfare recipients interviewed by someone of similar ethnic and socioeconomic background report greater distress about being on welfare. The logic of this reaction might be something like: "She's no different from me, and she's not on welfare. What's wrong with me?" Individuals with low self-regard are particularly sensitive to differential status and comparative success, attributing offers of assistance to their perceived incompetence rather than to the difficulty of the task.

## Summary

These four theoretical areas of research illustrate how care can be perceived by recipients as either predominantly threatening or supportive. When assistance threatens a recipient's self-esteem, it is accompanied by personal discomfort, burdens of reciprocity (i.e., inability to return the favor), constraints on freedom and personal control, negative self-evaluations, negative evaluations of the donor, and a refusal of aid. In contrast, when aid is perceived as supportive, it is accompanied by positive affect, a focus on task difficulty rather than the recipient's incompetence, freedom of choice, opportunity for reciprocity, positive evaluations of the donor, and gratitude.

Offers of care can seriously miss the mark when individuals, owing to limited reflective functioning, are unable to recognize relevant personal and situational factors. Failure to recognize specific dynamics of the donor–recipient relationship has undermined many well-intentioned offers of international aid, peer tutoring, counseling, legal aid, and health care advice. Within psychological clinical practice, for example, offering advice and too much assistance escalates levels of anxiety for both therapists and clients; robs clients of learning opportunities; and communicates to clients that they cannot resolve problems on their own, thereby confirming the clients' negative self-views. Beginning therapists who find themselves working too hard for their clients typically have difficulty with their own (often unrecognized) anxieties and insecurities. Similarly, parents and teachers may experience anxiety in response to their children's struggles and do too much for them. Struggle and disequilibrium are central to growth. An Aristotelian-based morality (i.e., doing the right thing, at the right time, toward the right people, for the right ends, in the right way, and with the right motives) requires that our understanding of persons must be rich, but it also suggests the importance of gaining sufficient clarity of one's own motives, and of whom one has become and values becoming. This is what was referred to above as "sorting oneself out" or of clarifying one's moral identity. A rich understanding of others is predicated upon a rich self-understanding, and vice versa. The ancient Greek aphorism to "know thyself" remains as an important moral imperative.

## Caregiving–Attachment Complementarity

The underlying resemblance that present relationships have with our earliest experiences of care within the parent–infant attachment bond complicates the caregiving–receiving dynamic, particularly within close relationships. For example, when people are offered solace or assistance, they may experience the offer as being made to feel like a child, the way their parents made them feel. More frequently, these connections are less explicit, even unconscious.

Within an attachment framework, an ethic of care can be viewed as a complementary relationship between support seeking and caregiving. Within early formative attachment experiences, internal models of sensitive caring and receiving care first form, likely directing information about and strategies for providing care to others. To understand the implications of self-knowledge in care and how care can go awry without such

knowledge, attachment theory can be recast as a guiding paradigm of
moral identity. After describing the central assumptions of how support
seeking and caregiving complement one another, this chapter outlines two
faces of care gone awry.

## Attachment Theory as a Guiding Moral Paradigm

Observations of infants across numerous studies have confirmed that
when children suffer insecurity within the early parent–child relationship,
the situational flexibility in range of expression and interpersonal behavior
becomes rigidly constrained. One style of interpersonal behavior comes to
dominate, and others are suppressed. In very young children, the human
attachment (or support-seeking) system aims at reducing the risk of harm
to the self by maintaining proximity to the primary caregiver (or caregivers). The complementary caregiving system aims at protecting infants
through sensitivity to their needs (i.e., through empathy) and by motivating responsiveness (i.e., sympathy). Grasping, smiling, crying, and gazing
into the caregiver's eyes are all innate signaling behaviors intended to enlist comfort from a recognized attachment figure. By age 6 weeks, infants
can recognize their mothers' smell and voice. By about age 6 months, infants begin displaying separation anxiety, signaling distress when the adult
upon whom they depend leaves.

The signaling behaviors of infants are ideally complemented by the
sensitive and comforting responses of parents, jointly forming the attachment relationship. In contrast to earlier views of parenting in which maternal responsiveness was assumed to produce dependency, the experience
of "felt security" within a responsive relationship is now viewed as providing infants with a "home base" from which to explore the environment.
Attachment *security* is associated with caregivers who respond promptly,
consistently, and appropriately to infants' distress signals. In contrast, the
mothers of *insecure* infants tend to dislike closeness or use the infant to
comfort their own distress; are awkward in handling their babies; behave
in a "routine" manner; and can be bitter, resentful, and rejecting. Such patterns may be elicited by ambiguous behaviors on the part of the infant or
by the mother's inability to perceive the needs of her children.

Distinct forms of insecure attachment can been identified and used
to infer "internal working models" used by infants to organize their experiences of themselves in relationship. Infants determine whether their
caregivers can be expected to be loving and, as a consequence, whether
they themselves are worth loving. These internal models not only direct
interpersonal behaviors but have also been linked to different styles of

emotion regulation. Secure attachment patterns facilitate greater positive affect, persistence in problem solving, and the capacity for ego resiliency and flexible responding in later years. Securely attached children are able to regulate negative emotions and impulses more effectively than insecurely attached children.

Insecurely attached infants encounter difficulty in consistently obtaining comfort from caregivers, which leads to protest behaviors, anxiety, anger, and sometimes sadness. Two primary patterns of insecure attachment have been identified from observations of parent–child interactions. The first pattern of insecure attachment arises when caregivers are intermittently caring. Infants cope by becoming hypervigilant and clingy, or *anxiously attached*, reacting with strong protests to any signs of abandonment. Anxiously attached individuals view themselves as unlovable and derive their sense of worth through significant others who are idealized. A second pattern of insecure attachment arises when caregivers are consistently unavailable or rejecting. The attachment system copes by deactivating itself in an effort suppress displays of anger or distress. Rather than defining themselves as unloved and unlovable, *avoidant* infants come to minimize the importance of relationships. They show little distress during separations with their caregivers, but when avoidant infants are monitored physiologically (e.g., heart rate, skin conductance), they actually show greater distress than highly anxious infants (Kobak & Sceery, 1988).

Anxious and avoidant attachment strategies used by infants to adapt to the family environment are only partially successful. Anxiously attached infants often become impulsive and dependent later in life and may become easily overwhelmed with their own emotions when witnessing another's distress. They have hyperactivated attachment systems, reacting more to their own distress than to the distress of others. Avoidant infants often develop problems with hostility in relationships and demonstrate little empathy when witnessing the distress of others (Kestenbaum, Farber, & Sroufe, 1989). Insofar as empathy involves "feeling with" another, avoidant children have strategically detached themselves from others and cut themselves off from their own emotions and self-understanding (Kestenbaum et al., 1989).

A rapidly growing catalog of longitudinal studies extending from infancy to the school years has supported the relative stability of these attachment patterns. Stability of attachment also extends across generations: anxiously attached parents frequently raise anxious children, and avoidant parents frequently produce avoidant infants. Unlike the behavioral indices that are used to classify infant attachment (e.g., proximity seeking, distress at separation, reaction at reunion), working models of adult attachment are assessed using a semi-clinical interview. Adults are asked to discuss attachment-relevant themes, including current and past relationships with parents, incidents of attachment separation, how these relationships have changed over time, and how they may have influenced current functioning. Adult attachment style is also visible within the interactions that emerge between interviewers and interviewees.

When *secure* infants are free to access the full range of their affective and behavioral responses, they grow up to be secure adults who value attachments and relationships, view them as formative, and are able to be objective in their recollections of past events. Having become integrated into a coherent self-understanding, secure adults are capable of freely exploring the negative and positive aspects of past events. Anxious adults typically have access to childhood memories but have difficulty organizing them into a coherent narrative. An extreme example is evident from a young woman in an abusive relationship who stated with some pride, after reporting parental abuse earlier, "My father made me who I am today." One is struck with the incoherence of such a remark. Anxious individuals appear "confused" about negative aspects of their experiences with their parents and continue to make great efforts to gain parental acceptance. These efforts to gain the approval of significant others are primarily associated with "care gone awry." Avoidant infants, who have cut themselves off from attachment-relevant information, grow up to be avoidant adults who have difficulty in recalling attachment-relevant information and discount the relevance of early experiences to present functioning. Specific experiences that are recalled tend to be negative, if not rejecting. Yet on a more general level, avoidant adults report positive relationships with their parents, even idealizing them.

Although secure adults possess a coherent narrative understanding of themselves, they have also been shown to possess greater nuance in their understanding of other people, including their own children. Sensitive and responsive parents engage their infants in a way that ascribes to them complex mental states and attributes. These adults view an infant's crying not merely as a behavior; the crying becomes meaningfully attributed to the infant's desires and intentions such as "wanting to come and see mama," or "feeling uncomfortable in a wet diaper." Wanting, feeling, and intending something that infants cannot carry out or be consciously aware of ascribes to infants a complex theory of mind. In treating infants as richly complex and aware beings, sensitive parents contribute to their infants' self-understanding and cognitive development. Through interaction with sensitive caregivers, children are able to find an image of themselves as a reflective functioning agents who act upon their own feelings, beliefs, and intentions.

The role of biological vulnerabilities should also be noted. Oppositional, hyperactive, and attention-deficit children, for example, provoke
situations of conflict, affecting the parent–child attachment relationship.
At the level of reflective functioning, children frequently do not know the
reasons for their misbehavior and operate on distorted understandings of
situations in which they find themselves. Responses from other children
that are otherwise benign may be viewed as malevolent (e.g., "He hit me
on purpose, so I whacked him back!"). Similarly, parental requests for an
explanation (e.g., "Why did you do that?") are all too frequently met with
the child's response, "I don't know." Parents (or teachers) who avoid a difficult child and angrily react to a child's adverse behavior are unable to
aid the child in rendering his or her behavior intelligible. Behavior made
intelligible can be submitted to high levels of cognitive control. The aim of
parental as well as educational intervention is to make the unintelligible intelligible. Sensitive parents who view a child's behavior as meaningful will
seek out explanations of the child's pattern of misbehavior and, through
appropriately timed discussions, communicate this back to the child. This
requires a sensitive parent (or teacher) capable of accurate reflective functioning. When children find no confirmation of their intentionality, including intentions lacking conscious awareness, they tend to lack a sense of
personal responsibility and moral agency, and they blame their problems
on others. Children who have suffered maltreatment do not lack language
skills per se; rather, they lack the language to represent their internal states
and rely on concrete context-bound representations (Beeghly & Cicchetti,
1994). These findings highlight the moral importance of and relationships
between reflective functioning and emotionally grasping what is relevant
within interpersonal situations.

An attachment model may not articulate the full breadth of the moral
domain, but secure attachment forms an important foundation. Particularly among the 40% of the population expressing insecure internal models
of attachment, moral development and the formation of a moral identity
may first require some sorting out of whom one has come to be before
determining whom one values becoming.

## The Two Faces of "Care Gone Awry"

Clinical observations have long noted the frequency with which an
individual's dominant style of relating becomes incorporated into an ideal
self. Karen Horney (1945) observed the tendency of individuals to ideal-
ize rigid modes of interpersonal relating. These findings closely resemble
attachment observations; her findings revealed that people either move

away, move toward, or move against others. Individuals whose style is to move away from others (i.e., avoidant) frequently overvalue their rugged independence, their ability to "go it alone," and their clarity of thought in the absence of perturbating emotions. Individuals whose adaptive strategy is to move toward others (i.e., anxiously preoccupied with relationships) form a self-ideal as being kind, caring, and self-sacrificing. Later social adjustments and gender roles can exacerbate these problems by associating female moral goodness with caring and self-sacrifice and male moral goodness with independence (for a review, see Cross & Madson, 1997). In both instances, what is defended as the perceived moral good life is a rigid and narrow distortion, a once adaptive strategy held over from childhood that now constrains fuller human functioning. What makes intervention difficult is that these constricted modes of relating are regarded as "egosyntonic" or consistent with how individuals prefer to view themselves.

From early shaming and neglectful environments, some children learn the adaptive advantage of turning off their caring emotions. Conversely, individuals who express traits of what otherwise might appear as benevolence and care may actually be expressing overly anxious forms of attachment. They become preoccupied with needing the approval of others, doubting their capacity as decision makers, silencing themselves, and becoming hyperresponsible for others while being underresponsible for themselves. Their *"caring" is neither accurate nor authentic* in that care fails to meet the needs of the situation.

In a series of studies, I have been seeking to integrate the findings of several independent investigators related to these two faces of care gone awry (Hennig & Walker, 2003). Existing research programs share the belief that *intrusiveness in caring* and *excessive other focus* are problematic for both benefactors and recipients. Results of these investigations indicate a clustering of questionnaire items into two groups, an *anxious concern* cluster and a *self-sacrificial care* cluster. The term "concern" rather than "care" to identify the first cluster is intended to throw ambiguity upon whether the object of concern is the distress of others or one's own distress. Not only have researchers been studying relatively similar forms of care gone awry, they have also glossed over a potentially meaningful distinction between two distinct "faces" of the problem. A sample item from the anxious concern cluster reads: "I keep silent if I think my opinions might create conflict." A sample item from the self-sacrificial cluster reads, "If I am not highly caring, I feel like a bad person."

*Anxious concern* is associated with timidity, self-doubt, fear of negative evaluation, and avoidance of social situations that involve challenge and authority over others. Anxious concern is particularly associated with a "false-self" orientation: Anxiously concerned adults report that if others accept them first, then they can accept themselves. For these individuals, concern and care are less motivated by a focus on the welfare of others than on the need to gain others' approval.

*Self-sacrificial care* is associated with an avoidance of interpersonal conflict and excessive feelings of obligation. Problems in saying no to other people can leave such individuals vulnerable to coercive sexual behavior and related problems with self-exploitation. Self-sacrificial care comes closer to genuine care than does anxious concern in that the former is moderately associated with the capacity to provide emotional support and empathy.

The long-term outcomes of these behaviors are often low self-regard, neuroticism, eating disorders, and depression. In another example, a mother, one of my clients, was doing everything she could to keep a fragmenting family situation together. When all her children were asleep, she retreated to the shower, where she could safely cry and give expression to her feelings of sorrow. She was lost in a labyrinth without any indication of who she was. High doses of antidepressants merely enabled her to continue in this self-defeating pattern. She spoke of love for her children but was entirely perplexed when asked if she could include herself on her list of people who need care. This form of caring is self-destructive, but there are also other reasons for thinking that she was missing the ethical import of her actions.

In another study (Hennig & Walker, in press), participants were asked to write two personal narratives. In the first, participants were instructed to "write a story about a time when a friend (or partner) went to someone *other than yourself* to get and receive assistance or care." In the second narrative, participants were asked to " write a story about a time when a friend (or partner) either ignored or refused your help or care." After completing each exercise, participants indicated the extent to which the reported incident made them feel distressed, upset, sad, irritable, and so forth. Levels of both anxious concern and self-sacrificial care predicted negative affect states and distress. The external focus and reliance on others for feelings of self-regard leaves these individuals very vulnerable to any signs of rejection in their role as caregivers. This vulnerability is particularly common for individuals who are preoccupied with self-sacrificial care; they are less upset that the other person sought and hopefully attained help than they worry about whether recipients come to *them* for help. Clinical observation shows that when recipients succeed on their own, donors who are anxious or self-sacrificing frequently feel resentment. These individuals require that recipients remain needy and are distraught when they assume or resume independence. In this study, women were significantly more likely than men to experience distress when they perceived themselves to be rejected as caregivers. Men, less stereotypically identified with the caregiving role, did not report distress when their friends went to someone else for assistance.

Our findings are consistent with other investigators. Individuals who report high levels of *ingratiation*, to use a recognized clinical term encompassing both anxious concern and self-sacrificial care, focus on others at the expense of self-regard (Helgeson & Fritz, 1998). Ingratiation is associated with low self-disclosure, low self-assertion, discomfort in receiving support, and a desire that others take their advice. These individuals' sense of themselves rests upon the judgments of others. Concerned with others, individuals high in ingratiation are reluctant to disclose their own problems. The avoidance of self-disclosure appears to arise from a concern over burdening others with their own emotional problems and anxiety over revealing personal vulnerabilities. Focus on others can also be a way of protecting oneself. The pattern of overintrusiveness in others' problems combined with little social support seeking leaves these individuals at risk for a variety of mental and health problems. The pattern of martyrdom accompanied by (or intermittent with) hostility is one that has received much investigation in the depression literature.

A common sense view of caring suggests that offers of aid and caring should be motivationally accompanied by empathy and sympathy, a *feeling with* the distressed followed by a desire to relieve the other's distress. Similar findings associated with anxious attachment seem to support the notion that individuals who report high levels of ingratiation are motivated not so much to relieve the distress of the others but to relieve their own distress. After hearing a research confederate discuss problems she was having with a boyfriend, individuals high in ingratiation reported greater levels of personal distress than did those who reported either low ingratiation or high levels of empathy. In more recent research (Hennig & Walker, in press), both faces of ingratiation (i.e., anxious concern and self-sacrificial care) have been associated with insecure attachment. Ingratiators report greater attachment anxiety and difficulties associated with their close relationships.

## Conclusions

A recent surge of interest in Aristotle's ethics and character education seems to take for granted that Aristotle and people in the twenty-first century share the same world. Some assume that, with Aristotle, we can optimistically take character education to involve the simple laying down of "correct" behavioral "habits" without considering (a) early parent–child attachment relationships, which inform our foundational and largely unconscious templates of giving and receiving care; (b) children's socioeconomic contexts (Aristotle presumes a patrician background); and (c) the complexities involved in correcting the effects of early relational damage.

Incorporating an attachment framework, this chapter has emphasized the formative and complementary relationship between the early parent–child relationship and later competencies in caregiving. Several implications emerge from the adoption of this framework. Insofar as a renewed focus on moral education is seen as a means of addressing disruptive or antisocial behavior in youths, an attachment framework suggests that intervention should focus on the foundations of human interactions by providing reparative relationships and fostering a healthy moral identity. In attachment terms, interventions should seek to move individuals from *insecure* attachments to *secure achieved* attachments. Change is always possible and is typically prompted when individuals experience themselves in new relationships. Creating healthy adult partnerships signals one such positive avenue for change; finding a special relationship with a teacher is another. When moral education is overly focused on rules and behavior with little consideration given to the (often unconscious) motivational and interpersonal components underlying behavior, problems may be exacerbated rather than alleviated. Just as the misuse of moral principles can be used to justify a range of paternalistic war atrocities, "niceness" can be its own self-destructive trap. The perversion of moral standards and ideas that takes place on a sociopolitical level has its counterpart on the interpersonal level; both may appeal to the use of moral systems to justify actions that might not otherwise be justifiable. An absence of reflective functioning constrains individuals to dehumanize others and view them as mere physical entities, social role members, or anonymous faces in a group. Reflective functioning is also needed to increase our awareness of automatic tendencies to perceive others not as they are, but as we incorrectly perceive them to be; perceptions based often on past experiences in personal relationships.

Glover (2000) listens attentively to the narrative of history in the same way that good parents, teachers, clergy members, and clinicians listen. They look with an insightful eye to the complexity and depth of what it is to be human, including the shadowy, less conscious regions. Character building is something wise caregivers do smoothly and automatically in the quality of their talk about emotions, in discussions precipitated by sibling and peer conflict or daily events, and in how they resolve their own disputes. Character building occurs in fleeting moments, perhaps just before going to bed at night, when children spontaneously express something that is troubling.

An analogy from clinical practice may be instructive. Several decades of psychotherapy research has concluded the same results: The precise content or type of therapeutic intervention does not predict outcome. It does not matter whether someone is a therapist from this school of thinking or that, or practices this type of intervention or that. A client's improvement is typically related to the quality of the relationship between the therapist and the client, or what is referred to as the "therapeutic alliance." Although not wishing to dilute the importance of sociopolitical reflections on the question of "How can we get along globally?" nurturing moral identity and the question of "How shall I live?" may best be served by reflecting again on the prototype of nurturance, the parent–child relationship.

# References

Beeghly, M., & Cicchetti, D. (1994). Child maltreatment, attachment, and the self system: Emergence of an internal state lexicon in toddlers at high social risk. *Development and Psychopathology, 6*, 5–30.

Cross, S. E., and Madson, L. (1997). Models of the self: Self-construal theory and gender. *Psychological Bulletin, 122*, 5–37.

Fisher, J. D., Nadler, A., & Whitcher-Alagna, S. (1982). Recipient reactions to aid. *Psychological Bulletin, 91*, 27–34.

Gerber, I. (1969). Bereavement and the acceptance of professional service. *Community Mental Health Journal, 5*, 487–495.

Glover, J. (2000). *Humanity: A moral history of the twentieth century.* New Haven, CT: Yale University Press.

Helgeson, V. S., & Fritz, H. L. (1998). Relation of agency and communion to well-being: Evidence and potential explanations. *Psychological Bulletin, 116*, 412–428.

Hennig, K. H., & Walker, L. J. (2003). *Mapping the care domain: Structural and substantive analyses.* Manuscript submitted for publication.

Horney, K. (1945). *Our inner conflicts.* New York: Norton.

Kestenbaum, R., Farber, E. A., & Sroufe, L. A. (1989). Individual differences in empathy among preschoolers: Relation to attachment history. *New Directions for Child Development, 44*, 51–64.

Kobak, R., & Sceery, A. (1988). Attachment in late adolescence: Working models, affect regulation and perception of self and others. *Child Development, 59*, 135–146.

Ladieu, G., Hanfman, E., & Dembo, T. (1947). Studies in adjustment to visible injuries: Evaluation of help by the injured. *Journal of Abnormal and Social Psychology, 42*, 169–192.

# Chapter 5

# Stereotyping, Prejudice, and Discrimination

## The Effect of Group-based Expectations on Moral Functioning

Jennifer Steele, Y. Susan Choi, and Nalini Ambady

American citizens are extremely fortunate to live in a democracy, and more specifically, a society that upholds egalitarian and meritocratic ideals. Americans have fought wars and faced internal struggles in order to establish this system and champion these values. Within the past two centuries, this nation has abolished slavery, given women the right to vote, and desegregated schools. In more recent years, the movement toward equal opportunity has been advanced even further; public and private schools have increased financial support for economically disadvantaged scholars, and affirmative action programs have been developed as yet another means of combating inequities. It would seem that as a society, the United States is moving toward the moral ideal of equality for one and all.

Yet disparities remain. Race continues to be inextricably linked to socioeconomic status and education level, with certain racial and ethnic groups such as White and Asian Americans reaping more societal advantages on average than others, including African Americans and Latinos. Women remain underrepresented in many prestigious and lucrative fields, such as engineering and business, despite seemingly equal access to opportunity. Additionally, a significant wage gap continues to exist between such historically disadvantaged groups and more privileged groups, even when controlling for differences in education and experience. Although this country is moving in the right direction, it is clear that the nation still has far to go to fulfill its moral ideals.

Perhaps not surprisingly, stereotypes, prejudice, and discrimination play an important role in maintaining these inequalities. This chapter outlines how stereotypes can impede people's better intentions and lead to inaccurate assumptions, perceptions, and judgments. It examines how and when children develop prejudice and the different forms that prejudice can take later in life. The chapter also touches on discrimination faced by women and minorities in schools and in the workplace and concludes with suggestions for how stereotypes, prejudice, and discrimination might be overcome.

The terms *stereotypes, prejudice,* and *discrimination* are generally used by social psychologists to refer to cognitive, affective, and behavioral biases, respectively. *Stereotypes* can be defined as an overgeneralized belief about a group of people, such as "African Americans are athletic" or "Asian Americans are smart." Stereotypes can be negative, positive, or fairly neutral statements about members of social category groups such as gender, race, or age.

*Prejudice*, on the other hand, is the expression or experience of a negative attitude or feeling toward another person or group based on a group-based characteristic. For example, statements such as: "I hate Jews" or "Homosexuals disgust me" are expressions of prejudice. Similar to stereotypes, prejudice can develop at a very early age, especially for children who are surrounded by friends and family members who express such negative beliefs.

Finally, *discrimination*, the behavioral component of bias, occurs when a person acts differently toward a person of a given group based on stereotypes or prejudice. Discrimination generally results in the denial of opportunities or resources to members of stigmatized groups. For example, choosing to promote a less qualified man over a woman would be a blatant instance of discrimination. However, discrimination often takes a more subtle form.

Stereotypes, prejudice, and discrimination can all serve to undermine the moral functioning of our meritocracy when individual efforts are often overshadowed by inaccurate perceptions and unfair expectations. In our effort to stay true to the ideals of our system, it is of paramount importance that we work to overcome the obstacles that group-based biases impose.

## Stereotypes

Stereotypes, or overgeneralized beliefs about the people in our social world, begin to form at a very early age. Many of children's first stereotypes are based on gender because gender is one of the first dimensions along which children are able to categorize the people they encounter. Between about ages 3 to 6 years, children are not only able to identify culturally based gender stereotypes, but they also endorse them quite readily. This is one particularly important aspect of children's early development of stereotypes: Unlike adults, who often view stereotypes as more *descriptive* of society, very young children view stereotypes as socially *prescriptive*. Essentially, preschool-aged children often believe that stereotypes explain not just the way the world *is* but also the way the world *should be*. And children use their stereotype knowledge to help dictate how they should behave. Accordingly, children generally show a preference for stereotypically gender-appropriate toys by 3 years of age and express a preference for stereotypically gender-consistent occupations by 5 years of age (Golombok & Fivush, 1994).

Slightly later in early childhood, children begin to categorize and form generalized beliefs based on race or ethnicity. Several different studies have shown that by the time they are 5 years old, most White American children attribute more positive characteristics to members of their own racial group and more negative characteristics to African Americans. Unfortunately, research has also shown that children's early awareness of racial stereotypes makes them susceptible to the same memory and inferential biases that adults encounter.

Although stereotypes were initially believed to reflect faulty mental processing, social psychologists have recently argued that stereotypes are actually necessary and quite normal for cognitive functioning. Stereotypes have come to be conceptualized as cognitive schemata that automatically provide us with expectations about new people and situations we encounter. The automatic nature of stereotyping has been revealed by work that has shown that simply reminding people of the category label "Black" can lead to quicker associations with words that describe commonly held stereotypes of Blacks.

Therefore, stereotypes can be seen as readily accessible associations between traits and a category group that have been built up over time through experience and exposure to culture. These associations can serve as "shortcuts" that help people to quickly know what to expect and how to act in a constantly changing world. When meeting an unfamiliar person, generalized beliefs based on the person's appearance, clothing, gender, ethnicity, and age can help ensure that the interaction runs smoothly. For example, if the person is elderly, it might be appropriate to speak more loudly, or if the person is from a foreign country, it might make sense to speak more slowly. The decision to act differently toward these individuals often occurs automatically and may be based entirely on stereotypes such as "elderly people are hard of hearing" or "foreigners have trouble understanding English".

Yet when applying group-based beliefs in interactions with individuals, we are bound to make mistakes: *All* elderly people do not have trouble hearing, and *all* foreigners do not have difficulty understanding English. Nevertheless, these heuristics often serve to guide our behaviors and sometimes lead us to make errors in judgment that are costly for individuals we encounter. For example, several studies have demonstrated how stereotypes can affect people's perceptions of others, their memories of events, and even their interpretations of ambiguous actions. In an often-cited study from the 1940s, one study participant was shown a picture of a well-dressed Black man on a subway train in conversation with a White man who was holding a razor blade (Allport & Postman, 1947). This participant was asked to describe the picture to another participant, who was then asked to describe it to another, and so on. Only the first participant had actually seen the picture. The researchers were interested in seeing whether the description would get distorted in line with societal stereotypes through this "broken telephone" type of game. By the time the description reached the sixth participant, the story had often changed in such a way that the razor was in the Black man's hand, consistent with the negative stereotype that depicts Black men as aggressive. This is one example of the ways that stereotypes can subtly—but powerfully—affect people's memories in a way that distorts reality and supports false beliefs.

In a more recent study, White American participants saw two men (one Black and one White) engaged in a disagreement that concluded with one person shoving the other (Duncan, 1976). Findings revealed that the shove was later described as more violent when the perpetrator was Black than when he was White. A conceptual replication of this study with children found similar effects (Sagar & Schofield, 1980). White sixth graders were presented with four stories depicting ambiguously violent acts. The picture accompanying each story presented the perpetrator of the ambiguous act as being either an African American or a White child. Consistent with societal stereotypes and with the previous findings with adults, children rated the acts as being more mean and threatening when an African American child performed them than when they were performed by a White child. This is not to say that the distortion of memories or the misinterpretation of behaviors will always occur; however, an important step in combating the effects of stereotypes is to identify these potential biases.

Even White American children have demonstrated memory biases consistent with stereotypes about African Americans. In one study, 4- to 9-year-old White American children who had little exposure to African Americans were presented with a series of stories that depicted both an African American and a White American child (Bigler & Liben, 1993). In some of the stories, either the White American (counterstereotypic) or the African American (stereotypic) child behaved in a manner consistent with negative stereotypes about African Americans. The goal of this study was to determine whether children's memories would be distorted in such a way that they would remember the counterstereotypic stories in a stereotypic manner.

When children were later questioned about which character behaved poorly, they often distorted their memories, believing that it was the African American who behaved in a negatively stereotypic manner even when it was actually the White American child who had behaved in that way. Thus, these children changed their memories of the story to fit their stereotypes.

## Stereotypes as Self-fulfilling Prophecies

Given the research described, it is perhaps not surprising that stereotypes can also serve as self-fulfilling prophecies. A self-fulfilling prophecy is said to occur when "an initially erroneous social belief leads to its own fulfillment" (Jussim & Fleming, 1996, p. 161). In one classic study, Rosenthal and Jacobson (1968) demonstrated just how these types of self-fulfilling prophecies could occur. After testing children in a variety of classes at the start of the school year, teachers were informed that a handful of students in their classes were "late bloomers." That is, the academic performance of these students was expected to improve dramatically throughout the year. Sure enough, when these "late bloomers" were tested at the end of the school year, their performance had improved more dramatically than that of other students, just as the researchers had predicted. It seemed as though the researchers had an accurate test to predict "late bloomers"—or did they? In reality, these "late bloomers" had not been identified based on test scores; instead, they had been randomly chosen. By identifying these students as having potential, the researchers induced positive expectations in the teachers; in the end, the students met these expectations. In short, the fact that these students had actually bloomed simply reflected a self-fulfilling prophecy.

Similar effects have been found in more controlled experimental settings (Word, Zanna, & Cooper, 1974). In one study, researchers asked White participants to interview one White and one Black high school student who had been trained to act comparably as job applicants. The researchers found that White participants were much more nonverbally negative toward the Black applicant than the White applicant despite the fact that the students had been trained to respond and behave comparably. Specifically, White interviewers sat farther away, had more speech errors, and spent less time with Black interviewees than with White ones. This demonstrated the interviewers' biases, but could this lead to a self-fulfilling prophecy?

This question was addressed in a second study in which interviewers were trained to nonverbally behave toward interviewees either as the White or Black applicant had previously been treated. Only White applicants were interviewed, and they were either treated more positively (as the White applicant had been) or more negatively (as the Black applicant had been). Consistent with self-fulfilling prophecies, participants treated more coldly subsequently interviewed more poorly. This helps to explain how stereotypes can allow White candidates to appear more qualified than Black candidates during job interviews—through the operation of self-fulfilling prophecies.

Researchers have since demonstrated that stereotypes based on gender, race, socioeconomic status, and even physical attractiveness can induce intrapersonal expectations in much the same way. For example, researchers have found that Korean immigrants in Japan, who are negatively stereotyped by the Japanese, score significantly lower on tests of intelligence than Korean immigrants in the United States, who are positively academically stereotyped as Asian Americans (Bruner, 1996). Such a finding could reflect a self-fulfilling prophecy or it could be the result of a process termed *stereotype threat*.

## Stereotype Threat

As already discussed, with self-fulfilling prophecies, perceivers treat targets differently based on a group-based expectation, which can lead targets to confirm the stereotype. Stereotype threat, on the other hand, can occur entirely in the mind of the target. Stereotype threat is the "sense that one can then be judged or treated in terms of the stereotype, or that one might do something that would inadvertently confirm it" (Steele, Spencer, & Aronson, 2002).

Studies of stereotype threat have demonstrated how these overgeneralized beliefs can directly affect the academic performance of members of negatively stereotyped groups (Steele & Aronson, 1995). For example, in one study, Black and White American students at a prestigious university took a challenging verbal test that was described as either being diagnostic or nondiagnostic of ability. It was hypothesized that describing the test as diagnostic of ability would make the negative stereotype about African Americans' intellectual abilities salient, which would lead to decreased performance by the African American students. Sure enough, African Americans in the diagnostic condition performed worse than White students (after controlling for differences in SAT scores), but those in the nondiagnostic group did not.

Similar results were found for women taking a challenging math test (Spencer, Steele, & Quinn, 1999). When the test was described as showing gender differences, women underperformed on the test relative to men. However, when the test was described as showing no gender differences, women no longer feared that their performance would reflect on their gender group, so they performed just as well as men did. Such stereotype threat results have been replicated with a host of other stereotyped group members, including Latinos, individuals with low socioeconomic status, and even elderly individuals.

Positive stereotypes have similarly been shown to enhance performance under certain conditions. In one study, Asian American women were asked to fill out a brief questionnaire before taking a challenging math test (Shih, Pittinsky, & Ambady, 1999). Some women filled out a questionnaire that reminded them of their Asian identity, which is positively stereotyped for mathematics, but other women filled out a questionnaire reminding them of their negatively stereotyped gender identity. Consistent with societal stereotypes, women reminded of their Asian identity performed the best on the math test, and women reminded of their female identity performed the worst relative to a control condition. In a follow-up study conducted with children, similar findings emerged (Ambady, Shih, Kim, & Pittinsky, 2001). For the younger Asian American girls aged 5 to 7 years, as well as for the older girls aged 11 to 13 years, performance on age-appropriate math tests was similarly influenced by their condition. Specifically, children reminded of their Asian identity before completing the test performed the best on the math test, and children reminded of their female identity performed the worst relative to a control condition.

Although these findings might seem to suggest that positive stereotypes can be a good thing, the evidence for this is still unclear. Asian Americans have been referred to as the "model minority" because many of the stereotypes they encounter, including being studious, hard working, musically gifted, and scientific, are very positive. Yet some research suggests that Asian Americans may experience undue stress in trying to live up to these stereotypes.

In sum, it is clear that stereotypes can influence the way group members are perceived, remembered, and treated. In addition, stereotypes can lead to depressed academic performance through self-fulfilling prophecies and stereotype threat. Although stereotyping is not an inevitable or necessarily malicious process, it is important to recognize that knowledge of societal stereotypes can lead to a distortion of reality, creating a moral issue that needs to be addressed. Perhaps not surprisingly, through similar yet often more conscious processes, prejudice can also result in negative outcomes for members of stigmatized groups.

## Prejudice

Unlike stereotypes, prejudice tends to be driven by emotion. Prejudice is often described as a negative feeling or attitude toward members of an outgroup. Although stereotypes might inadvertently distort people's memory and perceptions of others, prejudice can lead to the dehumanization of others, to intergroup hostility and violence, and sometimes even to mass murder and group destruction. One need only think of the millions of Jews murdered in the Holocaust; the recent genocide of Tutsis by the Hutus in Rwanda; the continuing conflict between Israelis and Palestinians; or even the terrorist attacks of September 11, 2001, to appreciate the horror that intergroup hatred can cause.

Prejudice within the United States has not taken such epic proportions in recent years, yet stories about homosexuals, Blacks, and Hispanics being beaten or murdered because of their group membership continue to emerge. For example, in 1998, Matthew Shepard, a University of Wyoming student, was brutally beaten and left to die in freezing temperatures simply because he was gay. And how can we forget the image of several White Los Angeles police officers severely beating African American Rodney King in an act that appeared to be racially charged? These are both examples of the acts of violence that are directed toward members of minority groups because of prejudice and hate. When do these attitudes form, and how do they develop over the years?

Children first show signs of prejudice at a very early age (Aboud, 1988). Children's prejudice levels are often quite high around 5 years of age and usually decrease or show greater flexibility as children grow older. Some studies suggest, however, that the prejudice displayed in early childhood returns as children reach the preteen years and beyond, particularly if prejudice is more noticeable in children's immediate social environment. For example, children's ethnic attitudes have been shown to be significantly related to the ethnic attitudes of their mothers, with more prejudiced mothers having more prejudiced children. Early studies have also found evidence that parents high in authoritarianism—which is characterized by greater rigidity, coldness, and intolerance for difference—had more prejudiced children. Although the exact causes of children's prejudice development are not currently known, recent research with adults suggests that children's expressions of prejudice usually shift to take on a more socially acceptable form as they grow older.

## Current Forms of Prejudice

Some 50 years ago, outward expressions of racial prejudice were much more acceptable than they are today. The expression of prejudice, particularly in urban settings, has changed to fit the times. With the growth of "political correctness" and the spread of egalitarian values, many people have become much more hesitant about expressing negative attitudes about members of different groups. Unfortunately, growing evidence suggests that some people's true attitudes and behaviors toward stereotyped others do not always match the less prejudiced views that they espouse. That is, when given the opportunity, some people are still capable of being prejudiced.

A great deal of this evidence comes from research on what has been called *aversive racism* (Dovidio & Gaertner, 1986). Aversive racism is found among a subset of White Americans who strongly endorse egalitarian values and who see themselves as nonprejudiced. Unlike those truly low in prejudice, aversive racists harbor negative attitudes toward Blacks, sometimes without even being fully aware of these beliefs. This negativity manifests itself as discrimination against Blacks in situations in which it is possible to attribute negative reactions to nonracial factors. For example, when asked to help individuals portrayed as being somewhat undeserving of help, aversive racists were less likely to help Black, compared with White, targets (Frey & Gaertner, 1986). In this case, the appropriateness of helping was unclear, and the failure to help could be attributed to the undeserving nature of the victim and, therefore, not race.

The results of numerous studies have demonstrated how seemingly well-intentioned individuals reveal their prejudices when it is clear that they will be able to avoid being accused of bigotry. Such findings are disturbing for many reasons, not the least of which is the suggestion that strongly endorsing egalitarian views outwardly is not enough to combat discrimination. In many ways, this form of racism is even more difficult to eliminate because it is often hidden to outside observers, as well as to aversive racists themselves. Nevertheless, it is important to be aware of this more subtle form of prejudice to begin to recognize and fight it through education and policy interventions.

A somewhat different kind of prejudice has been demonstrated by research that focuses on *modern racism*. In contrast to "old-fashioned" racists who readily endorse prejudiced beliefs, modern racists, similar to aversive racists, agree that racism is immoral. However, unlike aversive racists, they endorse the belief that discrimination against Blacks no longer exists because they believe that Blacks now have the opportunity to attain any success they are motivated to achieve. Modern racists further believe that African Americans push themselves too much into domains where they are not wanted and get more attention as a group than they deserve. Although these beliefs may sound racist to some, modern racists believe that these statements reflect a reality rather than prejudice. However, individuals who endorse such attitudes display their racism in other ways, such as voting against Black mayoral candidates who are running against White candidates and expressing opposition to busing designed to desegregate schools.

Recognizing that self-report measures of prejudice do not always reflect actual attitudes, researchers have taken to using more subtle measures of prejudice, such as nonverbal behavior and social distance. For example, research has shown that among Whites who verbally endorsed friendly attitudes towards Blacks, the less positive attitudes of some were revealed through more subtle cues, such as an unfriendly tone of voice. Along similar lines, measurements of social distance have revealed that prejudiced White study participants choose to sit farther away from Black individuals than White individuals.

Research examining aggressive behavior has also revealed a tendency for some White participants to deliver more intense and longer shocks to Black (compared with White) targets in learning experiments. Interestingly, the possibility for retaliation by the Black victim, censure for discriminatory behavior, and lack of anonymity affected the degree to which White participants aggressed against Black victims. Specifically, these types of conditions decreased direct aggression but increased more indirect forms of aggression. Another study found that whereas White participants angered by an insult gave more intense shocks to Black than White victims, those who were not insulted aggressed less against Blacks than Whites (Rogers & Prentice-Dunn, 1981).

These types of studies reveal the diverse ways that prejudice can manifest itself and the ways that researchers have studied these forms of bias. Although some people endorse nonprejudicial views both publicly and privately, there is a subset of the population for whom prejudiced beliefs appear only when measured indirectly. It is clear that the largely hidden nature of modern prejudice, as reflected by aversive and modern racism, has led to a focus on these indirect measures of negative attitudes and bias. However, old-fashioned forms of prejudice do still exist. The next section presents examples of how blatant prejudice takes its form in overt discriminatory behavior.

## Discrimination

Despite the advances that have been made in overcoming bias, examples of discrimination are all too commonplace, as a casual examination of the website for the American Civil Liberties Union reveals. For example, just a few years ago, the systematic mistreatment of African Americans by a national restaurant chain was exposed. And the recent furor over racial profiling reflects people's outrage toward practices that make Black Americans more likely to be targeted for investigation by police because of their skin color. Women are also subject to such discriminatory behavior. For example, women are more likely to receive different negotiation strategies by car sales personnel compared with male customers, with the result often being higher car costs for women. Girls are also targets of discrimination in the classroom, where boys often receive more attention and critical feedback from teachers.

Some sobering statistics describing recent conditions in the workplace and in educational settings for both women and minorities reveal the role played by discrimination. In 1992, one study found that equally qualified female managers lagged significantly behind their male counterparts in salary progression, even after controlling for factors such as self-selection, years in the workforce, and company tenure (Stroh, Brett, & Reilly, 1992). After ruling out other possible explanations for this discrepancy, the authors concluded that discrimination did, in fact, contribute disproportionately to this difference. Furthermore, gender-based complaints to the Equal Employment Opportunity Commission reveal that women have a difficult time in the workplace. It is disheartening to note that complaints have changed little from 1975 to 1989 and, in some cases, the number of complaints has increased sharply. Finally, in terms of wages, women currently earn 72% of men's income, a difference that has been attributed to low access to upper-level positions.

Similar disparities have been found among members of minority groups. In terms of education, more Black students are graduating from high school, but the relative number of those attending college is 25% less than Whites. Recognizing this disparity, affirmative action programs, or programs that preferentially select individuals based on minority status or gender, have worked to increase the numbers of Black college students. However, the debate surrounding the consequences of affirmative action for both beneficiaries and nonbeneficiaries has led some educational institutions to stop their affirmative action programs. A recent example of this can be seen with the University of California at Berkeley, which found a 43% reduction in the Black student population after the end of affirmative action.

In the workplace, Black job candidates are often the targets of systematic discrimination at all stages of the employment process. At the interview stage, employers have been found to interview minority candidates less frequently than nonminority candidates, despite equal qualifications. Beyond the interview, Black job applicants were also more likely to be given less information about positions and fewer referrals, sometimes being told that the jobs no longer existed. Even after a Black candidate gets a job, evidence suggests that discrimination persists. For example, the effect of discrimination has been found in wages, with Black men with professional degrees earning 79% of the salary of White men and Black women earning only 60% of the salary of White men. Black workers not only have lower salaries and fewer promotions, but they are also provided with less access to tools for advancement, such as training and development activities, regular performance evaluations, and opportunities for integration into the organization. The prevalence of high-profile suits against large corporations such as Home Depot, Microsoft, and Texaco reveals the widespread nature of such treatment.

As briefly described here, discrimination has many real-life consequences that are extremely detrimental to the lives and well-being of its targets. Therefore, it is incumbent upon us as researchers and practitioners to search for ways to reduce, if not eliminate, these biases and their negative effects. We describe below some of the ways that researchers have approached the problem of intergroup bias and try to provide some viable solutions.

## Overcoming Stereotypes, Prejudice, and Discrimination

Based on the research presented here, it is clear that stereotypes, prejudice, and discrimination can impede our ability to function in a moral fashion. Inequalities can be sustained and justified if we fail to acknowledge how our minds operate and if we choose not to take action. With this knowledge in mind, it is crucial to consider how each of us can help to combat the negative effects of assessing individuals based on their group membership. How can we as educators and policymakers work to reduce the biases we hold and strive to enhance moral development in those around us?

## Individual Awareness and Responsibility

Before making specific suggestions for individual approaches to bias reduction, we would like to offer two caveats. First, as mentioned earlier, stereotypes have been shown to arise automatically and to be rooted in normal, fundamental psychological processes. This is an important point to recognize when attempting to properly direct efforts toward stereotype, attitude, or behavioral change. The aim of this section is to suggest possible interventions that seek to reshape these fundamental processes rather than eliminate them entirely.

A second point that should be emphasized is that "automatic" does not necessarily mean "inevitable." We firmly believe that people are fully capable of exercising agency and personal responsibility over their responses to stereotyped others. For example, recent research has shown that the degree to which individuals think and act in a prejudiced manner is largely influenced by their personal beliefs and goals. In this spirit, we focus on ways to promote responsibility through individual thought and action.

## Making the Choice Not To Be Prejudiced

Although it may seem obvious, one of the best ways to avoid being prejudiced is to make a concerted effort not to be. However, as easy as this sounds, research has demonstrated that some approaches to this goal are more effective than others. For example, if a person decides that he or she no longer wants to be prejudiced or hold negative stereotypes, one strategy that might be adopted is to simply try to suppress the negative thought, essentially pushing it out of one's mind. Interestingly, research has demonstrated that this is not always a useful strategy. Trying not to think about a given stereotype can often lead to a rebound effect, in which the stereotype is actually thought about more often as soon as the individual stops making the effort to ignore it (Macrae, Bodenhausen, Milne, & Jetten, 1994).

Fortunately, several other strategies seem to be far more effective in reducing one's reliance on stereotypes. *Perspective taking*, or trying to mentally put oneself in another person's shoes, has been found to be one of the more effective ways to elicit empathy for stereotyped others and to decrease prejudice (Galinsky & Moskowitz, 2000). Perspective taking is a means by which another individual can be drawn closer to one's own self-concept through the realization of basic shared similarities. Studies that have focused on this technique have asked individuals to imagine a day in the life of another person, as if they were that person. The results of such perspective taking have been decreased use of stereotypes in making judgments of others, as well as a decrease in the degree to which people discriminate against stereotyped individuals. This type of thinking has been found to be especially effective in reducing prejudice when coupled with an effort during interactions to think of people less as members of a stereotyped group and more as unique individuals.

Researchers have also found that certain goals can help to combat stereotypes and prejudice. Specifically, when people have a strong commitment to egalitarian values, they work hard to prevent stereotypes from affecting their thoughts and behavior. Research on so-called *chronic egalitarians* has found that such individuals consider egalitarian goals to be central to their identities and feel a sense of incompleteness whenever they have violated these goals. These individuals stand in stark contrast to aversive racists because of the degree to which they have truly internalized their ideals. The key to becoming a chronic egalitarian is to focus on the practiced, goal-oriented nature of chronic egalitarianism. That is, consistently keeping in mind the goal of treating others fairly while repeatedly striving to fulfill that goal leads to a "blocking" of prejudiced responses that becomes automatic over time.

Being aware of our biases, whether they are based on stereotype knowledge or long-term prejudices, and making a concerted individual effort to overcome them are important first steps toward society's moral ideal. But as important as it is to identify our own potential biases, it is just as essential that we help others, especially children, to recognize these tendencies within themselves.

## Educational and Policy Interventions for Bias Reduction

It is easiest for intergroup hostilities and hatred to grow when we do not personally know the targets of our prejudice, when they are people passing at a distance on the street or living in far-off communities. When the potential targets of prejudice are our friends, however, it is much more difficult for the seeds of hatred to grow. With this in mind, it is perhaps not surprising that research has demonstrated the importance of childhood interracial friendships in buffering the development of prejudice. Such relationships should be fostered in the classroom and beyond.

INTERGROUP CONTACT.    As with adults, one of the precursors to cross-race friendship development in children is, quite simply, contact with members of other racial groups. For decades, social psychologists have argued that intergroup contact is critical in the battle against the development of prejudice and the formation of stereotypes (Allport, 1954). However, years of research have also demonstrated that there are caveats to this suggestion. For example, it has been shown that intergroup contact is most beneficial when members of different groups have equal status in the setting, cooperation is involved, opportunities are available for stereotype disconfirmation, and the potential exists for friendships to develop (Hewstone, 1996). The essential goal of intergroup contact, then, is to allow members of different racial or ethnic groups to realize that they share similar values and beliefs. It also allows people to reduce the amount of anxiety they might otherwise feel during interactions with members of unfamiliar or negatively stereotyped groups.

Intergroup contact can help to foster interracial friendships, and such relationships have been shown to be pivotal in the development of a more positive orientation toward others. In one retrospective study conducted by Wood and Sonleitner (1996), White students at the University of Oklahoma were asked about their interracial contact as children and their current attitudes toward Blacks. It was found that childhood interracial contact significantly decreased negative stereotyping and prejudice toward Blacks, suggesting that appropriate school desegregation is an effective force for fostering positive attitudes. Similar findings have been obtained with children and other adults. Even the formation of interracial friendships in adulthood can help to promote more positive attitudes toward racial minorities.

School programs designed to promote intergroup contact have been developed by psychologists and have met with mixed success. One early program made use of what is called the jigsaw technique (Aronson & Bridgeman, 1979). Jigsaw classrooms are designed to create interdependent learning environments that are conducive to positive cross-race interactions. Teachers must provide lessons that can be learned in small groups. Each group member is provided with information that must be shared with other group members in order for everyone in the group to learn all of the material. If students want to be successful, they are dependent on all of the members of their group because each member has a certain expertise to share. If this program is successfully implemented, it can lead to increased participation by minority students; increased empathy for other students; and when success is attained by the group, an increased feeling that all members of the diverse group are successful.

Another program that has received support for its promotion of interdependent cooperation is Teams-Games-Tournament (TGT; DeVries, Edwards, & Slavin, 1978). Similar to the jigsaw classroom technique, diverse teams are created in TGT to increase opportunities for cross-race interactions. Team members are taught to cooperate and help one another in the service of a common goal: performing well in a tournament played against other teams. In preparation for the tournament, which is composed of a set of skill games, team members tutor each other and work toward improving their skills. During the tournament, each individual team member then competes against a student from another team who is at a similar skill level. The winning team is determined by the total points accrued by all the members together over the course of the tournament. Several studies designed to evaluate the effectiveness of TGT have found that it is particularly effective in increasing the number and percentage of cross-racial friendships.

Teachers who seek to promote greater integration within the classroom need not follow these exact procedures. But both programs make use of several important principles, including interdependence, cooperation, and the pursuit of a common goal, in order to promote greater intergroup harmony in the classroom. Programs that make use of these principles while being tailored to meet the specific needs of a classroom will no doubt be the most effective for both students and educators.

CONTACT THROUGH ROLE MODELS.   In some racially homogeneous communities, providing the opportunity for interracial contact can be challenging at best. However, even in communities where intergroup contact is difficult because of a lack of diversity, a host of media are available that can provide positive interracial contact. One way for elementary school teachers to encourage some initial contact is through school pairing programs. Pairing with the same grade at more diverse schools can provide opportunities to initiate and foster cross-race friendships from afar. Children can be assigned pen pals or E-mail buddies, providing children from both communities with the opportunity to share their interests and beliefs. This, in turn, can allow the teachers to model positive interracial connections.

Even in the absence of direct intergroup contact, many opportunities exist to provide children with positive role models from all racial and ethnic groups. Posters, class projects, and relevant classroom activities can provide children with information about the accomplishments of people from all walks of life. *Sesame Street* is one educational television program for children that has taken this approach to heart. This program provides an incredibly diverse cast and often tackles issues of difference head on, with characters explaining their differences (i.e., why they are speaking a different language on the phone, why they are in a wheelchair) to another character, who emerges from the interaction with greater understanding. Cross-race friendships across multiple settings are frequently modeled and supported by friends and adults. One study demonstrated that White American children who had watched 2 years of *Sesame Street* expressed more positive attitudes toward African Americans and Latinos (Graves, 1999). Thus, it seems as though even television role models can have an effect.

In summary, although intergroup contact and role models may help in the reduction of prejudice, such approaches may not always be viable or effective. For this reason, specific educational programs have been developed in an attempt to challenge children's developing prejudices. In addition, because stereotypes have been shown to influence the academic performance of negatively stereotyped group members, programs have also been developed to help students overcome the limitations imposed by societally held beliefs.

INTERVENTION PROGRAMS.   Several educational programs have been developed in order to foster positive intergroup attitudes and decrease children's interracial prejudice. Unlike the programs mentioned earlier, which are designed to foster positive intergroup contact, educators have also attempted to create positive dialogues about race through antiracist education. Many of these programs are founded on the belief that socialization contributes significantly to the development of prejudice (Aboud & Levy, 2000). The effectiveness of these programs has not always been clear, although it seems that the outcomes are, overall, moderately positive. More research is needed to determine the conditions under which antiracist programs are most successful. However, it seems that such programs have some real potential for positive impact, especially when they are age appropriate and have strong teacher support.

Programs have also been developed to help promote academic success among racial minority group members, such as African Americans and Latinos, who are negatively stereotyped in this domain. As noted earlier, research on stereotype threat has demonstrated that becoming aware of a self-relevant negative stereotype can harm academic performance. In response to this, several "wise" schooling practices, designed for teachers, have been suggested (Steele, 1997). Teachers who provide an optimistic perspective on the students' potential, provide challenging work (instead of remedial work), and support the view that intelligence is malleable (as opposed to fixed) are more likely to be successful as mentors and champions for students striving to overcome the additional barriers that negative stereotypes can impose.

As much as these programs can have a positive impact, even the most effective education programs cannot always combat the effects of stereotypes, prejudice, and discrimination. Therefore, it is imperative that policies be created that reflect current social realities.

AFFIRMATIVE ACTION.    Affirmative action has been used in educational settings and workplaces as a means to compensate for past or present discrimination based on gender, race, or ethnicity. Institutions with affirmative action programs try to give special consideration to women and minorities through additional recruiting efforts and preferential selection. In practice, this means that to fulfill diversity goals, college admissions officers may choose a minority candidate over a White candidate when the candidates are similarly qualified.

Recent efforts aimed at evaluating the effectiveness of affirmative action have focused on its impact on leveling disparities in wages, employment, and college admissions (Murrell & Jones, 1996). On the positive side, affirmative action programs have led to a significant increase in workforce participation among minorities, especially Blacks. In education, affirmative action has provided funding for postsecondary education for minorities, which has helped to increase the number of minority students attending college. When the potentially lifelong effects of stereotypes and subtle discrimination on minority group members are considered, as well as the fact that many economically disadvantaged minority children are not provided with appropriate educational resources, there is little question that affirmative action programs make at least a concerted attempt to redress past wrongs. In addition, such programs may promote future equality by providing opportunities for intergroup contact and by increasing the visibility of minorities in workplaces and in classrooms.

Despite positive outcomes such as these, affirmative action does have some problems, as indicated by recent changes in policy by institutions such as the University of California at Berkeley and the ongoing court case involving the University of Michigan. The continued existence of disparities as outlined in this chapter casts into doubt the degree to which affirmative action has truly been successful in achieving its aims. Nonbeneficiaries of affirmative action have also objected loudly to what they see as "reverse discrimination," which seems to deny opportunities to majority group members in favor of potentially less qualified minority or female applicants.

Even those who benefit from affirmative action are subject to the negative consequences of preferential treatment. Research has shown that being the recipient of affirmative action can lead to academic underperformance, negative self-views, and an increased fear that any success achieved will be seen as undeserved or unearned (Brown, Charnsangavej, Keough, Newman, & Rentfrow, 2000; Heilman & Alcott, 2001). Recipients of affirmative action face a great deal of ambiguity in tracing the true cause of their success (e.g., "Was it my ability or preferential treatment that got me here?"), which may lead them to question their competence. It is clear that policymakers have a great deal to consider when weighing the costs and benefits of affirmative action programs because there is evidence for both sides of the debate. Nevertheless, it is clear from the research reviewed in this chapter that the implementation of policy may need to play a critical role in remedying current inequalities.

## Conclusions

Perhaps one of the greatest challenges facing the promotion of morality among today's youth is the question of how best to handle intergroup relations in an increasingly diverse society. Differences in ethnicity, gender, age, religion, sexual orientation, socioeconomic status, and political orientation—to name just a few—serve as the basis for group distinctions. Although such diversity can offer rich opportunities for learning and growth, differences between groups can also serve as fertile ground for stereotyping, prejudice, and discrimination. This chapter sought to provide an overview of current research in social psychology that may shed some light into ways of promoting moral approaches to group differences. With continued research and the application of findings, we hope to steadily approach a society in which differences do not lead to prejudice and discrimination but are instead valued and nurtured.

## References

Aboud, F. (1988). *Children and prejudice.* Oxford, UK: Basil Blackwell.

Aboud, F. E., & Levy, S. R. (2000). Interventions to reduce prejudice and discrimination in children and adolescents. In S. Oskamp (Ed.), *Reducing prejudice and discrimination* (pp. 269–293). Mahwah, NJ: Lawrence Erlbaum.

Allport, G. W. (1954). *The nature of prejudice.* Reading, MA: Perseus.

Allport, G. W., & Postman, L. (1947). *The psychology of rumor.* Oxford, England: Henry Holt.

Ambady, N., Shih, M., Kim, A., & Pittinsky, T. L. (2001). Stereotype susceptibility in children: Effects of identity activation on quantitative performance. *Psychological Science, 12,* 385–390.

Aronson, E., & Bridgeman, D. (1979). Jigsaw groups and the desegregated classroom: In pursuit of common goals. *Personality and Social Psychology Bulletin, 5,* 438–466.

Bigler, R. S., & Liben, L. S. (1993). A cognitive-developmental approach to racial stereotyping and reconstructive memory in Euro-American children. *Child Development, 64,* 1507–1518.

Brown, R. P., Charnsangavej, T., Keough, K., Newman, M. L., & Rentfrow, P. J. (2000). Putting the "affirm" into affirmative action: Preferential selection and academic performance. *Journal of Personality and Social Psychology, 75,* 736–747.

Bruner, J. (1996). *The culture of education.* Cambridge, MA: Harvard University Press.

DeVries, D. L., Edwards, K. J., & Slavin, R. E. (1978). Biracial learning teams and race relations in the classroom: Four field experiments using teams-games-tournament. *Journal of Educational Psychology, 70*, 356–362.

Dovidio, J. F., & Gaertner, S. L. (1986). *Prejudice, discrimination, and racism.* Orlando, FL: Academic Press.

Duncan, B. L. (1976). Differential social perception and attribution of intergroup violence: Testing the lower limits of stereotyping of Blacks. *Journal of Personality and Social Psychology, 34*, 590–598.

Frey, D., & Gaertner, S. L. (1986). Helping and the avoidance of inappropriate interracial behavior: A strategy which perpetuates a non-prejudiced self-image. *Journal of Personality and Social Psychology, 50*, 1083–1090.

Galinsky, A. D., & Moskowitz, G. B. (2000). Perspective-taking: Decreasing stereotype expression, stereotype accessibility, and in-group favoritism. *Journal of Personality and Social Psychology, 78*, 708–724.

Golombok, S., & Fivush, R. (1994). *Gender development.* Cambridge, UK: Cambridge University Press.

Graves, S. B. (1999). Television and prejudice reduction: When does television as a vicarious experience make a difference? *Journal of Social Issues, 55*, 707–725.

Heilman, M. E., & Alcott, V. B. (2001). What I think you think of me: Women's reactions to being viewed as beneficiaries of preferential selection. *Journal of Applied Psychology, 86*, 574–582.

Hewstone, M. (1996). Contact and categorization: Social psychological interventions to change intergroup relations. In C. N. Macrae, C. Stangor, & M. Hewstone (Eds.), *Stereotypes and stereotyping* (pp. 323–368). New York: Guilford.

Jussim, L., & Fleming, C. (1996). Self-fulfilling prophecies and the maintenance of social stereotypes: The role of dyadic interactions and social forces. In C. N. Macrae, C. Stangor, & M. Hewstone (Eds.), *Stereotypes and stereotyping* (pp. 161–192). New York: Guilford.

Macrae, C. N., Bodenhausen, G. V., Milne, A. B., & Jetten, J. (1994). Out of mind but back in sight: Stereotypes on the rebound. *Journal of Personality and Social Psychology, 67*, 808–817.

Murrell, A. J., & Jones, R. (1996). Assessing affirmative action: Past, present, and future. *Journal of Social Issues, 52*, 77–92.

Rogers, R. W., & Prentice-Dunn, S. (1981). Deindividuation and anger-mediated interracial aggression: Unmasking regressive racism. *Journal of Personality and Social Psychology, 41*, 63–73.

Rosenthal, R., & Jacobson, L. F. (1968). *Pygmalion in the classroom: Teacher expectations and student intellectual development.* New York: Holt, Rinehart & Winston.

Sagar, H. A., & Schofield, J. W. (1980). Racial and behavioral cues in black and white children's perceptions of ambiguously aggressive acts. *Journal of Personality and Social Psychology, 39*, 590–598.

Shih, M., Pittinsky, T. L., & Ambady, N. (1999). Stereotype susceptibility: Identity salience and shifts in quantitative performance. *Psychological Science, 10*, 80–83.

Spencer, S. J., Steele, C. M., & Quinn, D. M. (1999). Stereotype threat and women's math performance. *Journal of Experimental Social Psychology, 35*, 4–28.

Steele, C. M. (1997). A threat in the air: How stereotypes shape intellectual identity and performance. *American Psychologist, 52*, 613–629.

Steele, C. M., & Aronson, J. (1995). Stereotype threat and the intellectual test performance of African Americans. *Journal of Personality and Social Psychology, 69*, 797–811.

Steele, C. M., Spencer, S. J., & Aronson, J. (2002). Contending with bias: The psychology of stereotype and social identity threat. In M. P. Zanna (Ed.), *Advances in experimental social psychology* (Vol. 34, pp. 277–341). San Diego, CA: Academic Press.

Stroh, L. K., Brett, J. M., & Reilly, A. H. (1992). All the right stuff: A comparison of female and male managers' career progression. *Journal of Applied Psychology, 77,* 251–260.

Wood, P. B., & Sonleitner, N. (1996). The effect of childhood interracial contact on adult antiblack prejudice. *International Journal of Intercultural Relations, 20,* 1–17.

Word, C. O., Zanna, M. P., & Cooper, J. (1974). The nonverbal mediation of self-fulfilling prophecies in interracial interaction. *Journal of Experimental Social Psychology, 10,* 109–120.

# Chapter 6

# Conflict and Morals

## Susan Opotow

Youth conflicts can range from fleeting quarrels to more enduring antipathies expressed as violence toward individuals or groups. These conflicts can inflict physical and psychological harm, and when they fester, they can siphon off energy from more productive activities. However, conflicts also have positive potential. They can surface urgent concerns and motivate positive change by stimulating individuals, groups, or organizations to approach issues with fresh insight. Conflicts challenge us to be sufficiently attentive to learn from the dissonant understandings that give rise to conflicts and to be sufficiently skilled to resolve them constructively. This chapter argues that for adults and organizations that seek to nurture morality in youths, conflicts can be an underappreciated and valuable resource.

The first section of this chapter describes the constructs *conflicts* and *morals*, drawing on social science research, particularly social psychology. It then describes the application of these constructs to the conflicts of adults and youths. For both groups, conflicts have the potential to be constructive or destructive; are based on one's own particularly situated perceptions that may not be shared by others; and offer opportunities to rethink the status quo of relationships, groups, and institutions. The second section of this chapter describes research on two kinds of pervasive and ordinary youth conflict—peer conflicts among middle school students and conflicts surrounding class cutting for high school students. This section describes both kinds of conflicts in light of their moral meaning for youths. The chapter then offers practical suggestions for fostering constructive conflict processes that can nurture youths' moral development and stimulate self-reflection and change in organizations that serve youths.

## What Is Conflict?

Conflicts, which can be large or small, obvious or hidden, suffuse our lives at home, at work, in communities, and as a nation. A *conflict* exists when incompatible ideas, interests, or actions result in a struggle to neutralize, harm, or eliminate opponents. Incompatibilities, which are at the heart of conflict, result from each party's having distinctive interests, positions, goals, knowledge, culture, conflict skills, needs, values, and beliefs about fairness. As conflicts take shape, initial provocations and objectives can get lost as parties' attention shifts away from resolving initial incompatibilities to finding ways to inflict harm. Conflict is often associated with pain and losses that can accrue to one or all parties as the result of harsh tactics. Some conflicts have a clear winner and loser (i.e., *zero-sum conflicts*), but most conflicts concern a variety of issues and, as a result, each party can often achieve some, if not all, gains (i.e., *win–win conflicts*).

Although the word *conflict* can evoke a sense of foreboding or fear, not all conflicts take a competitive and destructive form. Conflicts also have considerable positive and constructive potential. They can spark creative energy, foster collaborative ties, and change the status quo (Deutsch, 1973; Table 6.1). In addition, conflicts generate a sense of discomfort and urgency that can focus attention on acute or festering problems. Youth conflicts, too, have constructive potential. They can not only help youths navigate the challenges of social living but they also offer participants, bystanders, and even the institutions that serve youths opportunities to understand multiple perspectives more deeply and solve immediate and intractable problems in creative and constructive ways.

Table 6.1. Constructive and Destructive Conflicts

|          | Constructive Conflicts | Destructive Conflicts |
|----------|------------------------|-----------------------|
| Goals    | Doing well<br>Being productive<br>Both sides gain | Harming others<br>Being destructive<br>One side wins; one side loses |
| Process  | Discussion<br>Cooperation | Harsh tactics<br>Competition |
| Outcomes | Satisfying<br>Mixed motive<br>　(some wins and losses for all parties) | Dissatisfying<br>Zero sum<br>　(there is a winner and a loser) |

## Types of Conflict

Conflicts among friends, classmates, families, institutions, and nations occur over countless issues that can be categorized as conflicts of interests, conflicts of resources, and conflicts of values. *Conflicts of interest* arise from miscommunication, the failure to understand another's perspective, and the failure to see the possibility for joint gain, as described in the popular book, *Getting to Yes* (Fisher, Ury, & Patton, 1991). In a classic conflict of interest, two parties fighting over an orange fail to realize that one wishes to eat the orange and the other wants to use the peel to flavor a cake. Conflicts of interest seem like zero-sum conflicts, but when parties discover each other's interests, they have the capacity to be to reconciled as win–win situations.

Not all resources can be shared. *Conflicts of resources* (also called *realistic* or *veridical conflicts*) are often at the heart of mild and severe conflicts. Squabbles in children's' daily lives, such as who will receive much-coveted attention or a favored seat in a vehicle, are resource conflicts. Resource conflicts also include intransigent, deadly conflicts throughout the world in which groups or nations seek control of land, water, petroleum, minerals, or other valued resources. Resource conflicts concern not only tangible resources (e.g., goods and money) but also such intangible resources as status, information, services, and caring. Although compromise is possible for some resources, it is not always possible to use, share, and conserve other resources, particularly those that are scarce. Time is one example of a resource that does not always lend itself to a win–win outcome because time spent on one task can mean that other tasks remain undone.

Although people with different values can live together peacefully, value differences can also spark disagreements and intransigent conflicts. *Conflicts of values* and differing worldviews are often salient in ethnic, religious, and political conflicts. Conflicts of values can escalate conflict and justify aggressive attitudes and violent behavior, particularly when one party views its adversary as having bad values (unaware that the adversary has a similar view). As Lewis Coser (1956) warned, "Expect more violence to the extent that participants perceive the issues at stake in terms of abstract values transcending the specific case" (p. 112).

Although it can be useful to categorize a conflict as primarily concerning interests, resources, or values and address it accordingly, many conflicts—large and small—are all three types. Conflicts of interests occur in virtually all conflicts as a result of the imperfect way we do things: We do not always listen carefully to understand others' needs or positions, nor do we express our own needs clearly or, on some occasions, recognize what we actually want. Conflicts over tangible and intangible resources also factor into virtually all conflicts because most conflicts concern the desire to attain particular things. Conflicts of values concern whose values should be most influential and trump others. Conflicts of values also enter into virtually all disputes, including those concerning interests and resources because all conflicts fundamentally invoke explicit or implicit moral beliefs about one's own and adversaries' entitlements, deserving, rights, and obligations.

## What Are Morals?

*Morals* encompass norms, rights, entitlements, obligations, responsibilities, and duties that shape our sense of justice and guide our behavior with others (Deutsch, 1982). They emerge from cultural expectancies about how particular people should behave in particular contexts. Morals help us differentiate between what is good or bad; right or wrong; acceptable or intolerable; helpful or harmful; and warranted, excessive, or insufficient. Morals operationalize our sense of fairness, orienting us to what we should do in particular situations. The perception that a person has violated social norms that are generally accepted within a particular social context, such as acting with excessive greed, selfishness, or aggression, can arouse a sense of injustice that then justifies efforts to restore a sense of moral balance and fairness.

Given the influence of morals in social relations, what is *not* moral? Deutsch (1982) advises that in addition to morals, cognitions and motives influence our relations with others. *Cognitions* are the mental work that provides us with rapid appraisals of what is occurring. Cognitions label people and situations, but because we inevitably have more information about the factors that affect our own behavior than about those that affect the behavior of others, our understanding of what is occurring in social relations is often fragmentary and depends on previously acquired expectancies and stereotypes that vary in their accuracy. *Motives* are goals, drives, needs, and incentives. Motives are our understanding of what we (and others) want and how we (and they) will get it. Motives can inspire individuals, groups, organizations, and societies to achieve positive goals, but motives can also be destructive, particularly in competitive contexts when reaching goals depends on preventing others from attaining the same goals. Motives can give rise to threats, coercion, and harmful tactics to achieve one's aims at any cost.

Cognitions, motives, and morals interact in conflict. Cognitions categorize conflict participants and contexts by identifying what is going on; morals inject these cognitions with questions of deserving and responsibility, including who deserves to get what. Motives are attuned to one's own and others' goals in conflict; motives in concert with morals can apportion blame for the failure to achieve desired ends. Morals can also moderate motives, designating what might be unreasonable objectives. Thus, morals exert an influence on cognitions and motives that ultimately affects perceptions about the conflict (e.g., what it is about, whether or not it is justified, how it should be waged) and, subsequently, on conflict processes and outcomes.

## What Is Moral About Conflict?

Coser (1956) defines constructive and destructive conflicts in terms of morals: Constructive conflicts do not contradict the basic assumptions upon which relationships are founded; in destructive conflicts, contending parties no longer share basic values. Constructive conflicts, therefore, have a constructive moral emphasis as parties seek out others' perspectives and ways to achieve joint gains (see Table 1). Destructive conflicts have a destructive moral emphasis that casts the conflict as righteous and seeks moral justifications for harmful tactics and injurious outcomes. Moral influences on conflict are evident in moral judgments, norm violations, moral exclusion, and apology.

### *Moral Judgments*

Moral judgments evaluate oneself and opponents in conflict and focus attention on the basis for conflict; conflict behavior; and conflict outcomes, including the nature, degree, and appropriateness of harm inflicted. Because each person's viewpoint results from a distinctive position, including one's stake in the conflict, one's conflict experiences, and one's ideological perspective, moral judgments in conflicts are subjective. One may see behavior as intentional, but another may not; one may see behavior as harmful, but another may not; and one may see injury, but another may not. Behavior abhorred by some may be hailed as positive social change by others. However, people in conflict may not recognize that their judgments about intent, behavior, and injury differ from those of their opponents.

As described, moral judgments concern fairness, responsibility, obligations, and deserving. However, moral judgments in conflicts can be sidestepped by viewing behavior with moral implications in nonmoral terms. Individuals can perceive their own or others' conflict-related behavior as occurring outside the moral domain; in the *conventional domain*, in which social conventions are salient; or in the *personal domain*, in which personal discretion is salient. For example, adolescents can view smoking or substance abuse as a moral question (i.e., right or wrong), as a matter of social convention (i.e., something to do while hanging out with friends), or as a personal issue (i.e., up to their own taste, preferences, and discretion) (Berkowitz, Guerra, & Nucci, 1991). Because conflict-related behaviors can be judged in moral or nonmoral terms, understanding a particular conflict depends on knowing how conflicting parties frame their own and others' behavior.

## Norm Violations

Morals also influence conflict through the shared social norms that guide our expectancies about how people should behave with one another. Social norms maintain group solidarity, provide a sense of belonging, and foster social coordination and communication because members of a social group can assume that their own normative understandings are shared and respected within the group. Although social norms are relatively stable and can be seen as enduring traditions, they also undergo change. Norms against violence, for example, weaken when they are continually assailed by difficult life conditions and strife.

Social norms can deter or escalate conflict. Social norms indicate the kinds of transgressions that can be overlooked (e.g., physical aggression by a young child), but they can also provoke and escalate conflict when norm-violating behavior is construed as insulting a person, family, community, or nation. They can then trigger a chain of linked attributions that focus on antagonistic interests and malevolent motives. This process can lead to hostile reactions, conflict escalation, and violent action. Norm violations are less likely to trigger this negative spiral when violations are seen as unintentional rather than intentional and transient rather than stable and when parties conflict (e.g., friends, community groups, nations) have well-developed informal and formal ways of redressing norm violations (e.g., a forum for airing grievances). Redress of norm violations can take constructive forms, such as a heart-to-heart talks, family meetings, and community mediation, but redress of violated norms also has the potential for destructive behavior such as mob violence.

## Moral Exclusion

Morals are evaluative and normative. They identify what we owe to whom and whose needs, views, and well-being count and whose do not. Moral rules and norms apply only to people we value and include in our *scope of justice* (or *moral community*) such as family members, friends, neighbors, compatriots, or co-religionists. Shared social norms designate who is included and excluded. We extend moral rules and norms to them by considering fairness in dealing with them, sharing valued social resources with them, and making sacrifices to foster their well-being (Opotow, 1990). Moral rules can also extend beyond humankind, such as when we respect and protect endangered animals or habitats.

When we see others as outside our scope of justice or as *morally excluded*, constructive moral rules and norms do not apply to them. Instead, those who are morally excluded are eligible for harm and exploitation that can seem normal, acceptable, and the way things are or should be. Those who are morally excluded are seen as inferior (e.g., poor or homeless people), as property (e.g., slaves, women, children), or as enemies. Although excluding some kinds of people from the scope of justice can seem morally reprehensible, everyone has boundaries for justice. Moral exclusion is an increasingly influential dynamic as conflict increases and becomes destructive. Because moral exclusion changes cognitions, motives, and moral obligations toward others, it can take considerable time to counter full-blown moral exclusion and reestablish cooperative and respectful interpersonal, intergroup, or international relationships.

## Apology

Conflict and morals also combine in apology. An *apology* is saying one is sorry, admitting that there is no excuse for one's behavior, and expressing the hope that the victim will offer forgiveness. An apology is a moral narrative about an acknowledged wrong that shifts power from a transgressor to a victim (Tavuchis, 1991). An apology is a straightforward verbal exchange with the capacity to restore moral balance to a damaged relationship. It can stop the destructive momentum of conflict and start a relationship on the slow path to rebuilding trust.

## Youth Conflict

What is the relevance of conflicts and morals to youth conflict? In recent years, some youth conflict has been deadly and violent. The 1999 Columbine High School massacre left 13 dead and caused widespread revulsion and shock. Youth perpetrators in this and similar massacres justified their norm-violating violence with spurious, self-serving moral judgments. They saw themselves as outside their peers' scope of justice and, as a consequence, excluded their victims—teachers, administrators, and fellow students—from their own scope of justice. These tragic, vivid acts of violence overshadow milder, ordinary conflicts that are an integral part of youths' daily lives.

My research has examined two kinds of ordinary conflicts that youths experience: peer conflicts and conflicts surrounding class cutting. Typically, these conflicts are understood from the adult (i.e., teacher, counselor, administrator, and parent) perspective, in which fostering safety, protecting individuals, and promoting institutional well-being are paramount concerns. From this perspective, these two kinds of conflicts have the potential to harm students and disrupt the institutions in which they occur; therefore, both kinds of conflicts typically prompt mandate administrative responses. My research suggests that youths' conflicts are not completely negative or destructive and that closer examination of issues in these conflicts yields constructive outcomes. From the perspective of youths, these conflicts have a moral core. I see the moral issues raised by youth conflict as opportunities; they are junctures in which adults can constructively engage with youths in ways that can nurture youths' growth, learning, and moral development.

## Peer Conflicts

In research on peer conflicts among seventh graders (i.e., 12 to 13 years old), 40 students described a conflict they experienced with a peer. Most described a conflict with a friend or classmate rather than with a stranger. For many students, peer conflicts left an unpleasant aftermath that could last days, weeks, or months and include feelings of humiliation, loss of status, and social isolation. One young man summarized the discomfort of conflict: "Everybody's looking at you. When you lose, everybody puts their backs to you." One young woman ruminated about her responsibility for ending a friendship:

> I'm not gonna say that it was all her fault. Because it might have been something else that I had done to her already and maybe with that on top of it, she said, "Forget it." I don't know. Maybe it might have been something else that I had already done and never realized that I did.

No longer talking with her ex-friend, this young woman remained puzzled about the conflict and feared that she might unknowingly commit a similar gaffe and end another valued friendship. After conflicts, students often continued to see former adversaries at school. When they did, they feared that the conflict might resume and they would again face rejection as their peers took sides. Consequently, after conflicts with peers, attending school could be more stressful for students.

Despite these negative aspects of conflict, students volunteered some positive aspects of conflict. One student said: "Without conflicts and fights you will never find out who you are and what type of person you like and what you want out of life." Another said: "You can find out how another person reacts to certain things.... You can find out more about persons. Sometimes, even, the fights help you establish a relationship with somebody." Conflicts also supported valued social norms. As a young man described: "Most kids who get jumped, they deserve it, though. They go around talking about mothers and messing with kids' girlfriends. Then a whole bunch of kids jump them." He essentially described some youth conflicts as collective actions that enforced valued social norms and addressed behaviors that youths find unacceptable.

For students in this research, peer conflicts had moral meaning because they caused prompted reflection on what was right and wrong and good or bad in their own and others' behavior. Students ruminated about moral judgments and social norms that influenced their own behavior, their adversaries' behavior, and bystanders' behavior. They also worried about moral exclusion as a consequence of the conflict. Students spontaneously remarked that they found it helpful to talk with me about their conflict as participants in this research project because they came to better understand the conflict and themselves. Possibly because students viewed these conflicts as their own, few students had discussed their conflicts with adults. Adult engagement, even with the best of intentions, was seen by students as reducing their options. It risked students' losing control over the course and outcome of the conflict, having the conflict dismissed as unimportant, and having adults take charge of the conflict in unpredictable ways.

School adults corroborated students' impressions that adults trivialized peer conflicts or dismissed them as fleeting and silly. A teacher said, "I think it [student–student conflict] is something that is bugging them about something else altogether. Nine times out of 10, they don't know why they got all worked up." A school administrator said:

> It doesn't have to be much for them to get into it: "He looked at me the wrong way," or "[he] made the wrong kind of comment that I didn't like," or "he pushed, touched me in the hallway and didn't say excuse me."

Conflicts that seem insignificant to bystanders, however, can have personal meaning for participants, can be part of a larger conflictual history, and can concern sensitive information about oneself or others. Youth conflict that seems to result from a "he-said/she-said" scenario or from an exchange of insults (e.g., "your mother ...") can signal a challenge to one's reputation or social standing that is unwise to ignore. One student said, "Fights are important because next time they'll think twice before messing with you because they know you'll defend yourself."

Peer conflicts that came to the attention of school adults often triggered enforcement of institutional rules and regulations. These responses were not designed to address the nuances of the conflict from the perspective of youths. Opportunities for student reflection about what was right and wrong or good and bad, together with interested adults, were lost at administrative hearings that were not structured as forums to help students thoughtfully air their lingering concerns, reflect on the bigger picture, and consider ways they hope to conduct their relationships in the future. Peer mediation programs can offer such a forum, but they are limited in scope. They are more appropriate for conflicts of interests or resources that lend themselves to compromise and concrete agreements rather than for addressing the moral issues in value conflicts that make peer conflicts difficult, interesting, and opportunities for personal growth. Additionally, peer mediation programs may not offer opportunities for in-depth reflection with supportive and knowledgeable adults.

## Institutional Conflict

In another research project on youth conflict, I studied class attendance decisions among high school students (i.e., 14 to 18 years old) using focus groups and individual interviews. I worked collaboratively with high school student co-researchers in two cities in the northeastern United States. I found that students who chose to cut class (i.e., selectively miss classes during their school day) often did so because of conflicts they experienced at school, particularly conflicts with the institution and how it did things. Students described cutting classes for a variety of reasons that they tied to pedagogy or to administrative policy, including onerous rules for class lateness, early morning classes, different substitute teachers each day, or the way their class schedule structured the school day (e.g., many short periods and academic transitions). Students also cut classes they experienced as alienating, too easy, or irrelevant to their interests and future goals. A young woman said:

> Well, for me, it's, like, the learning. There's only like a few classes I actually care about. Everything else is, like, pointless, because I'll never use it in my life .... If my teacher's not teaching me anything, then I'm gonna go to work. I'm not gonna sit here and waste my time and twiddle my thumbs when I could be doing something more productive.

Students who cut class expressed frustration because they understood that they could not change their own situation or school policy. They had little voice or power in the school hierarchy. A young woman said, "The difference between us going to school and having a job is you can quit the job and find another job. This school—we cannot go anywhere else." Lacking the ability to change how things are done and having few other options, students engaged in the self-help option of class cutting. Essentially, they addressed conflicts they perceived by redesigning their school days.

Although class cutting could be seen as conflicts of interests or resources, class cutting is a conflict of values for students. For them, class cutting involves a moral judgment, a discrepancy between what they should have and what they are offered. Students wanted and believed they deserved caring, knowledgeable, reliable teachers and a safe, individually attuned learning environment with pedagogical approaches and resources designed to entice them (Sanon, Baxter, Fortune, & Opotow, 2001). Students saw the school as responsible for providing them with this learning environment, but they expressed a more complex moral view that allocated responsibility for class cutting to both individual students and the institution. As one young man stated, "Kids have to motivate themselves instead of putting all the blame on teachers. It is a fifty-fifty thing from where I stand."

The conflicts students describe as causing class cutting did not seem valid or important to school adults, who characterized students' reasons for cutting class as excuses. Instead they described student immaturity, shortsightedness, poor decision making, and inadequate academic preparation and work habits as root causes of class cutting. Because institutional factors that students cited as underlying class attendance decisions were seen as spurious, they did not get addressed (Fallis & Opotow, 2003). The issues students raised, however, are not only amenable to change but they also do periodically change as policy initiatives. These initiatives, however, are top-down schoolwide or systemwide administrative efforts that occur without the benefit of student input. Institutional policies that do not work from the perspective of students are candidates for organizational and systemic change. Students' concerns about their schooling experiences—conflicts that prompt class cutting—may offer a productive way to rethink school policy. Students' concerns about schooling are opportunities for school adults—administrators, teachers, and counselors—to engage with students to design schoolwide and systemwide policies that can foster student attachment to and achievement in school.

## What Is Moral About Youth Conflict?

As described, morals encompass norms, rights, entitlements, obligations, responsibilities, and duties that shape our sense of justice and guide our behavior with others. In peer conflicts, moral questions about what was or should have been done were the elements that fascinated students and lingered long after conflict episodes ended. In class cutting, students saw morals as relevant in their obligations to do what was required of them as long as the institution met their expectations. It is disturbing that peer and institutional conflicts are pervasive yet invisible. Students promote this invisibility by navigating both kinds of conflict through self-help. This is problematic because these ordinary conflicts have the capacity to generate important personal, social, and moral learning about entitlements and obligations to oneself, others, and institutions. In both kinds of conflicts, adults were present but were not positioned to help students learn from their conflict experiences. This omission suggests that organizations that seek to nurture morality in youths can look more critically at how they position their staff members to engage with youths.

Adult engagement in youth conflict requires great sensitivity. If adults ignore these conflicts—as is common in both peer conflicts and class cutting—they leave students struggling alone. If, on the other hand, adults intervene, they do so as outsiders and risk coming down hard on students with the rules and regulations that students find onerous and unhelpful in addressing their conflicts. Adult engagement should allow students to maintain ownership of their conflicts yet encourage students to learn from conflicts. In my research on both peer and institutional conflicts, youths wanted to explore their conflict issues and options with adults they trusted. These adults were friendly, interested, and nonintrusive. They were willing to serve as sounding boards and function as "safety nets" yet let youths make their own decisions. Those who can offer this kind of help are endowed with insight, caring, and the time needed to be available to youths. The next section discusses how organizations that seek to nurture youths can foster in their staff members this orientation toward youth conflict.

## Implications for Practice

Youth conflict can be seen as disruptive, distracting, dangerous, and something to be disposed of expeditiously; however, it can also be seen as a resource that offers youths ways to learn, grow, and nurture morality. It is important to recognize that this learning and growth should not be limited exclusively to youths. Because conflicts pervade social living, both students and adults need to learn constructive conflict skills so they can understand and address conflicts in ways that nurture personal growth; cooperative relationships; and, as I will describe, constructive organizational change. (For effective approaches, see Bodine & Crawford, 1998; Cornelius & Faire, 1989; Deutsch & Coleman, 2000; Diaute & Fine, 2003; Killen & Hart, 1995; Opotow & Deutsch, 1999; and Rubin, Pruitt, & Kim, 1994.) Some practical

## Table 6.2. Conflict Styles

|  | Advantages | Disadvantages |
| --- | --- | --- |
| Compete | Clarity, naming, honesty. | May miss other side of argument and other factors.<br>Can alienate other parties and reduce the potential for an acceptable, stable outcome. |
| Collaborate | Can address each party's needs and interests.<br>Problem centered.<br><br>Outcomes can be win–win.<br>Everyone gets heard.<br><br>Parties feel better about the process.<br>Can lead to more stable outcomes. | Goals that benefit from a more competitive approach may suffer.<br>May take an inordinate amount of time and be inappropriate for quick decision making.<br>May require more interaction than desired.<br>The process may be perceived as "faux collaboration" and manipulative. |
| Compromise | Both parties gain something.<br><br>Can get a conflict "unstuck". | Both could lose things that matter to them.<br>Not all conflicts lend themselves to compromise. |
| Accommodate | Can demonstrate concern for others. | Can devalue own contribution or needs. |
| Avoid | Does not add to conflict or escalation.<br>Some conflicts simply end on their own. | Does not deal with problems, so they do not get resolved.<br>Gains or changes that could result from conflict may not occur. |

Conflict typology based on Thomas, 1976.

approaches that that can help adults and institutions engage constructively with youths in conflict are described below.

1. **Be flexible and cooperative in responding to conflict.** People often respond to conflict habitually, repeating prior responses such as fight or flight. In my research on peer conflicts, students could identify the "conflict seekers" and "conflict avoiders" among their peers (Opotow, 1991). School adults, too, describe taking on a habitual, rigid, authoritarian role when they intervene with students over school infractions, acting like a "bad guy" or "tough." These responses to conflict can be effective in some contexts but not in others. Kenneth Thomas' (1976) typology describes five types of conflict responses: compete, collaborate, compromise, accommodate, and avoid. As Table 6.2 indicates, each style has advantages and

disadvantages. Versatility in one's conflict response is a valuable resource. Because collaborative conflict styles are more likely to foster positive, co-operative conflict processes and outcomes than are more competitive styles (Deutsch, 1973), it is advisable to use collaborative approaches when addressing youth conflict because doing so is more likely to result in mutual understanding and constructive outcomes.

2. **Use soft rather than harsh influence strategies.** Five sources of social influence, from those that are softer to those that are harsher, are referent power (hoping to be similar to a particular person), expert power (having special knowledge or information), reward power (having the ability to provide something desired), legitimate power (having the right to lead and command), and coercive power (having the ability to mete out threats and punishment that influence one's behavior (Raven, 1993). The choice of particular influence tactics ultimately affects social relationships. When dominant parties in unequal power relationships (e.g., school administrators and students) use harsh tactics to elicit compliance—as is often the case for conflicts labeled "rule infractions" such as peer conflict and class cutting—they are likely to devalue low power individuals who comply (Kipnis, 1976). Compliance elicited through harsh influence tactics can make these tactics appear effective and appropriate, furthering their normalization as standard operating procedure. Using harsh tactics, however, can be shortsighted; using power to elicit compliance can have considerable long-term costs (Ury, Brett, & Goldberg, 1989). Moreover, harsh tactics are unlikely to foster cooperation and are more likely to yield rigid, destructive conflict processes and outcomes that can foster moral exclusion.

3. **Acknowledge whose conflict it is.** Our own conflicts often seem more complex and important than others' conflicts. Bystanders to conflicts lack participants' detailed knowledge of the dynamics that began and furthered the conflict. When the danger of physical or other injury exists, adult bystanders can prevent conflicts from escalating out of control. It is important that potential interveners can distinguish between helpful and unhelpful conflict interventions. When intervention is warranted, the type of intervention used should permit the parties themselves to shape their own experience and learning, albeit with a safety net in place if subsequent events do not work as expected.

Youths have little organizational power, and some conflicts they experience are those of the organization. In other words, organizational conflicts can be projected onto the students. To use conflicts experienced by organizational members as resources, organizations themselves must be willing to be learning organizations characterized by critical self-reflection. From this perspective, acute and chronic conflicts experienced by those within the organization or those affected by the organization can serve as an impetus for organizational growth and change.

4. **Model constructive conflict skills.** Adults who work with youths are especially well placed to help youths learn important conflict skills. Adults who are available to talk with students about conflict should themselves be comfortable with conflict and knowledgeable about its complexities, even for seemingly simple conflicts. Adults can model conflict skills by taking youths' conflicts seriously; addressing conflicts in respectful, friendly, nonintrusive ways; and modeling constructive conflict skills and processes that engender cooperative processes and constructive goals in their own conflicts. When adults advise youths to "talk it out" with their adversaries, they underplay the difficulty of conflict talk, which many adults avoid in their everyday lives at home, at work, and in the community. For example, conflicts among school staff members are often quite apparent to students. If staff members handle these conflicts forthrightly and cooperatively, they offer students powerful lessons on constructive approaches to conflict. Similarly, when organizations view conflicts as opportunities and resources that can renew stale or outmoded processes or policies, they suggest to students that they, too, can find conflicts useful to refresh their perspectives and that the organization will listen with interest to their observations and concerns. Specific skills that may benefit adults and youths include recognizing that cognitive biases can foster conflict, increasing listening and perspective taking skills, learning self-esteem–preserving and honest ways to acknowledge to oneself and others the extent to which one is responsible for harmful actions, and learning ways for those who have acted harmfully to explain their behavior and the circumstances that led to it or to offer sincere apologies.

## Conclusions

Conflicts have a raw power that can bring to the surface the complexity and ambiguity of social living. Conflict and its aftermath offer an opportunity to improve communication, develop better perspective-taking skills, and engage in creative problem solving. However, because conflicts can generate discomfort and pain, the urge to control, manage, and resolve conflicts can seem urgent. Rather than try to subdue, conquer, or dispose of conflicts, we might approach them more gently. Each conflict is an opportunity to disturb our assumptions, expectancies, and stereotypes. Youth conflicts, which are often stereotyped as irrational and negative, offer opportunities to connect with fundamental moral issues that underlie conflict. If we, in our roles as teachers, administrators, counselors, parents, and professionals, are attuned to the challenges that face youths as they engage in conflict, we can be better positioned to help them. By disturbing social routines, conflicts offer us junctures for collaboratively, cooperatively, and constructively approaching the challenges that youths face. This kind of help can nurture morality in the moments when morality is most crucial and salient.

# References

Berkowitz, M. W., Guerra, N., & Nucci, L. (1991). Sociomoral development and drug and alcohol abuse. In W. M. Kurtines & J. L. Gewirtz (Eds.), *Handbook of moral behavior and development: Vol. 3. Application* (pp. 35–53). Hillsdale, NJ: Lawrence Erlbaum.

Bodine, R. J., & Crawford, D. K. (1998). *Conflict resolution education: A guide to building quality programs in schools.* San Francisco: Jossey-Bass.

Cornelius, H., & Faire, S. (1989). *Everyone can win: How to resolve conflict.* West Roseville, New South Wales, Australia: Simon & Schuster.

Coser, L. (1956). *The functions of social conflict.* New York: Free Press.

Deutsch, M. (1973). *The resolution of conflict.* New Haven, CT: Yale University Press.

Deutsch, M. (1982). Interdependence and psychological orientation. In V. J. Derlega & J. Grzelak (Eds.), *Cooperation and helping behavior* (pp. 15–42). New York: Academic Press.

Deutsch, M., & Coleman, P. T. (Eds.). (2000). *The handbook of conflict resolution: Theory and practice.* San Francisco: Jossey-Bass.

Diaute, C., & Fine, M. (Eds.). (2003). Youth perspectives on violence and injustice [Special issue]. *Journal of Social Issues* 59(1), 1–14.

Fallis, R. K., & Opotow, S. (2003). Are students failing school or are schools failing students?" Class cutting in high school. *Journal of Social Issues,* 59(1), 103–119.

Fisher, R., Ury, W., & Patton, B. (1991). *Getting to yes: Negotiating agreement without giving in* (2nd ed.). Boston: Houghton Mifflin.

Killen, M., & Hart, D. (Eds.). (1995). *Morality in everyday life: Developmental perspectives.* New York: Cambridge University Press.

Kipnis, D. (1976). *The powerholders.* Chicago: The University of Chicago Press.

Opotow, S. (1990). Moral exclusion and injustice: An overview. *Journal of Social Issues,* 46(1), 1–20.

Opotow, S. (1991). Adolescent peer conflicts: Implications for students and for schools. *Education and Urban Society,* 23, 416–441.

Opotow, S., & Deutsch, M. (1999). Learning to cope with conflict and violence: How schools can help youth. In E. Frydenberg (Ed.), *Learning to cope: Developing as a person in complex societies* (pp. 198–224). Oxford, UK: Oxford University Press.

Raven, B. (1993). The bases of power: Origins and recent developments. *Journal of Social Issues,* 49(4), 227–251.

Rubin, J. Z., Pruitt, D. B., & Kim, S. H. (1994). *Social conflict: Escalation, stalemate, and settlement* (2nd ed.). New York: McGraw Hill.

Sanon, F., Baxter, M., Fortune, L., & Opotow, S. (2001). Class cutting: Perspectives of urban high school students. In J. Shultz & A. Cook-Sather (Eds.), *In our own words: Students' perspectives on school* (pp. 73–91). Lanham, MD: Rowman & Littlefield.

Tavuchis, N. (1991). *Mea culpa: The sociology of apology and reconciliation.* Stanford, CA: Stanford University Press.

Thomas, K. W. (1976). Conflict and conflict management. In M. D. Dunnette (Ed.), *Handbook of industrial and organizational psychology* (Vol. II, pp. 889–935). Chicago: Rand McNally.

Ury, W., Brett, J. M., & Goldberg, S. B. (1989). *Getting disputes resolved: Designing systems to cut the costs of conflict.* San Francisco: Jossey-Bass.

# Institutional Supports for Moral Functioning

Although there is relatively little research on parental socialization of moral reasoning, some tentative conclusions can be drawn. Children with higher levels of moral reasoning tend to have parents who are supportive and encourage autonomous thinking, stimulate their children's moral thinking by involving their children in moral discussions, and use inductive rather than power-assertive modes of reasoning.

*—Nancy Eisenberg*

To contribute to society, most individuals move beyond exclusive preoccupation with moral conduct and character to consider how institutional practices facilitate or undermine moral functioning. Schools can contribute to this development by helping young people expand their knowledge of personalities and by fostering a greater awareness of how societal institutions influence thoughts, feelings, and actions.

*—Theresa A. Thorkildsen*

Religion's influence on moral identity formation is likely to be most beneficial under three conditions: (a) moral issues are discussed in ways that incorporate worldviews and moral intuitions, (b) the synthesis of the self's aspirations with moral goals is supported, and (c) opportunities for prosocial action are regularly provided.

*—Daniel Hart and Robert Atkins*

Community-based youth organizations incorporate younger generations into the polity. They stabilize democracies to the extent that their practices develop democratic dispositions in youths. If community-based youth organizations were widely available, they could play a role in redressing class inequalities in political participation.

—*Constance A. Flanagan*

# Chapter 7
# Prosocial and Moral Development in the Family

## Nancy Eisenberg

People are not born moral or immoral. Normal children have the capacity to develop empathy and positive behaviors such as helping and sharing, as well negative behaviors such as stealing and aggression. But how do children become moral individuals? Evidence suggests that heredity plays some role in the development of moral behavior in children. Researchers have found that identical twins are more similar to one another in their empathy and prosocial behavior than are fraternal twins (see review in Eisenberg & Fabes, 1998). It is likely that aspects of children's temperament that are heritable (e.g., their tendencies to experience emotions such as sadness and anger and their ability to regulate their emotions and related behavior) provide an avenue through which genetics affect children's moral behavior. In addition, children's temperaments affect how their parents interact with and attempt to socialize them. Thus, it is likely that children's genetic inheritances affect their moral development in multiple ways. Nonetheless, it appears that socialization within the family is an important contributor to children's moral development.

Parents are likely to affect their children's moral development in numerous ways, and these ways may differ somewhat for different aspects of morality. Before turning to specific parental practices, let us consider an interesting real-life example of how parents might influence the development of prosocial behavior.

In their book *The Altruistic Personality*, Samuel and Pearl Oliner (1988) compared rescuers of Jews in Nazi-dominated Europe in World War II with people from the same regions who did not act as rescuers. Of course, providing help to Jews in countries controlled by Germany during the war was a very risky course of action that could easily cost helpers and their families their lives. The Oliners were interested in the factors that differentiated rescuers from their less altruistic neighbors.

Through extensive interviews with rescuers and nonrescuers, the Oliners found that an important factor was the training that people received in their families. For example, one difference was the values that were expressed through parents' verbalizations and actual behavior. Values of equity—that is, notions of fair procedures, fair allocation of goods, and impartiality in regard to the administration of justice—were emphasized in many of the homes of both rescuers and nonrescuers; however, rescuers were more likely than nonrescuers to report that they learned generosity and caring from their parents or another influential adult. For example, three rescuers reported:

> I learned generosity, to be open, to help people.
> I learned to be good to one's neighbor, honesty, scruples—to be responsible, concerned, and considerate. To work—and work hard. But also to help—to the point of leaving one's work to help one's neighbor.
> To be good and caring, to love people. Mother always said to remember to do some good for someone at least once a day (Oliner & Oliner, 1988, pp. 154–165).

When recalling the values they had learned from parents (or occasionally another very influential person in their life), 44% of rescuers mentioned caring or generosity compared with only 21% of bystanders (Oliner & Oliner, 1988).

Of equal importance, rescuers learned to be more inclusive than did nonrescuers in regard to ethical obligations. Nonrescuers reported that their parents emphasized ethical obligations to family, friends, elders, the church, and country but not to other groups of people. In contrast, 39% of the rescuers (compared with 13% of bystanders) reported that their parents emphasized that ethical values applied to interactions with all people. They said things like:

> They taught me to respect all human beings.
> He taught me to love my neighbor—to consider him my equal whatever his nationality or religion.
> He taught me especially to be tolerant (Oliner & Oliner, 1988, p. 165).

This orientation was reflected in the reasons that rescuers gave for their helping of Jews. Approximately half of all rescuers reported that a universalistic obligation was one reason for their helping, and the reports of the Jewish survivors they rescued were consistent with those of the rescuers. For example, one rescuer reported helping for the following reason:

> The reason is that every man is equal. We all have the right to live. It was plain murder, and I couldn't stand that. I would help a Mohammedan just as well as a Jew. We have got to live as humans and not as beasts (Oliner & Oliner, 1988, p. 166).

Parents of rescuers and nonrescuers also differed in the discipline practiced by their parents. For example, rescuers, in comparison with bystanders, reported that their parents used less physical punishment and more reasoning in their discipline. However, the two groups did not differ in the degree to which they recalled being disciplined for disobedience and behaviors such as aggression, lying, or stealing. In addition, more nonrescuers perceived that parental punishment had been routine and gratuitous—"a cathartic release of aggression on the part of the parent and unrelated to their behavior" (Oliner & Oliner, 1988, p. 180). Finally, and of considerable importance, rescuers reported that their families were closer than did nonrescuers.

Thus, rescuers and their less altruistic neighbors reported different experiences with their families when growing up. Rescuers had closer relations to their parents than did nonrescuers, which suggests that parents of rescuers were relatively warm and supportive. Parents of rescuers, more than parents of bystanders, tended to emphasize caring and the extension of ethical obligations to all people, reasoned with their children in disciplinary encounters, and used relatively little physical punishment. Parents of rescuers also modeled caring behavior with people both in the family and with others whom they did not know well. They did not indulge their children and did discipline them when they exhibited antisocial behaviors.

The Oliners' findings pertaining to the socialization of rescuers and nonrescuers are very similar to the research findings regarding the socialization of children's prosocial behavior in everyday life. But before summarizing the findings in this body of research, the next section briefly summarizes some of the research regarding the early socialization of a conscience and guilt. After an examination of the relationship of parenting to prosocial behavior, the relationship of parenting to the development of children's moral reasoning is discussed.

## Development of Conscience

The notion of a conscience (i.e., the voice inside us that causes guilt and pushes us to behave in moral ways) is familiar to most people in

American culture. In research on children, the term "conscience" is often used to refer to an internal regulatory mechanism that increases children's tendencies to conform with standards of conduct accepted in their culture. It is likely that young children's consciences often primarily reflect parental standards that have been taken on as their own (i.e., internalized). At older ages, values derived from other people and sources likely contribute to the development of a conscience. The conscience restrains antisocial behavior or destructive impulses and promotes children's compliance with adults' rules and standards, even when no one is monitoring their behavior. The conscience can also foster prosocial behavior by causing children to feel guilty when they engage in uncaring or hurtful behavior or do not live up to internalized values regarding helping others (Eisenberg, 2000; Hoffman, 2000).

Children are more likely to take on their parents' moral values if their parents do not use excessive physical punishment but instead use discipline that deemphasizes parental power. For example, parents' use of explanations that help children understand and learn parental values appears to enhance children's internalization of parental standards, although primarily when parents' messages are clear and consistent, perceived as appropriate by children, and motivate children (e.g., arouse concern for others; Hoffman, 2000). Furthermore, a secure, positive parent–child relationship provides the basis for young children's openness to parental communications about and enforcement of parents' values (Kochanska & Thompson, 1997).

Children may develop a conscience in different ways according to their temperamental emotionality. For fear-prone infants, the development of conscience seems to be promoted by their mothers' use of gentle discipline that deemphasizes power (e.g., reasoning with the child, making polite suggestions, using nonmaterial incentives). When mothers use gentle discipline, fearful children do not become so apprehensive and emotionally overaroused that they cannot learn from their parents. Gentle discipline is believed to arouse fearful children just enough that they pay attention to and remember the content of their mothers' socialization messages. In contrast, gentle discipline seems to be unrelated to the development of conscience in fearless young children, perhaps because these children are insufficiently aroused by gentle discipline. Fearless children benefit from a positive parent–child relationship that includes cooperation and a secure attachment. When mothers of fearless children are consistently available, supportive, sensitive, and empathic toward their children, the children tend to be cooperative, compliant, and eager to accept parental demands and values (Eisenberg, 2000; Kochanska & Thompson, 1997).

## The Socialization of Empathy-related Responding and Prosocial Behavior

*Empathy* has been defined in numerous ways. For our purposes, it is an affective response that stems from the apprehension or comprehension of another's emotional state or condition and that is similar to what the other person is feeling or would be expected to feel. Thus, if a girl views a sad person and consequently feels sad herself, she is experiencing empathy (Eisenberg & Fabes, 1998).

Empathy often evolves into sympathy. *Sympathy* is an emotional response that stems from the apprehension or comprehension of another's emotional state or condition; however, rather than being the same as the other's state or condition, sympathy consists of feelings of sorrow or concern for the other. Thus, if a girl sees a sad peer and feels concern for the peer, she is experiencing sympathy. Such a sympathetic reaction often is based on empathic sadness (Eisenberg & Fabes, 1998).

Children who experience sympathy or are prone to experience it are more likely than other children to engage in prosocial behavior (Eisenberg & Fabes, 1998; Hoffman, 2000). *Prosocial behavior* is voluntary behavior intended to benefit another. Prosocial behavior can be motivated by a variety of factors, including egoistic concerns (e.g., the desire for something in return, a concrete reward, or social approval), other-oriented concern (e.g., sympathy), or moral values (e.g., the desire to uphold internalized moral values). *Altruistic behaviors* are prosocial behaviors motivated by other-oriented or moral concerns rather than by concrete or social rewards or the desire to reduce aversive affective states. Often one cannot tell if prosocial behavior is altruistic or not, although socializers generally want to foster an other orientation rather than self-interested or approval-seeking orientations.

Consistent with the Oliners' findings in their study of rescuers, children who are sympathetic and prosocial tend to have secure attachments with their parents, and their parents tend to be warm and supportive. Moreover, these parents tend to model and value prosocial behavior and use disciplinary practices that promote the development of conscience and sympathy for others.

### Quality of the Parent–Child Relationship

Toddlers and preschoolers who show concern for others and engage in prosocial behavior tend to have secure, positive relationships with their parents. Thus, a positive relationship between parent and child seems to provide the foundation for moral development, including prosocial and empathy-related development. Moreover, maternal expression of positive emotion in the home and mothers' tolerance of children's negative emotions (when they do not harm others) have been linked to higher sympathy in children (Eisenberg & Fabes, 1998).

However, as children get older, parental warmth and support are only weakly associated with children's generosity and helping, and high levels of parental permissiveness combined with warmth are not associated with children's prosocial behavior. In childhood, the relationship of parental warmth with children's prosocial behavior seems to vary as a function of the child-rearing practices used by parents. When parents are supportive *and* use effective practices such as modeling and reasoning, their children are likely to be relatively prosocial. Children are less likely to be socially responsible and prosocial if their parents are nurturant but fail to set high standards, model prosocial behaviors themselves, or use practices that induce their children to consider others' needs and perspectives. The cycle seems to be mutually reinforcing in that children with warm parents seem to feel good about their parents and are receptive to parental influence, increasing the effectiveness of parents' child-rearing practices. Children's prosocial behavior can also elicit warm and supportive behavior from parents who might otherwise seem cold and nonsupportive. Moreover, because children tend to be close to warm parents, they seem to acquire a greater capacity to care about others' feelings and welfare. And because their own emotional needs are more likely to be met, children of positive, warm parents seem less likely than those of cold, negative parents to focus on their own needs (Eisenberg, 1992; Hoffman, 2000).

In summary, it appears that parental nurturance can foster the development of children's prosocial tendencies if parents also use other effective child-rearing techniques. However, parental nurturance combined with high levels of permissiveness does not appear to encourage the development of altruism.

## Modeling and Preachings

Children imitate the behaviors of other people, especially important, powerful, and nurturant people (e.g., parents). Although it is not entirely clear why this is true, children seem to identify with significant people close to them and want to be similar to them. In addition, most children want to behave in a competent manner and may believe that adults' behaviors are good examples. Children are sometimes rewarded for imitating adults and may learn new ways of helping or prosocial norms by imitating models. In any case, children tend to imitate the moral—or immoral—behaviors of their parents, as well as those of peers and other adults (Eisenberg & Fabes, 1998).

What kind of evidence supports the importance of modeling prosocial behaviors? In laboratory studies of the effects of modeling on children's prosocial behavior, a child and an adult typically play a game in which they earn prizes or tokens that can be traded for prizes. The adult either donates or does not donate some or all of his or her earnings to a needy person or group. Then the child is left alone, at which time his or her donating is monitored. In general, children imitate the prosocial or selfish behavior modeled by the adult (Eisenberg & Valiente, 2002).

The findings of nonexperimental studies generally are consistent with those from laboratory studies: Children tend to imitate the prosocial tendencies and empathic behavior of their caregivers (and their siblings), both at home and at school (Eisenberg & Fabes, 1998). For example, in a study of Freedom Riders—people who were involved in civil rights activities in the South in the 1960s, often at risk to themselves—the activists who were most fully committed in terms of their time and effort reported having parents who explicitly modeled altruistic behavior. These activists, referred to as the "Fully Committed," were most committed in terms of their time and energy rather than monetary donations.

One of the Fully Committed reported that "my father carried me on his shoulders during the Sacco-Vanzetti parades"; another described how his father fought on the side of the Loyalists in the Spanish Civil War. Finally, another respondent's father was outraged by the Nazi atrocities and, though overage and apparently disqualified on grounds of health, was finally accepted into the military during the Second World War. In short, we seem to have found the presence of altruistic models in the backgrounds of Fully Committed altruists, models whose very behavior apparently influenced the course of their offspring's activities (Rosenhan, 1970, pp. 162–163).

In general, adults' modeling of altruism seems to have a greater influence on children's behavior if there is a close bond between the adult and the child. Recall that Oliner and Oliner (1988) found that rescuers' parents modeled and preached caring behavior and that rescuers felt close to their parents. In the study of the civil rights workers, the most committed, altruistic workers reported not only that their parents frequently were models of altruism but also that they had warm and respecting relationships with one or both parents (Rosenhan, 1970).

Adults can also model prosocial behaviors symbolically—that is, through their discussion of prosocial activities or the value and importance of helping others. Oliner and Oliner (1988) found that parental preachings about caring and the universality of ethical standards appeared to influence the rescuers' own value systems. In that group, parental modeling of prosocial behavior and their preaching seem to have occurred simultaneously.

Nonetheless, the wording of adults' preaching influences the degree to which children take those preachings to heart (Eisenberg & Fabes, 1998). In laboratory studies, if children are exposed to adults who merely state general norms regarding altruism (e.g., "People should give"), they are not particularly likely to share. In contrast, preaching increases children's donating when it pertains to the effects of sharing on other people (e.g., "They will be very happy if they could buy food and toys") or highlights the needy state of a potential recipient of assistance (e.g., "If everyone would help these children, maybe they wouldn't look so sad").

In summary, socializers can foster prosocial behavior in children through their own words and deeds. Children are especially likely to imitate warm models, such as supportive parents. Preaching that capitalizes on children's capacity for empathy and sympathy seems to be particularly effective. Furthermore, the combination of words and deeds is important: Socializers who are hypocritical—who preach altruism but do not model it—may have little positive effect on children's prosocial development (see Eisenberg & Fabes, 1998).

## Instructions to Help and Practice by Doing

Children are more likely to help or share with others if adults instruct them to do so. In laboratory research, young children instructed to share tend to do so even in private, and the effects of the instructions may last for weeks. However, the effectiveness of more directive instructions (i.e., simply telling the child what he or she must do) may decrease somewhat with age during the elementary school years.

Instructing children to assist others may promote prosocial behavior because it induces them to rehearse or practice performing prosocial behaviors. Children who are induced to help others through encouragement (e.g., to donate some gift certificates to needy children or collect toys for children in the hospital) are more helpful on subsequent occasions. Such laboratory findings are consistent with cross-cultural studies of children in their families and neighborhoods. Children brought up in cultures in which they are routinely assigned responsibilities that involve caring for or helping others are more prosocial than children in cultures in which they are not. Children who have opportunities to help others may learn new helping skills, receive social approval or helping, and discover that they often feel good when they produce positive outcomes for other people.

They may also come to think of themselves as being helpful people and, consequently, engage in more prosocial behavior in other contexts. However, children are unlikely to think that they really wanted to help if they feel that they were forced (rather than induced) to assist others. Constraining instructions, which give children little choice, seem to become less effective as children grow older (Eisenberg & Fabes, 1998).

## Discipline and the Development of Sympathy and Prosocial Behavior

When children misbehave or do not engage in behavior desired by adults, parents can take a variety of approaches. Consider a situation in which parents observe their son refusing to share his toys with his younger sister, who then becomes upset. His parents may do nothing at all, scold the boy and send him to his room, or spank him. Alternatively, they may try to talk to him about his behavior; perhaps saying things such as, "How would you feel if your sister wouldn't share her toy with you?"

REASONING (INDUCTIONS). Researchers have found that some disciplinary techniques are more effective than others at promoting sympathy and prosocial behavior. The most effective disciplinary technique appears to be the use of reasoning (often labeled *inductions*). Such reasoning frequently, but not always, consists of the parent pointing out the consequences of the child's behavior for another person (e.g., "See, you made her cry") or highlighting another person's emotional state (e.g., "Now she feels bad"). Parents' use of inductions frequently tends to be associated with higher levels of both sympathy and prosocial behavior in children (Eisenberg & Fabes, 1998; Hoffman, 2000).

Inductions appear to be effective with older children, as well as children as young as 1 to 2 years old, if the inductions are simple and delivered with some affective force. Inductions that highlight others' feelings and needs, call attention to harm done to others, or encourage children to correct harm that they have done may be especially effective in promoting prosocial development (Hoffman, 2000). However, inductions seem to be effective only if they are used by parents who are not overly punitive or have a history of using this sort of discipline (Eisenberg & Fabes, 1998).

Inductions may promote prosocial development for a variety of reasons. By directing children's attention to others' needs and emotional states, parents encourage their children to take other people's perspectives and to sympathize with them. In addition, when using inductions, parents often provide reasons for behaving—or not behaving—in prosocial ways. Children can remember and apply these reasons in new situations.

Of related importance, parents' use of inductions likely creates an optimal learning situation. Children learn best when they are not overly frightened, aroused, or angry. When parents use inductions, children are unlikely to be too emotionally aroused to attend to the content of the induction and to the consequences of their behavior. Furthermore, parents' inductions frequently communicate that children are responsible for their own behavior, and parents who reason with their children rather than yelling, demeaning, or spanking them provide regulated, caring models for their children to imitate (Eisenberg, 1992; Hoffman, 2000).

POWER-ASSERTIVE OR PUNITIVE DISCIPLINE. Power-assertive discipline includes physical punishment, the deprivation of privileges, or threats of either of these. As previously discussed, such discipline undermines the development of conscience. In some research, it has also been associated with low levels of sympathy and prosocial behavior.

Whether or not power-assertive discipline is associated with low sympathy and prosocial behavior likely depends on quality of the parent–child relationship and on the severity of the discipline. Parents' excessive use of power-assertive techniques is generally associated with low levels of moral development in children, and such discipline may be especially harmful if parents are cold and punitive as a general rule. Power assertion may have little or no negative effect if used infrequently in a measured and rational way by warm, supportive parents who typically use other forms of discipline (Eisenberg & Fabes, 1998; Hoffman, 2000).

Excessive use of power-assertive discipline may be harmful to prosocial development because parents who consistently use this type of discipline model aggressive behavior for their children to imitate. Moreover, harsh punishment likely undermines children's motivation to attend to their parents or try to please them. In combination with the high level of arousal that harsh punishment can induce in children, this disincentive creates a situation in which it is unlikely that children will learn or internalize reasons to care about others' needs. Indeed, when they receive harsh punishment or threats thereof, children are likely to be scared and, consequently, may focus on their own needs rather than on those of other people. Thus, children who are frequently exposed to punitive discipline are unlikely to learn to sympathize with other people and may instead learn that the primary reason to engage in prosocial behaviors is to avoid punishment. Consequently, they generally will not be motivated to help others when there is no threat of punishment.

REINFORCEMENT. Many parents, educators, and developmental scientists believe that an effective way to increase the frequency of desired behaviors, including helping and sharing, is to reward these behaviors. Thus, parents may try to encourage prosocial behaviors by giving their children a treat or money when they have performed helpful deeds. They may also praise their children for their comforting, sharing, or helping behaviors.

In fact, material and social rewards do promote prosocial actions, at least in the short term. However, it is unclear if the effects of rewards, especially material rewards, are enduring. Social rewards such as praise may have stronger long-term effects on children's prosocial behavior than do material rewards; praise that attributes children's behavior to their kindness or internal motives may be more effective than praise that merely labels a behavior as positive (Eisenberg & Fabes, 1998).

Moreover, material rewards for children's prosocial actions sometimes undermine the development of altruism. Children who are frequently rewarded for their prosocial behaviors may come to believe that they assist others primarily to receive a reward. For example, in a study of second to fifth graders, some children were told that they would be rewarded for performing a task to help hospitalized children (or saw other children being told that there would be a reward), but others were not told that they would receive rewards. The participants' mothers were questioned regarding the degree to which they valued rewards and used them with their children. Children who were told that they would be rewarded assisted more in that context than did children who were not told that they would be rewarded. However, the rewarded children helped *less* in a subsequent situation in which rewards were not mentioned and they were left alone during the time they could help. The association of rewards with helping was detrimental only if the children's mothers reported that they valued and used rewards relatively frequently. Mothers who felt more positive about using rewards also reported that their children tended not to engage in prosocial behavior. Thus, children who were frequently exposed to rewards in the home seemed to be less intrinsically motivated to help when there were no rewards for doing so (Fabes, Fultz, Eisenberg, May-Plumlee, & Christopher, 1989). Such findings suggest that providing children with material rewards for their prosocial actions is not an effective way to promote an altruistic orientation in children.

In summary, prosocial children tend to have socializers who use reasoning rather than punishment or material rewards for discipline and provide opportunities for children to engage in prosocial actions. Socializers may also model and value prosocial behaviors and encourage perspective taking, empathy, and sympathy. Such techniques may be even more effective when children have warm, secure relationships with their caregivers.

## The Socialization of Moral Judgment

A commonly used measure of children's moral development is their moral reasoning. In research of this type, children are typically asked to resolve hypothetical (or occasionally real-life) moral conflicts and to provide reasons for their decisions. Their reasoning is coded on the basis of its level of moral maturity. For example, whereas decisions based on self-gain or fear of punishment are viewed as relatively low in moral maturity, reasoning based on moral principles is seen to be more advanced. Much of the moral reasoning research is based on Kohlberg's (1984) system of scoring moral judgment, although some rely on other systems such as Eisenberg's levels of prosocial moral reasoning (see Eisenberg & Fabes, 1998).

Socializers have typically been assigned a circumscribed role in moral development by cognitive developmental theorists such as Kohlberg. Thus, until recently, researchers had not paid a great deal of attention to the contributions of parenting to the development of moral reasoning. Furthermore, because cognitive developmentalists have emphasized the role of taking another's perspective in the development of moral reasoning, much of the relevant research on the socialization of moral judgment concerns parental practices that would be expected to foster perspective taking. With these caveats, some conclusions about the role of family in nurturing morality remain adequately supported.

### The Promotion of Autonomous Thinking

The available research provides some support for Kohlberg's (1984) assertion that providing opportunities for children to construct their own moral ideas fosters children's moral reasoning. Some evidence suggests that parents who encourage their children's participation in discussions and decision making by asking questions are more likely to have children who reason at relatively high levels of moral reasoning. Specifically, parental behaviors such as eliciting children's opinions, drawing out children's reasoning with appropriate probing questions, paraphrasing, and checking for understanding, all in the context of emotional support and attentiveness, have been associated with children's development of higher level reasoning. In contrast, simply providing information or critiquing and directly challenging children (especially in a hostile manner) have not been associated with children's moral growth. Moreover, parents' presentation of higher level reasoning predicts the development of children's higher level moral judgment. In brief, parental practices that promote consideration of higher level moral ideas—but do so in a supportive rather than heavy-handed manner—tend to be associated with children's moral growth (Eisenberg & Valiente, 2002; Walker & Hennig, 1999).

## Disciplinary Practices

Consistent with the findings for conscience and prosocial development, children who exhibit relatively high levels of moral reasoning tend to have parents who favor inductive (i.e., reasoning) discipline and use relatively little power-assertive, punitive discipline. However, parents' overall styles of parenting, more than any one disciplinary practice, may be associated with children's moral reasoning. Parents who use an authoritative parenting style (e.g., give explanations or suggestions, try to engage children in finding moral solutions, use a combination of reasoned control and support) are more likely to have children who exhibit high-level moral judgment than are parents who are less authoritative in their discipline (e.g., controlling and nonsupportive; see Eisenberg & Valiente, 2002).

## The Emotional Environment

As noted previously, parental warmth likely provides an optimal environment for socialization because children are more likely to attend to their parents and care about pleasing them when the relationship is generally close and supportive. In fact, the limited research suggests that parental warmth is associated with higher level moral reasoning in children (Eisenberg & Valiente, 2002). As was discussed in regard to prosocial development, it is possible that parental warmth does not exert a direct effect on children's moral reasoning. Rather, parental warmth may simply enhance the effectiveness of other constructive parental practices in fostering the growth of moral reasoning. Moreover, it is likely that parental warmth encourages children's involvement in productive moral discussions.

## The Relationship Between Parents' and Children's Moral Reasoning

A number of investigators have examined whether parents' level of moral judgment is related to the level of children's moral reasoning. A positive relationship between the two could be caused by a number of factors, including similarity between parents' and children's cognitive abilities and the idea that parents with higher level moral reasoning promote their children's moral reasoning by stimulating their cognitive conflict or using optimal child-rearing practices. Although findings have been rather inconsistent, a weak positive relationship appears to exist between children's and parents' moral reasoning, such that parents who are higher in their moral judgment have children who also have relatively high judgment (Eisenberg & Valiente, 2002; Walker & Hennig, 1999).

In summary, although relatively little research has been done on parental socialization of moral reasoning, some tentative conclusions can be drawn. Children with higher level moral reasoning tend to have parents who are supportive and encourage autonomous thinking, stimulate their children's moral thinking by involving their children in moral discussions, and use inductive rather than power-assertive modes of reasoning. In addition, a weak relationship may exist between parents' and children's moral reasoning.

## The Importance of Empathy Training

In the aforementioned study of rescuers of Jews in Nazi-dominated Europe, Oliner and Oliner (1988) found that rescuers were higher than nonrescuers in a measure of the tendency to experience empathy. Furthermore, sympathy and caring were the most common motives that rescuers gave for helping, and rescued survivors similarly reported that their rescuers appeared to be motivated by sympathy.

Parental techniques that foster children's ability to sympathize with others likely play an important role in the socialization of prosocial behavior. As previously discussed, inductions and preachings that point out others people's feelings and the effects of a child's behavior on others appear to be effective at enhancing children's conscience, prosocial behavior, sympathy, and (most likely) moral reasoning. Based on findings of this sort, numerous researchers and clinicians have argued that one of the most effective ways to enhance children's prosocial responding, reduce aggression, and promote social competence is to use child-rearing practices that help children understand the perspectives of other people and to empathize and sympathize with them.

In their book *Bringing Up a Moral Child*, Schulman and Mekler (1985, p. 67) suggest a number of methods for encouraging children to develop empathy and sympathy. They include the following:

1. Draw children's attention to people's feelings. Ask them to imagine how they would feel in the other person's place.
2. Let children know the impact of their actions on the feelings of others, including yourself.
3. Explain why people feel the way they do.

4. Make clear (or encourage children to discover) actions they can take that would be more considerate.

5. Let children know that you expect them to be considerate and that it is important to you that they are.

6. Let children know that you understand and care about *their* feelings and try to offer them a way to get at least some of what they want—if not now, then in the future.

7. Don't expect children to read minds. Take the time to explain your reasoning to them.

8. Help children understand other people's feelings by reminding them of similar experiences in their own lives.

9. Help children resist the influence of people who discourage or ridicule their empathic feelings.

10. Give children approval when they are considerate; show disappointment when they are not.

11. Use self-control empathy training to teach children to imagine themselves in someone else's place whenever they are inclined to hurt that person.

12. Share your own empathic feelings with children.

13. Point out examples of people who are empathic and those who are not, and communicate your admiration for kindhearted people.

14. Stress the good feelings that come from caring about other people.

15. Encourage children to consider people's capacity for empathy when selecting friends.

To this list, I would add: "Model prosocial behavior, including in your interactions with children."

## Facilitating Empathy Training

How do parents, teachers, and other socializers implement Schulman's and Mekler's (1985) suggestions? Many opportunities arise in everyday activities. For example, news stories and special shows often discuss people who have helped other people in emergency situations (e.g., earthquakes) or in other distressing conditions (e.g., famine) or discuss people who have protected and helped animals. The tragic events of September 11, 2001, for example, included extreme acts of courage and altruism by firemen and other people who tried to rescue victims of the attack on the World Trade Center in New York City. Highlighting such bravery, as well as others' everyday acts of kindness, can help children see that their parents are not the only people in their social world who frequently engage in kind and caring actions. Socializers can point out examples of people who are sympathetic, communicate that these people are admirable, and discuss reasons that people might want to help others.

In addition, disciplinary situations provide excellent opportunities for encouraging children to take others' perspectives and sympathize with them. Consider the following example of a dialogue that could ensue when a preschool child has refused to share a swing with her sister, even after she has used it for a long time:

> *Parent*: I know that you are having a lot of fun on the swing, but your sister also likes to swing. She would like a turn.
> *Child*: But I don't want to get off.
> *Parent*: We know. But sometimes your sister lets you use the swing and her toys. And she has been waiting for a long time. So it's only fair to let her use the swing sometimes.
> *Child*: But I had it first.
> *Parent*: Yes, you did. But do you remember how you felt when your sister was watching TV first and wouldn't let you watch anything you wanted? You felt it wasn't fair, and she feels the same way now (Eisenberg, 1992, p. 104).

This kind of discussion helps the preschooler to understand *how* her sister feels and *why*. Thus, the child is likely to better understand what her sister is feeling and to take that into account.

These are just a few concrete examples of ways that adults can foster children's perspective taking, empathy, and sympathy. Such techniques enhance the development of sympathy and prosocial behaviors based on caring rather than the desire to avoid punishment or for rewards or approval. Moreover, parents and other socializers can talk about their own feelings and perspectives and their own reasons for caring and helping others. All of these techniques likely contribute to the development of children's conscience, sympathy, and prosocial behavior and perhaps even their moral reasoning (Eisenberg & Fabes, 1998).

## References

Eisenberg, N. (1992). *The caring child*. Cambridge, MA: Harvard University Press.

Eisenberg, N. (2000). Emotion, regulation, and moral development. In S. T. Fiske, D. L. Schacter, & C. Zahn-Waxler (Eds.), *Annual review of psychology: Vol. 51* (pp. 665–697). Palo Alto, CA: Annual Reviews.

Eisenberg, N., & Fabes, R. A. (1998). Prosocial development. In W. Damon (Series Ed.) & N. Eisenberg (Vol. Ed.), *Handbook of child psychology: Vol. 3. Social, emotional, and personality development* (5th ed., pp. 701–778). New York: Wiley.

Eisenberg, N., & Valiente, C. (2002). Children's prosocial and moral development. In M. Bornstein (Ed.), *Handbook of parenting: Vol. 5* (2nd ed, pp. 111–142). Mahwah, NJ: Lawrence Erlbaum Associates.

Fabes, R. A., Fultz, J., Eisenberg, N., May-Plumlee, T., & Christopher, F. S. (1989). The effects of reward on children's prosocial motivation: A socialization study. *Developmental Psychology, 25,* 509–515.

Hoffman, M. L. (2000). *Empathy and moral development: Implications for caring and justice.* Cambridge, UK: Cambridge University Press.

Kochanska, G., & Thompson, R.A. (1997). The emergence and development of conscience in toddlerhood and early childhood. In J. Grusec & L. Kuczynski (Eds.),*Handbook of parenting and the internalization of values: A handbook of contemporary theory* (pp. 53–77). New York: Wiley.

Kohlberg, L. (1984). *Essays on moral development: Vol. II. The psychology of moral development.* San Francisco, Harper and Row.

Oliner, S. P., & Oliner, P. M. (1988). *The altruistic personality: Rescuers of Jews in Nazi Europe.* New York: Free Press.

Rosenhan, D. L. (1970). The natural socialization of altruistic autonomy. In J. Macaulay & L. Berkowitz (Eds.), *Altruism and helping behavior* (pp. 251–268). New York: Academic Press.

Schulman, M., & Mekler, E. (1985). *Bringing up a moral child.* Reading, MA: Addison Wesley.

Walker, L. J., & Hennig, K. H. (1999). Parenting style and the development of moral reasoning. *Journal of Moral Education, 28,* 359–374.

# Chapter 8

# Moral Functioning in School

## Theresa A. Thorkildsen

To contribute to society, most individuals move beyond an exclusive preoccupation with moral conduct and character to consider how institutional practices facilitate or undermine moral functioning. Schools can contribute to this development by helping young people expand their knowledge of personalities and by fostering a greater awareness of how societal institutions influence thoughts, feelings, and actions. In schools, students are able to interact with people whose families differ from their own, and they are exposed to new group norms and institutional practices. Schools are primarily responsible for helping young people learn to read, write, and compute, but many educators also intentionally accept responsibility for nurturing wisdom and fairness (e.g., Battistich, Solomon, Kim, Watson, & Schaps, 1995).

Some of the common discoveries made in school by students whose moral choices and behavior are guided by internal norms are outlined in this chapter. Conclusions focus on the fact that young people learn to differentiate between features of personality (conduct, conscience, and identity) and institutional structures (epistemological and justice concerns) to construct complex representations of schooling. Findings concerning students' knowledge of conscience, conduct, and identity offer information on individual differences in personality. Findings about young people's knowledge of how schools are and should be organized focus on age-related differences in students' commitment to educational practices. This evidence supports the idea that students coordinate knowledge of personality differences and the nature of institutional structures in a force that drives their classroom participation. Details of some collective agendas educators use to strengthen students' social knowledge and stimulate high levels of moral functioning are also integrated with information on development to illustrate how educators nurture morality.

## Imagining Life in School

Most children enter school ready to comply with their teachers' expectations. They have learned how to differentiate between their own interests and those of others and to influence events to achieve short-term goals. These are necessary skills for regulating personal conduct and developing enough of a conscience to think about the role of personality in moral functioning (Aronfreed, 1968). Experts disagree on whether the social knowledge necessary for moral agency evolves from repeated cycles of correction and encouragement, the imitation of models, or newly invented solutions to life's dilemmas. Yet it is easy to agree that individual differences in personality co-occur with age-related differences in moral knowledge to influence behavior in school. Even when students cannot talk about their knowledge, they elicit different kinds of emotional responses from their teachers that reveal various approaches to school.

The process of identifying aspects of experience, comparing observations with internal norms, and determining a course of action is currently being called *moral agency* (e.g., Bandura, 1999). Internal norms serve as a knowledge-driven force that compels social participation; the ethical features of this force are labeled *moral engagement*.

Having spent most of my research energies labeling common norms that are integral to students' moral engagement, it seems as though the commonly studied moral and motivational choices that influence conduct and identity reflect only some aspects of students' moral knowledge. Other internal norms that are not so easily understood reflect students' understanding of the nature and purpose of schooling and the fairness of educational practices. Research on beliefs about personal and institutional standards suggests that students' moral knowledge is as central to their intellectual functioning as their academic knowledge. That is, students' knowledge of what makes them feel successful (conduct and identity), what information is of most worth (epistemology), and how school should be organized (fairness) contains sufficient overlap that it seems safe to predict the coexistence of this knowledge in a force that compels classroom participation.

While exploring children's academic functioning, for example, the influence of their beliefs about how school should be organized and which ethical values they find most important was certainly evident in their daily reasoning and classroom behavior (Thorkildsen & Nicholls, 2002). In formal structured interviews, most students accepted the educational materials teachers introduced but reported different fairness and motivational beliefs depending on whether the information was controversial or widely accepted (Nicholls, Nelson, & Gleaves 1995; Nicholls & Thorkildsen, 1989; Thorkildsen, Sodonis, & White-McNulty, 2004). Students differentiate between learning, test, and contest situations and raise different fairness and motivational concerns for each type of situation (Thorkildsen, 2000). Furthermore, students' interest in particular forms of knowledge and preoccupation with particular kinds of fairness differ depending on whether they are concerned with issues of competence, self-determination, or affiliation.

Determining which aspects of moral engagement are central to daily functioning is a daunting task, but most educators listen carefully to their students. Learning where particular students may benefit from guidance can be commonly elicited in reflective conversations comparing problem students with others who show similar characteristics. One teacher, for example, was struggling to understand how Earl, a second grader, might view school. Earl could not talk about his assumptions, but his teacher was consistently reminded of her own son. This reflection helped the teacher realize that Earl was eliciting parenting as well as teaching behaviors and took this as a sign that he was struggling to understand the norms of school.

*Teacher*: It seemed like when [my son Jim] went to kindergarten, I sent this incredibly creative kid ... He had never lifted up a pencil because he didn't want to. But he was in a tree, and he would make a fort, and he would make inventions, and he would be totally into stuff I wouldn't understand. But he would explain it to everyone. He was fascinated with taking a hammer and opening acorns and spreading it for the birds ...

I used to say that every year [at school] he got less creative. He got dumber. They worked it out of him. Except that now he's pulled it all back together. In those early few years, he was so scattered in his thinking ... He'd have these ideas but he'd go nowhere with them.

*Investigator*: But he was scattered when he was little? Did he watch to see if the birds came [for the acorns]?

*Teacher*: No. I also noticed that when I used to read, once the action stopped, he'd pull [the book] out of my hand. "I don't need that part. I only want the action." And then in second grade, he kept a journal, and ... not one entry had a reflection; it was all planning. What I'm going to do next ... But it was, again, very fragmented ... Then I found, at second grade, he pulled back, and he really wasn't interested in anything.

*Investigator*: Even at home?

*Teacher*: Even at home. I think this was his hardest year at school. The teacher would complain to me: "The disorganization!" She had never seen anything

like it ... The social worker there said, "You know I think you've got to structure up his life more." So I pulled in a little ... And his teacher was very
structured. You know, ditto after ditto after ditto. The woman drummed it
into him. And now he does a beautiful project. He'll experiment and he'll
follow it through ... So, when I see the school providing the basics—I'll call
them the basics—I don't mind, because at home where he is free and able to
structure his own time and I can provide many more experiences that they
can't do at school, he's off and running ...
*Investigator*: And ... you started getting him to organize or frame things?
*Teacher*: At about the same time ... I just had this feeling, like, I've got this
really creative, bright kid, but he's going to walk under a truck! So I just
thought that it's my position as his mother to get him to that level.
*Investigator*: And that's what [your student] Earl misses now?
*Teacher*: Right. I feel a lot of times [although I am his teacher] I'm mothering
him ... And in schoolwork he has to be able to say, "I finished something. I
started it and I finished it like everyone else," which is something he never
does—sits down and reads something from start to finish on his own. He
pages through things, looks at the pictures, and then looks at everybody
else's stuff, and then into his desk, and so on.

These educators knew that most second graders could reflect on
their experiences, finish assignments, and remain committed to intellectual projects over several months. Earl's deviation from this norm elicited
frustration from his teacher. By exploring her frustration, Earl's teacher
was able to imagine how much difficulty Earl had coordinating his personal interests and others' expectations in school. To "become less scattered
in thinking" and understand others' expectations well enough to become
morally engaged in a classroom, students like Earl eventually learn to identify the features of particular situations, accept the goals associated with
those situations, and find ways to participate in classroom activities.

Children are less likely than adolescents to understand that their perceptions of school are legitimately influenced by their personal interests
and agendas. Nevertheless, all students, regardless of their age, look for
cues about the expectations of their teachers and classmates. They weigh
their observations against an internal set of norms to determine whether to
comply or take shortcuts. Looking more closely at common age-related patterns in how students learn about behavior, and the relationship between
personal choices and identity, reveals one essential component of moral
engagement. Looking at age-related patterns in students' understanding
of academic knowledge and the fairness of classroom practices offers a
second essential dimension. The coordination of these forms of personal
and school knowledge can become a force that compels participation in
classroom activities when students coordinate their own needs with others'
expectations.

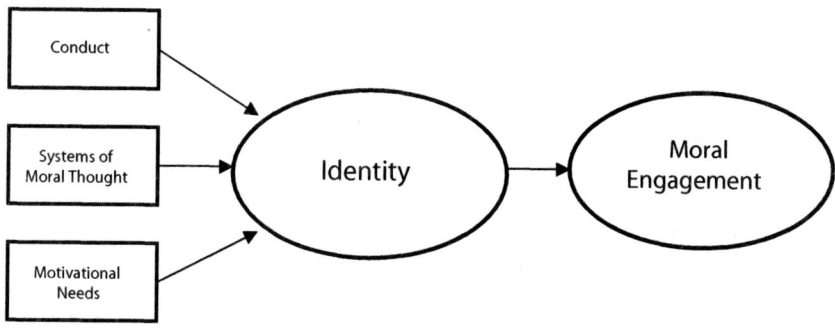

Figure 8.1. Identity and moral engagement in school.

## Learning to Differentiate Between Conduct and Identity

Young people's knowledge of conscience, conduct, and identity develops slowly even though observers are able to see individual differences in personality at all ages. In early childhood, individuals are usually more preoccupied with issues of conduct and compliance than with issues of identity or the fairness of institutional practices (Turiel, 1998); children are aware of the extent to which they correctly comply with others' requests, but they often remain dependent on educators to help them identify interesting projects and ideas. Somewhere in middle childhood, students begin to understand their own authority and value their interests enough to challenge the views of educators (Thorkildsen & Nicholls, 2002); they usually begin to explore the stability of their identities by observing others' reactions while altering behaviors that reveal their interests (e.g., handwriting, clothing, reading preferences). In middle school, the preoccupation with identity often dominates students' attention while forming, maintaining, and evaluating groups, and they use feedback from others to help them imagine possible lives (Peebles, 1995). By the time most students reach adolescence, they are able to reflect on the abstract qualities of identity as well as on the concrete aspects of conduct, offering clear representations of who they are and who they would like to become (Hart & Fegley, 1995). The details of students' views may be dynamic, but over time, they learn about the transient nature of conduct and the more stable features of personality.

Despite these age-related differences, common patterns are evident in how students define and respond to the moral features of their identity as a student (Figure 8.1). Information about such patterns is helpful to educators who are striving to organize classrooms that encourage exemplary forms of moral functioning.

## Common Systems of Moral Thought

Most children and adolescents show evidence of at least one of three approaches to moral reasoning. They may focus on a moral system that involves *obedience for its own sake* and the search for evidence that rules are enforced. Students may also rely on an *instrumental system of doing good* to get something in return or a system of *interpersonal conformity* in which they are concerned with doing good to please others. Each system of thought affects how individuals respond to requests for compliance and their reflections on how moral norms are expressed in behavior.

These approaches to moral problem solving have been apparent over numerous samples and were initially characterized as stages of justice reasoning that individuals eventually outgrow as they come to understand reasons for societal structures and moral principles (e.g., Colby, Kohlberg, Gibbs, & Lieberman, 1983). Currently, researchers disagree on whether individuals progress from one form of reasoning to another or whether these approaches coexist and are called forth by the demands of particular situations. Theoretically, these approaches call for progressively more complex levels of thought, but when individuals encounter situations that pull for primitive forms of reasoning, they seem to react to those expectations.

Rather than participating in theoretical debates, many educators accept the existence of all three approaches to morality. They usually devote their energy to helping students construct more elaborate notions of moral functioning by encouraging students to imagine multiple conceptions of moral authority and justifications for behavior.

## Common Motivational Needs

Systems of moral thought seem to interact with motivational needs in students' moral engagement (e.g., Thorkildsen & Nicholls, 2002). Just as adults do, children and adolescents experience an internal striving for self-determination, competence, and affiliation with others, and these strivings emerge from their personality. They also adopt different motivational orientations for locating their interests in the environment. Similar to the moral systems, these needs and orientations are forces that organize how individuals perceive, define, and evaluate their experiences. Whereas moral systems seem to emphasize the evaluation of conduct, common motivational needs emphasize students' internal strivings as they relate to the establishment of a comfortable identity.

The need for *self-determination* is essential for moral agency because it requires individuals to imagine whether they can succeed at assigned tasks and to select their own identity-enhancing interests. Self-determination impels young people to learn how to regulate their own behavior, make responsible choices, and avoid relying exclusively on the edicts of powerful others. In school, students typically comply with others' expectations, but some activities are organized to help them identify and sustain identity-enhancing interests. Finding meaning in some features of the world while feeling comfortable ignoring other features can enhance students' commitments to particular ideas and values.

Educators often nurture students' feelings of self-determination by noticing themes in students' schoolwork. They also encourage students to spontaneously select activities and label the values they find in the chosen activities. Young people eventually learn that self-determination involves freedom to act in accordance with their values as well as freedom from subjection to others.

The need for *competence* involves the satisfaction of demonstrating moral and intellectual expertise. Most students are learning to define and master a wide variety of tasks, only some of which are defined by their teachers. When learning something new, most students look to others in their environment for information on the task demands, approaches to task mastery, and consequences of performance. Students' orientations toward particular tasks reveal their definitions of competence (Nicholls, 1989). Some students feel competent when tasks are intrinsically meaningful and emphasize their interests, effort, and ideas; they find learning to be a valuable end in itself. Students can also feel competent when they outperform others or avoid appearing incompetent; these students usually find learning a means to the end of pleasing others or demonstrating superiority.

Despite these commonalities, age differences exist in how individuals interpret information obtained through social comparison. Such information can foster disengagement as easily as engagement. Even young children are able to compare their own performance with that of others well enough to take delight in feeling superior and experience shame in feeling inferior about their achievement. As young people develop a richer understanding of attributions for their success and failure, they also construct a more elaborate understanding of the thrills and pitfalls of competition.

With too much competition, a state of disengagement can emerge when individuals realize that their relative positions in social and intellectual hierarchies cannot meet their expectations. Before becoming disengaged, students may feel successful while avoiding schoolwork, withdrawing from others' expectations, and excluding themselves from social interaction. After becoming disengaged, students realize that they may never feel successful and withdraw or otherwise minimize opportunities for success. Students who feel successful are able to affirm a positive moral identity that those who feel unsuccessful cannot.

Educators usually facilitate feelings of success by remaining sensitive to variations in students' definitions of competence. They encourage students to make appropriate attributions for their successes and failures, imagine strategies for improving performance, and focus on task mastery rather than competitive goals.

A third *affiliation* need involves the frequency and quality of interpersonal relationships. At school, students regularly meet individuals who differ from themselves, and they are encouraged to establish many different kinds of relationships. Classroom structures pressure students to take initiative and become skilled at social interaction as they learn to discriminate new interpersonal expectations. Determining how teachers differ from parents, for example, involves the ability to establish, maintain, and restore positive relationships while sharing ideas and interests with others. Individuals do so in an impersonal way when they exchange information and resources without forming strong attachments. They may also find high-quality friendships in school, establishing a kind of intimacy that differs from close connections with family members. Intimacy in school usually involves warm, close, and communicative interactions that tap into shared intellectual and social interests.

Educators typically encourage students to feel successful when forming strong relationships and accept variation in students' preferences for social exchange and intimacy. Issues of trust, for example, are more salient in the collaborations of some students than others (Thorkildsen & Jordan, 1995). Similarly, students differ in the kinds of attention they seek from educators and in which forms of feedback they find encouraging (Thorkildsen & Nicholls, 2002).

## Convergence of Conduct, Moral, and Motivational Norms

The three moral systems of thought and three basic motivational needs commonly interact as young people come to distinguish between conduct and identity. Students differ in whether they are concerned with obedience for its own sake, instrumental exchange, or pleasing others. They also differ in the degree to which they strive for self-determination, competence, and affiliation and may or may not be aware of these orientations. Despite these differences, moral and motivational orientations are features of the internal norms that guide moral functioning in school. Students differ in their ability to talk about their emerging social knowledge, but these personality characteristics converge to drive their social participation.

Although particular situations can elicit common reactions, most educational activities are ambiguous enough that students' needs and orientations influence how they perceive, define, and evaluate their experiences.

Older students are usually more aware of their dispositions, but most educators readily see individual differences in personality among all age groups. Educators do so by observing students' behavior and labeling the emotions students elicit from others as well as by looking at themes in students' schoolwork.

When students obey rules without reflecting on the rules' purpose, they are likely to remain unaware of the forces that direct their behavior and may require coaching on how to interpret their own and others' conduct. Most children enter school with some willingness to reflect, but some children resist systematic inquiry into how their behavior affects others. For example, after his teacher found Jack hiding under his desk, claiming he could not find friends, two adults executed a class discussion and determined a course of action. The second graders easily identified why Jack struggled to find friends, labeled his problematic behavior, and offered compassionate suggestions for responding to such behavior. Unfortunately, Jack was unable to do this for himself.

*"Have you ever thought that there are some people who have trouble figuring out how to be friends?"* the instructor asks.
"For me, it's more like people don't like me, but I don't know why."
"I like you, Earl." (The discussion continued on this personal note.)
*"There's someone in class who has trouble making friends... He's not here right now."*
"Jack!"
"One time on the bus..." started Gillian. "Jack and a friend decided to say that, um, that he loved me. I knew he didn't mean it. Then one time, he left a message on my message machine, and he said that love stuff was a joke."
"Yes, well he once said to Tom that I didn't like him," said Matt. "And I know why he did it.
He wanted me to have him as his only friend."
*Encouraging reflection, the teacher asks,*
*"Why do you think he wanted that?"*
"Because he doesn't have friends." The conversation continued with students offering several additional stories about Jack's social transgressions.
*"Well, doesn't all that show he doesn't understand how to talk to people and make friends? He does these things that seem a bit silly to you."*
"It seems sad," said Fiona. "It's hard for us to understand him because he doesn't understand us."
*"Can we think of things to help Jack?"*
"When he does something you can't understand, you can tell him you don't understand."
"I think it would be nice to go through the rest of the day and try to make him feel more that he is a friend."

Despite this enthusiasm from his peers and numerous attempts to help Jack learn to interpret social cues, Jack's difficulty finding friends persisted

(Thorkildsen & Nicholls, 2002). His confusion was compounded by the fact that his needs for self-determination, competence, and affiliation remained unmet in school. Jack confused issues of intimacy and exchange, withdrew from social situations, and was unable to step outside his subjective experience well enough to accept his own moral authority.

In contrast, students who are dependent on instrumental forms of moral reasoning may search for exchange opportunities more often than intimacy, feel competent when they receive as much as they give, and prefer opportunities that directly align with their interests. This was apparent when two girls interviewed one another about collaboration:

*Jamika*: Latoya, when you working on a report, who do you choose to work with?
*Latoya*: I will choose someone that is like in the fourth or fifth grade and someone who works really, really nice.
*Jamika*: What if you think that person is gonna work really, really nice and they don't? What will you do?
*Latoya*: I will at least stop working with them and go somewhere else and find someone else to work with.

Jamika continued her line of questioning, hoping that Latoya would talk about the role of trust in collaboration. Latoya offered only instrumental reasons for choosing collaborators, a task orientation toward competence, and a strong sense that she was free to change collaborators at will (Thorkildsen & Jordan, 1995, p. 155). Differences in their orientations toward affiliation led these girls to emphasize different criteria for successful collaboration.

When students are preoccupied with adhering to social norms and exploring common notions of good and bad behavior, they can be uncomfortable when their conduct disappoints others and may value social comparison over affiliation. One group of junior high school students, for example, tended to undervalue their own needs, engage in mean-spirited forms of social comparison, and offer harsh criticism of their peers (Peebles, 1995).

*Teacher*: What's it like to be in junior high school?
*Dan*: I think it's tough because you've gotta have certain friends and you have to be with certain people, and if you're not with those certain people, then you're like an outcast. People won't treat you right or something. You gotta look a certain way. If you're different, they might say something about you and stuff like that.
*Teacher*: Is there a particular group here that is the popular group?
*Dan*: There's like three groups of people, really popular people, normal kids, and then there's the unpopular people.
*Teacher*: What makes the difference between the three groups?

*Dan*: If you have a lot of friends, I guess you're popular. That, and the way they dress and the way they act. You know, like you have to wear Guess and Esprit clothes, and the real expensive shoes. You know, like you hear about kids getting beat up for their shoes? Well, that's what I mean.

These snatches of conversation illustrate some of the complex social judgments students learn to make in school as they coordinate information concerning moral systems of thought and motivational needs. Marked differences exist in students' abilities to reflect on how their choices and behavior are indicators of their identity. Oriented toward the concrete aspects of behavior, younger students often focus on conduct and have difficulty defining their own and others' identity-enhancing interests. As late as junior high, students still rely on concrete representations of their social knowledge even though they are quite skilled at labeling features of their identities, negotiating complex social situations, and writing thoughtfully about their emotions. Something about the nature of school encourages students to suppress the subtle aspects of their social knowledge, but if encouraged to acknowledge individual personalities, even young children are capable of doing so.

Educators commonly encourage students to reflect on the reasons for their behavior and imagine rules that can facilitate greater levels of self-regulation. Educators also encourage students to reveal their personalities when choosing assignments and particular work habits. In doing so, educators acknowledge young people's developing moral acumen without deviating too far from the manifest purpose of school. Nevertheless, if educators rely only on practices that direct students' attention to personal needs they may minimize important opportunities for reflection on the role of societal practices in moral functioning.

## Learning About Epistemology and Institutional Practices

Even if educators do not always acknowledge it, most students are busy learning about the forms of knowledge to be acquired, definitions of particular situations, and consequences implicit in educational practices. When making judgments about how to respond to particular events, persons, or requests, students usually integrate their knowledge of conduct and personality with knowledge of how schools are organized. They respond to actual situations by coordinating personal and contextual aspects of moral knowledge and interpret ambiguous situations by relying on assumptions about how people should behave and how schools should be organized. The resulting internal norms can take many forms, but some

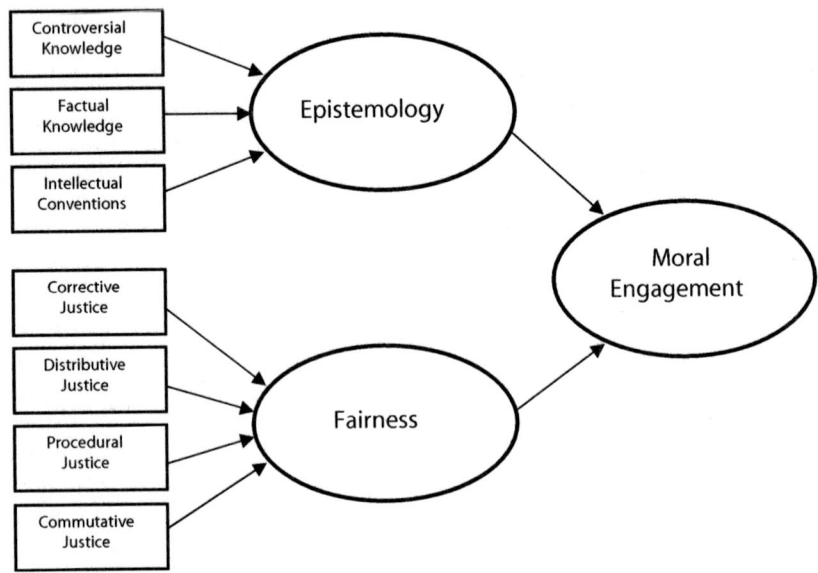

**Figure 8.2.** Epistemology, fairness and moral engagement in school.

questions related to educational norms can be identified. In interview studies, students have coordinated information about epistemology, fairness, and motivation to evaluate life in school (Figure 8.2). Details from more complex accounts are isolated here to call attention to specific features.

## *Identifying Valuable Knowledge*

Students' awareness of epistemology is evident in their critiques of school curricula. They quickly learn that the ideas they discuss in school contain moral content, either because educators call attention to such themes or out of natural curiosity. In structured interviews, most respondents agree that all forms of knowledge are important, but they prioritize the forms differently (Nicholls, Nelson & Gleaves, 1995; Nicholls & Thorkildsen, 1989; Thorkildsen, Sodonis, White-McNulty, 2004). More children than adolescents take pleasure in the certainty associated with learning *intellectual conventions* and *noncontroversial facts*. But more adolescents than children take pleasure in exploring *controversial topics* that involve no accepted position. Regardless of their age, students introduce issues of motivation and fairness when justifying their beliefs about which forms of knowledge are of most worth. Many students refer to the self-determination inherent in selecting positions on controversial issues and the feelings of competence associated with getting answers right. As one 10-year-old boy explained:

> I like to find out about how people treated other people, and I like to find out what they did wrong and what they should've done. [One of my favorite authors] writes how things really happened. He doesn't weed out things . . . like when in the fall they had to kill all the animals and he . . . thought some of them were wrong, like when they killed the pigs they just let them bleed to death . . . Most of the stories you read in class are pretty short and they leave out some things . . . At school, they think some things are too violent and they don't want to talk about it . . . And also, you know, sometimes you only read half of a story, like with Christopher Columbus. Everyone says he's so good, but he killed Indians when they didn't bring back enough gold, and used them as slaves.

This boy found pleasure in reading materials that challenged the ideas found in his schoolwork. He found a moral theme in his reading preferences, noticed the limited materials available at school, and imagined educators' reasons for limiting the flow of information on violent topics. Children and adolescents who are engaged in school often delight their teachers with such thoughtfulness when given the opportunity to express their emerging knowledge. Students who are less successful have difficulty connecting the ideas they learn in school with other parts of their personal and intellectual experience (Thorkildsen & Nicholls, 2002).

Educators can encourage students to think about the moral content of the materials they are expected to learn. They can also offer direct instruction about the assumptions that underlie particular disciplines and reveal controversies in their fields of expertise. Such conversations, when generated at opportune moments, call attention to the ethical features of how knowledge is acquired, shared, and valued. These conversations can also encourage students to integrate school-related knowledge with other internal norms to enrich their moral engagement when acquiring new insights.

## Understanding Educational Situations and Classroom Practices

Conversations about what knowledge is of most worth invariably include critiques of *how such knowledge should be taught* in school. In exploring institutional practices, it is helpful to determine if readily identifiable structures are present in school. Children, adolescents, and adults typically see that school involves *learning*, *test*, and *contest situations* and share common definitions of these educational structures (Thorkildsen, 2000). When asked to prioritize the situations, most people see learning as more important than tests or contests but recognize that all three types of situations serve important purposes (Thorkildsen & Weaver, 2003). Despite these commonalities, marked age differences exist in students' evaluations of classroom practices. Young people hold a complex understanding of fairness that is elicited when they solve particular moral dilemmas. Each type of justice problem offers different intellectual challenges, but determining if classrooms are well organized involves the consideration of corrective, distributive, procedural, and commutative justice themes.

*Corrective justice* involves the regulation of conduct, and age-related differences in young people's reasoning are parallel to differences in their understanding of intentionality and authority. Younger children are less able to draw accurate inferences about people's intentions than are their elders and are more likely to suggest harsh punishments. Younger children are also more likely than their elders to assume that authority resides in adults rather than in the work to be accomplished or in themselves. Knowledge of these issues constrains young people's reasoning about punishment, reward, and reconciliation.

Educators assist students in developing a richer understanding of how conduct should be regulated by involving students in the decision-making process. They sometimes form discipline committees in which peers determine how best to correct misbehavior or ask students to generate rules for regulating their behavior in school. Involvement in the regulation of conduct also facilitates comparisons among different personalities and can facilitate greater levels of self-awareness in students.

*Distributive justice* involves the allocation of resources, and age-related differences in young people's reasoning are parallel to differences in their understanding of privilege, equity, equality, and need. Children as well as adolescents and adults often recognize that situations lead to different distribution rules. Nevertheless, children are more easily confused than their elders by problems that involve complex logical mathematical reasoning. Most children seem to focus on simple equality first and then alter their reasoning to reflect the demands of the situation. Older students tend to focus on merit and alter their reasoning to compensate for social inequality. Young people who have experienced prejudice or observed marked levels of social inequality tend to use more complex language than their peers for representing privilege, need, and equity.

Educators can facilitate greater awareness of the challenges of distributing resources by asking students to imagine how to share materials. In some classrooms, teachers ensure that resources are scarce so that students will be required to negotiate when and how to use them. In classrooms with ample supplies, involving students in short- and long-term planning also facilitates new knowledge about distributive justice.

Reasoning about fair ways to organize learning, tests, and contests has been documented in studies of *procedural justice* for educational contexts. Age-related differences in reasoning about fair teaching practices are typically parallel to differences in reasoning about motivational attributions such as intelligence, current ability, effort, luck, and skill. Younger children confound some of these ideas and may use vocabulary words differently from adults. For example, before age 10, the terms *effort* and *ability* are often used interchangeably by children. Similarly, younger children assume that effort can cause success on a task in which the outcome is determined by luck as often as when the outcome is determined by skill. These confusions seem to influence students' ability to determine which procedures will ultimately lead to successful goal attainment.

Educators facilitate greater awareness of procedural issues by explicitly labeling the agendas inherent in their choices of practices and the various attributions that are appropriate for labeling success and failure. Labeling task difficulty and the appropriateness of help seeking in learning and test situations, for example, can call attention to the necessity of effort for optimal performance. Establishing guidelines for judging competitions can help students differentiate between test and contest situations. Students tend to abide by the procedural norms introduced by their teachers but recognize the high degree of ambiguity in some educational situations.

Reasoning about the role of school in society falls under the purview of *commutative justice* because it involves a perspective that is more general than the day-to-day events associated with corrective, distributive, and procedural justice dilemmas. Nevertheless, these considerations are important for organizing fair classrooms. Young people's reasoning about the purposes of school has rarely been explored systematically, but a few conclusions can be supported. Age-related differences in students' reasoning seem to be associated with their understanding of how particular institutions function in society. Young people seem well aware that the primary purpose of school is to teach reading, writing, and mathematics. They can respond to questions about how learning, testing, and contests should be prioritized; how to sustain motivation; and what kind of knowledge is valued in school. However, marked differences exist in young people's abilities to imagine a society without schools or the various societal expectations for schools, churches, legal systems, and neighborhood organizations. Many adults also find it difficult to imagine such a world, so it should not be surprising to find that children experience such difficulties.

Educators can encourage students to reflect on the nature and purpose of school by engaging them in conversations about why particular agendas are important. Busy with more immediate concerns, most educators over-look this aspect of helping students understand the role of schooling in society. Nevertheless, as students progress through school, they learn how different teachers balance educational concerns to promote equal opportunities; teachers place different priorities on learning, test, and contest situations in ways that reveal different assumptions about commutative justice.

Working with four different teachers, for example, I found three distinct approaches to fairness. Teachers emphasized *equality in academic attainment, equality in self-determination,* or *equality in communication* (Thorkildsen & Jordan, 1995; Thorkildsen & Nicholls, 2002). Their classrooms were exemplary and were selected because students typically showed marked improvement in academic performance and average achievement levels were well above national norms; the manifest purposes of school were not overlooked in the service of promoting moral functioning. Each classroom had an internally coherent set of norms that served as a guide for student reflection, even if teachers did not always discuss these norms with their students.

Although multiple forms of justice are relevant to questions of equal educational opportunity, even adults have difficulty thinking about all forms simultaneously. Adults as well as young people find it easier to critique the appropriateness of particular practices for use in particular situations. For example, individuals can evaluate fair ways to distribute tests (e.g., quizzes, standardized tests), organize tests (e.g., using peer tutoring or solitary work), or punish students who cheat on tests. Children can also determine whether tests should be used to classify students into certain programs. Nevertheless, children and adolescents have difficulty simultaneously coordinating all of the dilemmas that educators are asked to consider.

To effectively drive social participation, moral engagement involves the coordination of details about these structural aspects of school as well as of personal conduct and identities, but individuals are likely to differ in which details attract their attention. Educators can nurture moral functioning by helping students gain the necessary information for constructing complex internal norms. Internal norms that are grounded in knowledge of the moral concerns relevant to personalities and institutional structures are most likely to be called forth when moral engagement compels action. When the representations of particular educational situations are concrete, students can also elaborate on the psychological features and consequences of educational practices to make wise decisions. Promoting class discussions on epistemology and ways to prioritize different situations and teaching practices can encourage students to improve their knowledge of how schools are structured.

## Coordinating Personal and Collective Agendas

Describing moral engagement in educational settings is difficult because individual differences in personalities are coordinated with variation in students' knowledge of educational structures. Educational activities occur regardless of whether students fully participate in them, but students' *moral engagement* serves as a drive that influences their likelihood of doing so. Educators would like to find ways to help all students become engaged in learning, not just those who understand the complexity of educational situations. Collaborations with teachers have led me to identify three collective agendas that, if considered in combination, can help students coordinate knowledge of their personal needs and others' expectations to sustain high levels of moral engagement.

First, definitions of equal educational opportunity that emphasize a level motivational playing field are more likely to nurture social development than are those that emphasize equality of test scores. Students sustain motivation if they can consolidate the complex features of their experiences in personal standards that guide behavior. Educators can label the connections they notice and encourage students to share their discoveries. In such classrooms, conversations focus more on identity-enhancing interests than on who is superior or inferior in the social hierarchy. Confidence flourishes when students feel empowered to make moral and intellectual choices, understand their competence, and feel connected with one another.

Second, educators can create stimulating environments and encourage everyone to label the educative features of those environments. When educators label the features of particular tasks, they help students determine where to direct their attention. Watching students' frustration, boredom, or excitement and labeling the relationships between these emotional states and particular tasks can help students learn about task difficulty, their own interests, and the expectations of others in school. Encouraging students to think of themselves as educational theorists can help them draw connections between their internal states and aspects of their concrete experiences that are easily observed. Challenging students with perspectives they had not considered can encourage richer states of reflection than ignoring students' thoughts, yet such challenges require humor, tact, and compassion.

The final cluster of suggestions involves calling attention to moral agency. When students and teachers talk through daily moral dilemmas, virtuous behavior is validated. Highlighting the moral content of the manifest curriculum, labeling students' fairness judgments and caring behavior, and negotiating classroom practices offer opportunities to invent and practice moral languages. Recognizing the moral lessons evident in resistance as well as compliance can help students identify their own and others'

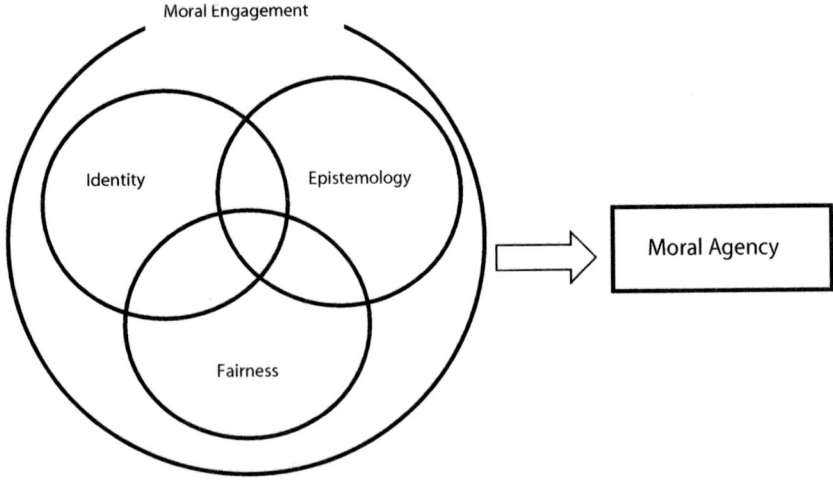

Figure 8.3. Moral engagement and moral agency in educational contexts.

frustration, forms of miscommunication, and forms of disrespect that can then be challenged. Playfully comparing word and deed can help students work through conflicts rather than seethe with anger and resentment from feeling helpless, incompetent, or lonely.

Young people are obligated to attend school, but their commitment to educational agendas is often beyond the direct control of the adults who structure the school day. If educators offer too much structure, their management strategies can easily be misunderstood as a form of dominance. But if educators offer too little structure, their strategies seem like a form of neglect. As is the case in other contexts, modeling can be an outstanding form of support for morality, but preserving freedom of inquiry in a stimulating environment can foster moral development.

## References

Aronfreed, J. (1968). *Conduct and conscience: The socialization of internalized control over behavior.* New York: Academic Press.

Bandura, A. (1999). Moral disengagement in the perpetration of inhumanities. *Personality and Social Psychology Review, 3,* 193–209.

Battistich, V., Solomon, D., Kim, D., Watson, M., & Schaps, E. (1995). Schools as communities, poverty levels of student populations, and students' attitudes, motives, and performance: A multilevel analysis. *American Educational Research Journal, 32,* 627–658.

Colby, A., Kohlberg, L., Gibbs, J., & Lieberman, M. (1983). A longitudinal study of moral development. *Monographs for the Society for Research in Child Development, 48,* 1–96.

Hart, D., & Fegley, S. (1995). Prosocial behavior and caring in adolescence: Relations to self-understanding and social judgment. *Child Development, 66,* 1346–1359.

Nicholls, J. G. (1989). The competitive ethos and democratic education. Cambridge, MA: Harvard University Press.

Nicholls, J. G., Nelson, J. R., & Gleaves, K. (1995). Learning "facts" versus learning that most questions have many answers: Student evaluations of contrasting curricula. *Journal of Educational Psychology, 87,* 253–260.

Nicholls, J. G., & Thorkildsen, T. A. (1989). Intellectual conventions verses matters of substance: Elementary school students as curriculum theorists. *American Educational Research Journal, 26,* 533–544.

Peebles, M. (1995). Social alienation in the junior high school: Five case studies. (Doctoral dissertation, University of Illinois at Chicago, 1995). *Dissertation Abstracts International, 56–06,* A2194.

Thorkildsen, T. A. (2000). Children's coordination of procedural and commutative justice in school. In W. van Haaften, T. Wren, & A. Tellings (Eds.), *Moral sensibilities and education II: The schoolchild* (pp. 61–88). Bemmel, The Netherlands: Concorde Publishing House.

Thorkildsen, T. A., & Jordan, C. (1995). Is there a right way to collaborate? When the experts speak can the customers be right? In J. G. Nicholls & T. A. Thorkildsen (Eds.), *Reasons for learning: Expanding the conversation on student-teacher collaboration* (pp. 137–161). New York: Teachers College Press.

Thorkildsen, T. A., & Nicholls, J. G. (with Bates, A., Brankis, N., & DeBolt, T.). (2002). *Motivation and the struggle to learn: Responding to fractured experience.* Boston, MA: Allyn & Bacon.

Thorkildsen, T. A., Sodonis, A., & White-McNulty, L. (2004). Epistemology and adolescents' conceptions of procedural justice in school. *Journal of Educational Psychology.*

Thorkildsen, T. A., & Weaver, A. (2003). *Developing conceptions of the role of school in society: Prioritizing learning, test, and contest situations.* Presented at the biennial meeting of the Society for Research in Child Development, Tampa, FL.

Turiel, E. (1998). The development of morality. In N. Eisenberg & W. Damon (Eds.), *Handbook of child psychology: Vol. 3. Social, emotional, and personality development* (5th ed., pp. 863–932). New York: John Wiley & Sons.

Chapter 9

# Religious Participation and the Development of Moral Identity in Adolescence

## Daniel Hart and Robert Atkins

Religion's connection to morality may currently be of greater interest than it has been in any previous period of American history. Scarcely a week goes by without headlines in the newspaper and stories on television news concerning religion and its role in the ethics of education, public life, international relations, and so on. The salience of religion and morality has resulted partly from the clash of background assumptions about religion with current events. Most Americans presume that religion contributes to the public good and to ethical life. In a recent national poll (Public Agenda, 2001), 70% of Americans reported that they wanted religion's influence on the country to grow. Particularly surprising was the same poll's finding that most (76%) of those advocating for greater religious influence on public life claimed that denominational affiliation did not matter. In other words, Americans seemingly believe that those connected to a religious community—whatever that community's practices may be—are more ethical than those without membership in a religious group. This belief probably underlies the American public's support for nondenominational school prayer as an effective strategy for moral development (Public Agenda, 2001).

World events of the first 2 years of the 21st century have made it difficult for Americans to leave unexamined the presumption that religion inspires only ethical action. The terrorists who destroyed New York's

World Trade Center in September 2001, killing thousands of people, were motivated by their religious beliefs (Sullivan, 2001). Osama bin Laden's campaign of terror against the United States had the protection of Islam as its ideological goal. Wide agreement exists among those knowledgeable about Islam that bin Laden's views of religious doctrine were inconsistent with the thrust of Islamic thought and with Islamic practice. Nonetheless, the attack on the World Trade Center raised into the consciousness of the American public the possibility that religious belief can be recruited to justify immoral action. Although that attack is the single event that reverberates most in public discourse on religion and morality, conflicts elsewhere (e.g., between predominantly Hindu India and Islamic Pakistan) and legal debates within the United States (e.g., over the inclusion of "under God" in the Pledge of Allegiance and subsidies to children attending religious schools) have also served to keep the conjunction of religion and ethical behavior in the forefront of the American consciousness.

The goal of this chapter is to examine how religion influences moral development—specifically, the formation of moral identity—in the context of the United States. The chapter proceeds in three steps. First, the chapter explores some interesting findings that illustrate a powerful association between religious participation in adolescence and one index of moral identity, community service. Next, the chapter presents a model of moral identity development. This model of development structures the third section, which seeks to locate the sources of connection between religious participation and moral identity within a theoretical model. The hope is that the chapter will contribute to a constructive public debate on the role of religion in fostering the moral development of America's youth.

## Does Religious Participation Increase Moral Behavior?

*Community service*—voluntary action to benefit others—is generally considered to be morally worthy. Those who volunteer to serve the hungry in soup kitchens, drive the sick and elderly to doctors' appointments, raise funds for neighborhood playgrounds, and so on are judged to be working to benefit others because these activities have no apparent benefit to the self. What gives rise to the motivation to work on behalf of others? Does religion contribute to this motivation? The answer to this latter question, at least in the United States, is yes (the answer to the former question is discussed in the next section).

Figure 9.1 depicts the relationship between religious participation and the likelihood that adolescents are involved in voluntary community service. This graph is based on data from the Children of the 1979 National Longitudinal Survey of Youth (Children-NLSY, 2000) dataset. In 1998, more

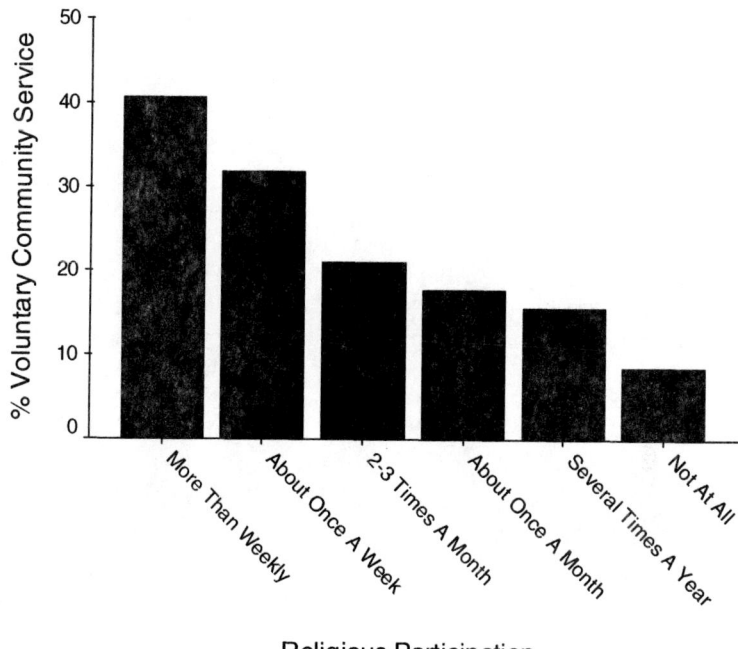

**Figure 9.1.** The percentage of adolescents involved in voluntary community service in each of six levels of religious participation.

than 1,800 participants in this national survey, all between ages 14 and 17 years, responded to the questions relevant for this chapter's purposes. They were asked if they were involved in community service, and, if so, if the service was completely voluntary (i.e., not done as a condition of probation or to satisfy a school requirement). Only those who answered affirmatively to both questions were judged to be participating in voluntary community service. The participants were also asked about the frequency of their participation in religious activities on a six-point scale, ranging from "once a week or more often" to "not at all." The graph illustrates the association between the two measures.

Figure 9.1 shows that religious participation is a potent predictor of community service. Adolescents who report weekly or more frequent religious participation are four times more likely than those who do not attend religious functions at all to be involved in community service. This is a very strong relationship. Participation in community service is related to a number of other factors, some of which are described in the next section. But probably none of these other variables shows the strength of connection to community service that the correlation illustrated in

Figure 9.1 does. For example, more girls than boys are involved in community service, but the difference is relatively small (60% vs. 40%, meaning that girls are 33% more likely than boys to be involved in community service).

The data from the Children-NLSY (2000) do not allow good estimates of the influence of religious denomination on community service. This is because in a national sample of several thousand youths, most of the participants belong to the most common denominations and relatively few report membership in others. This was true in the Children-NLSY sample: Although participants reported affiliation with numerous Christian religions, Judaism, Buddhism, and Islam, just a few of the religions were commonly selected. However, there were enough participants in three denominations—Roman Catholic, Baptist, and traditional Protestant (i.e., Episcopal, Lutheran, Methodist, and Presbyterian)—to allow for meaningful group comparisons. Figure 9.2 depicts the relationship of voluntary community service to religious affiliation. A relationship between religious affiliation and voluntary community service does exist, but it is

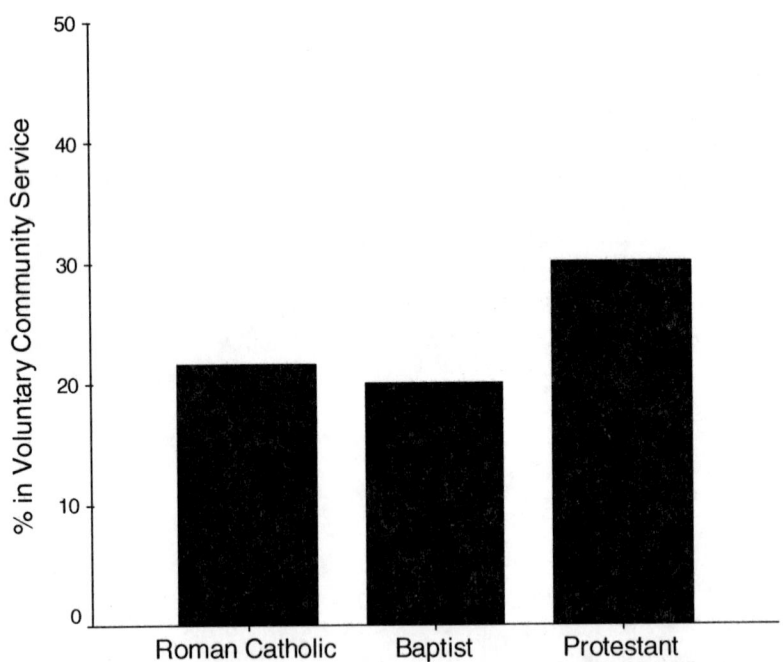

**Figure 9.2.** The percentage of adolescents involved in voluntary community service in three Christian religious traditions.

not as strong as the powerful connection between religious participation and community service. Consistent with the view of Americans captured by recent polls, then, it appears that religious participation in adolescence does increase one form of moral behavior (i.e., community service), and this effect seems largely independent of the religious tradition in which the adolescents participate (at least among the three Christian denominations that are compared in Figure 9.2).

Why is religious participation such a powerful predictor of community service? The answer to this question requires a model of moral identity development, one marker of which is community service. This chapter discusses this model and then explores how religion affects the model's components and their interactions.

## The Development of Moral Identity

In the authors' view, moral identity is defined by a set of commitments consistent with one's sense of self that advance the welfare of others. This definition of moral identity probably does not exhaust the full domain. For example, one can imagine moral lives filled by commitment to safeguarding the natural world (perhaps some animal rights activists might be in this category) or to developing personal integrity and virtue (one of the apparent goals of some hermits). This chapter does not focus on these areas because these moral qualities are more difficult to assess from both philosophical and psychological perspectives.

Figure 9.3 presents a schematic representation of the authors' theoretical model of how moral identity (i.e., commitments to action on behalf of others consistent with the sense of self) develops. According to the model, moral identity has both distal and proximal sources. The distal sources are on the left side of the figure and include personality and temperamental factors (the upper left quadrant) as well as location in the relatively stable structure of culture and class (the lower right quadrant).

## Distal Influences on Moral Identity Development

### Personality and Temperament

Considerable evidence indicates that personality and temperamental factors influence moral judgment, moral emotion, and moral action (for a review, see Hart, London, Burock, & Miraglia, 2003). Briefly, the evidence suggests that children and adolescents who are capable of regulating their emotions and who are sympathetic to others are more likely to develop the moral features upon which moral identity rests. However,

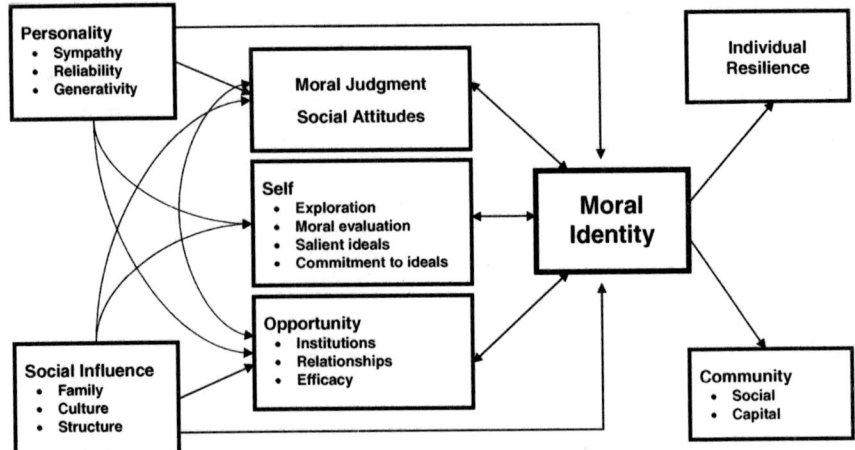

Figure 9.3. A developmental model of moral identity.

the connection of personality or temperament to an enduring commitment to work on behalf of others is neither straight nor strong. Many people with friendly personalities do little to aid others, and many who have been judged by history to be moral saints had disagreeable personalities.

Culture and social class also shape the constituents of moral identity. Jensen (1997, 1998) has thoughtfully addressed the role of culture in framing moral life. According to Jensen (1997, p. 326), cultures organize thinking about four ontological questions: "Who are we?" "Where are we?" "Why are we suffering?" "What is the remedy?" In a series of studies in India and the United States, Jensen has demonstrated that a culture's answers to these four questions influences individuals' moral judgments on a variety of issues.

Particularly important for the goals of this chapter, Jensen (1997, 1998) has suggested that religion is a type of culture. Jensen uses the dimension of fundamentalism–progressivism as an analytic perspective for inferring commonalities among religions and to characterize religion's connections to the moral domain. Fundamentalist religions assume that "God has revealed moral truth to humans," reject "a strict distinction between public and private spheres," and deny "the freedom of the individual to pursue diverse goals" (1998, p. 91). Progressivists, on the other hand, believe that morality is "subject to change and progress"; as soon as a change in morality is a possibility, certainty in any single moral rule is reduced, relativism is increased, and authority accorded to individuals to make moral decisions for themselves grows (1998, p. 92).

Jensen has used the fundamentalism–progressivism dimension to identify fascinating similarities in moral judgments between fundamentalists in India (i.e., orthodox Hindus) and the United States (i.e., fundamentalist Baptists) as well as among progressives (i.e., liberal Hindus, mainline Baptists) in the two countries. These findings are quite remarkable because it is ordinarily assumed that the differences between the two countries are so vast that Americans should resemble Americans more than they should Indians. Jensen's research demonstrates that similarities in religion can produce similarities in moral judgment, even among individuals from very different countries.

To summarize, culture—and, specifically, religion—can frame the ways in which youths and adults think about moral issues. Fundamentalism–progressivism may be helpful for understanding religion and its relationship to morality. This issue is included later in a discussion of other features of the model.

## Social Structure

The authors' work (Atkins & Hart, 2003; Hart & Atkins, 2002; Hart, Atkins, & Ford, 1998, 1999) has focused on the relationship of social class and race on the development of moral identity. The findings from many of the analyses support the conclusion that the neighborhoods in which poor, urban, minority youths live provide much less support for the development of moral identity than the neighborhoods that are home to affluent suburban youths. In the authors' view, this happens because poor, urban neighborhoods—disproportionately inhabited by minority children—tend to have relatively few adults, and adults are essential for providing the structure for the clubs, associations, youth groups, and teams that provide important opportunities for ethical and civic development.

# Proximal Influences on the Development of Moral Identity

The proximal influences on moral identity development, shown in the second column of Figure 9.3, can also be considered constituents of moral identity.

## Moral Judgment and Social Attitudes

Moral identity rests partly on moral judgment and social attitudes. This is both a conceptual and an empirical claim. On the conceptual side, ordinary understanding of moral identity would be distorted if it did not rest on the judgment that action on behalf of others has the features of a moral judgment (e.g., prescriptiveness, universality). For example, it is possible to imagine that a robot could be programmed to provide assistance to humans and that it could perform this function without the capacity for moral cognition. A robot that performs such actions could not be considered to be a moral actor, and could not, for that reason, have a moral identity.

Although moral judgment is necessary for moral identity, those with deeply moral identities typically do not necessarily exhibit the moral reasoning characteristic of philosophers. Colby and Damon (1995) interviewed people who had shown unusual moral character and although these individuals were found to be aware of the moral dimensions of their work, they did not reason about moral issues in ways that were dramatically more sophisticated than ordinary adults. Gandhi, for example, is often thought of as a man of heroic moral stature, and he had an articulated perspective of moral judgment and social attitudes concerning individuals, relationships, and civil behavior. Although Gandhi's philosophy served him well in a lifetime of leading the Indian peoples to liberty, it could lead to absurd conclusions when applied to contexts different from those in which it developed. Gandhi is reported to have claimed that German Jews should have committed mass suicide rather than resisting forcibly the Nazis' efforts to exterminate them (Orwell, 1949). Although Gandhi's view may have derived from his valuing of nonviolent resistance, a key element in his religious philosophy, its application to moral issues in the Nazi genocide had implications for ethical life that are counterintuitive. Consequently, we can claim that moral judgment is essential for a moral identity but that this moral judgment need not be sophisticated by the standards of moral philosophy.

Empirically, moral judgments and social attitudes are linked to moral behavior. An enormous amount of literature exists on this topic (for a review, see Turiel, 1983) that cannot be reviewed here. It is sufficient to conclude that this vast literature demonstrates conclusively that moral judgments and social attitudes are constitutive of moral behavior and, by extension, moral identity.

## The Self

Our definition of moral identity includes components of the sense of self. Working on behalf of others can be extraordinarily difficult; abandoning commitments to such work can be tempting. Previous research on adolescents dedicated to prosocial action (Hart & Fegley, 1995) has demonstrated that moral commitment is sustained partly by a prominent ideal self that has moral content. In other words, individuals who aspire to be fair and compassionate and for whom these aspirations are prominent in daily life are more likely to behave prosocially than those whose ideals are either nonmoral in content or peripheral to psychological functioning. A salient ideal self with moral content leads to moral evaluation of oneself (e.g., "I am a success if I fulfill my moral goals and a failure if I do not"). Salient moral ideals for oneself, partly regulating self-esteem, are central components of moral identity.

## Opportunity

Moral identities do not rise wholly out of moral judgment and the sense of self; they are not born solely of internal psychological processes. To develop a moral identity, individuals must witness others with sustained commitments to action on behalf of others and must have the opportunity to explore such lines of action themselves. Those identified as moral exemplars (e.g., Christians who harbored Jews in Nazi-occupied Europe) typically report that their parents led lives evidencing considerable concern for others (e.g., Oliner & Oliner, 1988). The authors' research on the precursors to community service regularly reveals that neighborhood social institutions link adolescents with opportunities to explore prosocial action (Atkins & Hart, 2003; Hart et al., 1998). Indeed, adolescents who belong to clubs and teams are more than twice as likely as those who do not to volunteer for community service.

## Summary

The proximal influences and constituents of moral identity—moral judgment, the sense of self, and opportunity—are influenced by each other, distal influences (e.g., personality, social structure), and immediate social context. With the developmental influences of moral identity outlined, we turn now to the third issue, religion's influence on the development of moral identity.

# Paths of Influence from Religion to Moral Identity

Religion is associated with many of the components of the model of moral identity development outlined in Figure 9.3. This section begins with a discussion of religion's influence on the bedrock of moral identity formation, personality, and social structure.

## Religion and Personality

Religion (at least as practiced in the United States) probably has relatively little direct influence on broad personality traits and temperamental qualities. In adulthood, the magnitude of relationships between religious participation and broad personalities is very small. Using data from the National Survey of Midlife Development in the United States (Midus; 1995–1996), the current authors calculated the correlation of frequency of self-reported religious participation to each of the five traits, measured via self-report, represented by the Five-Factor Model of personality (i.e., neuroticism, extraversion, openness, agreeableness, and conscientiousness). The frequency of religious participation did not account for as much as 4% of the variation in any of the traits. This set of findings demonstrates that religious participation is largely independent of personality. Moreover, even this extremely weak relationship might not be a result of religious participation's influence on personality; instead, it could reflect personality's influence on religious attendance (e.g., agreeable people are probably more interested in attending church and seeing others than are disagreeable people). The small magnitude of the associations of religious participation to personality traits, combined with the ambiguity of causality in these associations, leads to the conclusion that religion probably has little influence on personality and temperament. Consequently, religion's influence on the development of moral identity probably does not occur for those characteristics in the upper left quadrant of the model in Figure 9.3.

## Religion and Social Structure

One of the most frequently explored explanations for the association of religious participation with other variables is that those who are religious come from higher social classes than those who are not. For example, an association exists between religious participation and mortality in adulthood (McCullough, Hoyt, Larson, Koenig, & Thoresen, 2000). Those who attend church regularly die at older ages than those who attend infrequently. It is possible that the explanation for this correlation is that those who attend church on a regular basis have higher incomes than those who attend infrequently, and earning higher incomes is associated with improved nutrition and better access to healthcare, with these two benefits responsible for the lower rates of premature mortality. Indeed, some health studies indicate that this explanation accounts for part of the relationship between health and religious participation (McCullough et al., 2000). However, income differences between those who are deeply religious and those who are not are relatively minor, and they do not fully explain differences in mortality or—more important for the purposes here—differences in community service (see Fig. 1). In other words, the current authors do not believe that income or social class mediates religion's association with moral identity development.

## Religion and Moral Judgment

Religion has an enormous influence on the development of moral identity as one type of cultural context. It is likely that this influence occurs along several paths. First, religion highlights moral issues: Adolescents attending church or religious instruction are regularly exposed to moral claims (i.e., prescriptions for action that are judged necessary for all). This exposure is likely to make salient the moral dimension in life, and it can prepare religious adolescents to discern moral issues in contexts in which other adolescents perceive only issues of social convention or self-interest.

Second, religious participation can be a context in which thoughtful reflection about moral issues can take place. This reflection can be essential for the development of moral judgment. Moral judgment can be understood to consist of a set of cognitive processes that regulate social behavior according to principles of prescriptivity and universality. In many social contexts, moral problems arise, and the best resolution of these problems is not obvious. Sophisticated moral judgment requires imagining different hypothetical resolutions to these problems, their consequences for the individuals involved in the moral conflict or problem, evaluations of consequences in light of efforts to maximize prescriptivity and universality. This is a complicated process that draws on reflection and imagination in ways that deciding, for example, whether a particular food tastes good does not. If reflection on moral problems and consideration of the implications of different resolutions for them are fundamental for moral judgment sophistication, then discussion with others about moral claims can be useful because it clarifies reflection and widens consideration. Indeed, a wealth of evidence suggests that children and adolescents who regularly discuss moral issues acquire sophisticated moral reasoning at an earlier age than do youths without such opportunities (Rest, 1983). Religious instruction and participation can provide exactly this sort of context, allowing children and youths to discuss important moral issues with each other and with adults.

However, religious participation does not *guarantee* that sophisticated moral judgment will emerge. An earlier section noted that Gandhi's religious views resulted in moral judgments—his advocacy of mass suicide for European Jews as a means of drawing attention to the Nazis' genocidal intentions—that are at odds with our ethical intuitions. As this example from Gandhi's life suggests, religion and moral judgment may not always be mutually reinforcing.

Ideally, the worldview provided by religion is interactively linked with moral judgment, so that worldviews inform moral judgments, which, in turn, produce adjustments in the worldviews (see Jensen, 1997, 1998, for an exploration of this issue). But the worldviews offered by religion can become so embedded in people's thinking that no adjustments are possible; the consequence is that moral judgments cannot be finetuned by experience in social relations. Research has demonstrated that fundamentalist religious affiliation influences the quality of moral judgment. When moral judgment is characterized in terms of a developmental scheme such as Kohlberg's (1987), those with fundamentalist religious beliefs are less likely than those with progressive affiliations to reach the higher stages (see Rest, 1983, for a review). This is because the higher stages require the belief that moral judgments are based on principles that are socially negotiated among autonomous moral agents; as noted earlier, this belief is contrary to the essential tenets of fundamentalist religions.

Religion's effects are seen clearly in areas of social judgment that may combine moral issues with issues of social convention. For example, American adolescents can have attitudes about dress, sexual relationships, treatment of parents, the use of drugs and alcohol, and so on that have direct links to religious practices. The attitudes and social judgments that overlap the moral domain but are largely concerned with social conventions and self-interest are probably very important for understanding adolescent lives, but they are probably peripheral for tracking the development of moral identity.

## The Self

The fusing of moral goals with the sense of self is key to the development of a moral identity. The pursuit of moral goals is often accompanied by some hardship and self-sacrifice; consequently, these goals must be viewed as fundamentally important if they are to continue to motivate behavior. Moral goals that are psychologically salient and linked to one's evaluation of oneself have this quality. Colby and Damon (1995) found that moral exemplars whose adult lives exemplified moral commitment exhibited this connection between goals and the sense of self; this connection also emerges in Hart and Fegley's (1995) work with adolescents.

Religion can forge bonds between moral goals and the sense of self. Because each religion constitutes a worldview that offers answers to the existential questions of meaning and purpose of life (as discussed in connection with Jensen's work earlier), moral goals that are aligned with the worldview can become synthesized with basic elements of identity. For this reason, individuals devote their lives to missionary work: A missionary's religious worldview is the framework within which the belief that working to advance the welfare of others—the moral goal—is connected to the sense of self. Unfortunately, however, no systematic psychological investigations have been conducted in this area.

## Religion and the Opportunity for Exploration of Moral Action

Much of the research on religion's influences on successful adjustment has focused on the social benefits that accrue as a consequence of
membership in a community. As mentioned earlier, considerable evidence
indicates that those who are religious live longer than those who are not
(McCullough et al., 2000). Two points from this body of research are relevant for the discussion here. First, the evidence suggests that the frequency
of church attendance is a better predictor of mortality than are measures of
denominational affiliation or spirituality (McCullough et al., 2000). In other
words, how often a person goes to a place of worship matters more than
what goes on in the religious setting. This pattern suggests that the benefits
of religion for health must occur in congregating with others rather than
in doctrinal knowledge or spirituality. The same literature (McCullough
et al., 2000) suggests that those who participate in religious activities tend
to have more friends and social contacts than those who are not religious;
this pattern seems to explain many of the health benefits enjoyed by religious individuals.

The same pattern can be found in adolescence. Furrow and Wagener
(2000) examined the benefits of religious participation in a large (nearly
100,000 participants) study of adolescents. They found that problematic
behavior in adolescence is lower in religious youths than it is in nonreligious youths. Furrow and Wagener determined that this benefit is a consequence of a greater number of supportive social relationships among
religious youths.

In the context of the model in Figure 9.3, these findings suggest that
religious participation greatly increases the number of opportunities available to youths for social relationships. Religiously active adolescents regularly attend meetings with peers and adults who share some of the same
beliefs as the adolescents. This consistent interaction with a compatible
social network provides the foundation for the formation of meaningful
relationships.

Most importantly for the purposes of this chapter, the relationships
formed as a consequence of religious participation provide a context in
which adolescents can witness and explore lines of prosocial action. Many
religious communities are deeply involved in charitable work and expect
their members to contribute to these efforts. For example, a church may
agree to cook and serve Sunday dinners at a soup kitchen, a responsibility
that is shared by its members. Adolescent members of such a church are
drawn into the activity of preparing meals through the relationships they
have formed in religious practice: Their friends in the religious youth group
may already work in the soup kitchen, the adult leader of the group may ask
the members to participate, or a respected religious leader's willingness

to work at the soup kitchen may inspire the adolescent to volunteer in the activity. Relationships formed in religious practice form a bridge to exploration of opportunities to work on behalf of others.

In the authors' judgment, the provision of opportunities to witness and to explore prosocial activity makes religious participation such a powerful influence on the formation of moral identity in adolescence. All of our research (Atkins & Hart, 2003; Hart & Fegley, 1995; Hart & Atkins, 2002; Hart et al., 1998, 1999) suggests that dedicated commitment to working toward the welfare of others is not fully determined by enduring static qualities of the adolescent: No temperamental qualities ensure such action, and no social class history prohibits it. Instead, sustained prosocial action can be overlaid by most configurations of traits and social structure, if initiated and sustained by social relationships. Religious participation in adolescence provides this social context.

## Summary and Implications

It is customary for researchers to conclude a review with a call for additional research. A particular need exists for additional research on religion's influence on moral development, a topic about which public opinion is deep and varied and social science is largely absent. In his chapter on the psychology of religion, Gorsuch (1988) noted that researchers have largely ignored the systematic study of the effects of religion on psychological functioning. The consequence is that the field is confronted with powerful connections between religion and adolescent behavior (see Fig. 1) without being able to offer satisfying explanations for them. However, in the authors' judgment, enough is known to move ahead with practice (as the leaders of a youth development program, we understand the need to apply what is known). Several conclusions are warranted.

First, as a culture, we should care about the development of moral identity in adolescence. Moral identity has consequences for psychological and social functioning. Figure 9.3 shows that moral identity in adolescence is linked to individual resilience and to social capital in the community. Previous research has demonstrated that adolescents who have markers of moral identity are less likely to be involved in problem behaviors, and, by definition, they are involved in prosocial activity. This is certainly consistent with our notions of psychological resilience. Equally important are the contributions that prosocial activity has for the communities in which it occurs. Other research (Hart et al., 1998) has suggested that many impoverished cities in the United States could benefit enormously from the contributions of their adolescent populations.

Second, the findings suggest that religion's influence on the formation of adolescent moral identity is likely to be most beneficial when (a) moral issues are discussed in ways that incorporate worldviews and moral intuitions, (b) the synthesis of the self's aspirations with moral goals is supported, and (c) opportunities for prosocial action are regularly provided. This third condition most likely offers the most direct route for religious groups to promote moral identity development. Religious groups can contribute directly to the development of moral identity by recruiting their adolescents to work on behalf of others. If asked by people they care for and who care about them, most adolescents are willing to lend a hand. After they become involved in charitable action on behalf of others, many adolescents find that such efforts can be incorporated into their identities.

The third implication is that providing adolescents with opportunities to join groups in which they can form relationships with peers and adults that, in turn, facilitate exploration of prosocial activity can provide much of the benefit of religious participation for moral identity formation to nonreligious youths. Many groups already provide these opportunities. The Boy Scouts and Girl Scouts, for example, have traditionally emphasized community service. However, all clubs and organizations serving adolescents should provide opportunities for the exploration of prosocial activity. Providing such opportunities would contribute significantly to the development of moral identity in American youths.

This chapter began by noting that American public interest in the intersection of religion and morality is at an all-time high. It is an opportune time to explore the influence of religion on moral development and to seek to understand this influence's powers to both facilitate and to retard the acquisition of moral identity. The complexities of the issue support neither fears that civic life will be subverted by religious affiliation nor that adolescents can be transformed by the recitation of prayers in school. Ethical development is both more robust and more difficult to shape than these threads of public discussion suggest. Our goal—to help adolescents become ethical adults—is best advanced through reflective exploration and application of the system of elements that together constitute moral identity.

# References

Atkins, R., & Hart, D. (2003). Neighborhoods, adults, and the development of civic identity in urban youth. *Applied Developmental Science, 7,* 156–165.

Colby, A., & Damon, W. (1995). The development of extraordinary moral commitment. In M. Killen & D. Hart (Eds.), *Morality in everyday life: Developmental perspectives.* (pp. 342–370). New York: Cambridge University Press.

Furrow, J. L., & Wagener, L. M. (2000). Lessons learned: The role of religion in the development of wisdom in adolescence. In W. S. Brown (Ed.), *Understanding wisdom: Sources, science, and society*. (pp. 361–391). Philadelphia: Templeton Foundation Press.

Gorsuch, R. L. (1988). Psychology of religion. *Annual Review of Psychology, 39*, 201–221.

Hart, D., & Atkins, R. (2002). Civic competence in urban youth. *Applied Developmental Science, 6*, 227–236.

Hart, D., Atkins, R., & Ford, D. (1998). Urban America as a context for the development of moral identity in adolescence. *Journal of Social Issues, 54*, 513–530.

Hart, D., Atkins, R., & Ford, D. (1999). Family influences on the formation of moral identity in adolescence: Longitudinal analyses. *Journal of Moral Education, 28*, 375–386.

Hart, D., & Fegley, S. (1995). Altruism and caring in adolescence: Relations to moral judgment and self-understanding. *Child Development, 66*, 1346–1359.

Hart, D., Burock, D., London, B., & Miraglia, A. (2003). Moral development in childhood. In M. H. Bornstein, L. Davidson, C. L. M. Keyes, & K. A. Moore (Eds.), *Well-being: Positive development across the lifespan* (pp. 355–370). New York: Lawrence Erlbaum Associates.

Jensen, L. (1997). Different worldviews, different morals: America's culture war divide. *Human Development, 40*, 325–344.

Jensen, L. (1998). Moral divisions within countries between orthodoxy and progressivism: India and the United States. *Journal for the Scientific Study of Religion, 37*, 90–107.

Kohlberg, L. (1987). The development of moral judgment and moral action. In L. Kohlberg (Ed., with collaborators), *Child psychology and childhood education: A cognitive developmental view* (pp. 259–328). New York: Longman.

McCullough, M. E., Hoyt, W. T., Larson, D. B., Koenig, H. G., & Thoresen, C. (2000). Religious involvement and mortality: A meta-analytic review. *Health Psychology, 19*, 211–222.

National Survey of Midlife Development in the United States (Midus) [Computer file]. (1995–1996). ICPSR version. Ann Arbor, MI: DataStat, Inc.

Oliner, S., & Oliner, P. (1988). *The altruistic personality*. New York: Free Press.

Orwell, G. (1949, January). Reflections on Gandhi. *Partisan Review*. Retrieved July 27, 2002, from http://www.online-literature.com/orwell/898/.

Public Agenda. (2001). *For goodness' sake: Why so many want religion to play a greater role in American life*. Retrieved July 27, 2002, from http://www.publicagenda.org/specials/religion/religion.htm

Rest, J. (1983). Morality. In J. Flavell & E. Markman (Eds.), *Handbook of child psychology: Cognitive development*. (Vol. 3, 4th ed., pp. 556–629,). New York: Wiley.

Sullivan, A. (2001, October 7). This is a religious war: September 11 was only the beginning. *The New York Times Magazine*. Retrieved July 27, 2002, from http://www.andrewsullivan.com/thewar.php?artnum=20011007/

The National Longitudinal Survey of Youth—Children of the NLSY79 [Data File]. (2000). Washington, DC: Bureau of Labor Statistics.

Turiel, E. (1983). *The development of social knowledge: Morality and convention*. Cambridge, UK: Cambridge University Press.

# Chapter 10

# Institutional Support for Morality
## *Community-based and Neighborhood Organizations*

## Constance Flanagan

*Rational choice predicts that few people will be active in community affairs when, in fact, many are* (Verba, Schlozman, & Brady, 1995).

In their study of the factors that explain Americans' participation in collective action, Verba and his colleagues question the logic of rational choice theories that hold that citizens will refrain from activity on behalf of a collective good. Because individuals reap the benefits of collective goods whether or not they participate in the political process, rational choice theory suggests that it is smart for citizens to save their resources and abstain from community involvement, to "take a free ride." Verba et al. state: "The puzzle of participation, thus, becomes: how are we to explain the fact that millions of citizens, in apparent defiance of this elegant logic, vote or take part in various kinds of voluntary activity on behalf of collective ends?" The authors' answer is that the benefit of participation includes the satisfaction gained from "doing one's share to make the community, nation, or world a better place." This chapter argues that participation in community-based or neighborhood organizations (hereafter referred to as CBOs or CBYOs for community-based youth organizations) nurtures a civic ethic in young people. By engaging in such groups, youths learn that "bearing the cost becomes part of the benefit" (Verba et al., 1995, pp. 100–103).

This realization does not occur for the first time in adulthood. Rather, it is learned through practice during the formative years of youth. Opportunities for nonformal learning in CBOs may play a key role in this process. A host of studies have shown a connection between young people's involvement in CBOs and extracurricular activities and their involvement in community affairs later in adulthood. We know less about the mechanisms that might explain this association. This chapter discusses three reasons for the role these groups play in civic engagement and shows that each is a way in which CBOs nurture morality. First, CBOs provide a structured outlet for leisure time, including a prosocial reference group of peers and adult mentors who are typically models of moral behavior.

Second, CBOs provide opportunities to work toward goals that are collectively defined in a context where the status of all members is relatively equal. When they engage in group projects, peers hold one another accountable to the group, and individuals see that their interests are realized in those of the group. The habits that develop through these practices become integral to the youths' evolving identities and are the basis from which moral actions flow (Youniss & Yates, 1999). Virtues of loyalty, team spirit, trust, and trustworthiness—dispositions that are foundational for citizenship—are nourished (Flanagan, 2004).

Third, CBOs develop social trust. Their potential for extending the radius of humanity that youths trust and for whom they feel responsible depends on how much diversity exists within the organization and on the range of other groups in the community with which members of the organization interact.

## Prosocial Reference Group and Constructive Use of Leisure Time

Whether or not we believe that idle time is the devil's workshop, the evidence is clear that the after-school hours from 3:00 to 6:00 p.m. are the times when most juvenile misdemeanors occur and, therefore, are times of greatest need for community supervision. That niche is filled by many after-school clubs and neighborhood organizations. These programs play a role in informal social control insofar as youths who participate in structured youth groups are less likely to be involved in antisocial activities or substance abuse. In some studies, sports participation is an exception to this rule, possibly because of its status in the hierarchy of social cliques at school and the inclination of jocks and the popular crowd to drink alcohol. Additionally, as the Positive Coaching Alliance (Thompson, 2000) has pointed out, many sports programs are characterized by competition, an absence of team spirit, and uneven enforcement of the rules. The relationship between sports and moral development may also depend on the participant's motivation for participating and on the importance of winning to his or her self-esteem.

However, in general, CBOs share some common features that nurture identities that transcend the self. For example, compared with schools, CBOs' nonformal and less hierarchical organizational structure is better suited to nurturing the affective ties of young people to fellow members of their communities. In one study of African American youths in low-income urban communities, Kahne and his colleagues found that in CBOs, compared with schools, youths felt more respected by adults, more comfortable with and trusting of peers, and generally more accepted (Kahne, Nagaoka, Brown, O'Brien, Quinn, & Thiede, 2001). Affective or emotional ties to a community are a foundation for nurturing morality. When young people feel wanted and believe that they count in the affairs of the community, they are less likely to violate its norms. The absence of such affective ties is a problem for individuals as well as communities. Terms such as "disaffected" and "alienated" point to the significance we accord to a "sense of place" in youths' identities. When youths feel a "sense of place" in their communities, they come to see that their interests are realized in the interests of the whole. By extension, as adults, they will see that contributing to the community is not just an option; rather, they will believe it is simply the right thing to do.

The opportunities that CBOs offer for social incorporation and connection to prosocial outlets may be especially important for youths who, for one reason or another, have been marginalized from mainstream society. For example, the concept of social reintegration into the community figures prominently in the restorative justice approach to juvenile crime. In contrast to a retributive framework in which juvenile offenders are held accountable to the state, restorative justice practices emphasize youths' obligations to repair the harm done to their victims and to the broader community. Practices such as victim–offender mediation, community service, and conflict resolution are designed to repair relationships. But it is not only the offender who engages in reparation; community members also are made aware of ways that they may make the youths feel more included (Bazemore & Walgrave, 1999). Although few controlled studies of this approach to juvenile justice have been conducted, some evidence suggests that community service is more effective than detention in reducing recidivism. Community service in combination with group discussion and reflection on the experience is also effective in risk prevention programs. Community service may be one of the few opportunities that many young people have to demonstrate the contributions they can make to their communities. The role of community service in nurturing morality is discussed in detail later in this chapter.

## Membership and Solidarity

Aristotle described the polis as a network of friends bound together by the pursuit of a common good and an isolate as either a beast or a god who is unable or has no need to share in the benefits of political association. CBOs are organizations neither of beasts nor of gods but of people. They are settings where young people can explore communities of membership beyond the boundaries of their families. And whereas membership in families is a given, membership in CBOs is earned. In fact, in the give-and-take of what are, in principle, horizontal relationships among equals, democratic dispositions (e.g., tolerance, trust, and commitment to the collective) develop.

In CBOs, youths often work in groups, defining together the projects they plan to do. Peers hold one another accountable to those projects. Youths learn that they should keep promises they make to the group or risk "losing face" in the eyes of their friends. If they do not carry their weight or do their part, projects may not get done, and the whole group suffers. If they are loyal to the group, they demonstrate allegiance by doing their part. These practices shape character. If others count on us, we are held to that standard and we internalize it. The reciprocity between trust and trustworthiness is evident: Peers trust that members will come through for the group; if they do come through, they are trustworthy. Ultimately, these virtues of trust, loyalty, and responsibility are the bases of citizenship or loyalty to the polity (Flanagan, 2004).

However, group solidarity is not a given. It is achieved by working through differences and finding common ground. The egalitarian, peer-like structure of CBYOs suits them for this task. Compared with families or schools, in which relationships of power and authority are more asymmetrical, the status of the members in CBYOs is roughly the same. The consequences of disagreeing with others and of voicing opposing opinions are the same for all members of the group. Thus, such groups afford opportunities to practice democratic skills, including engaging in civil debate, asserting one's own and listening to others' perspectives, and deliberating and accommodating together. In the process, youths gain the skills of democratic citizens. They learn to make informed judgments, voice autonomous opinions, and hear other points of view. They realize that each member of the group cannot always get what he or she wants but that it is worth speaking up because their views often resonate with those of others. They may also decide that the social interaction and the feeling of solidarity itself are rewarding and that the group product is better than that which the individuals could have accomplished separately.

In democracies, citizens are expected to make decisions free from control by the state. A "good citizen" is not merely one who follows the rules but one who deliberates on the rules and questions them when they are unjust. For example, during the civil rights movement, good citizens challenged laws of segregation. Because deliberation and the exercise of judgment are virtues of good citizens, opportunities for self-determination, perspective taking, and deliberation are important in the formative years. Families and schools do provide such opportunities, and a sizable literature on authoritative parenting styles and democratic school climates shows that encouraging young people to voice their opinions promotes positive development, partly because of the reflection and deliberation that are involved in the process. But the role of adults is different in these settings compared with their role in CBYOs. In schools and families, adults provide structure. In CBYOs, youths are in charge.

Successful CBYOs have been described as partnerships between youths and adults characterized by mutual respect and equality. Respect for young people is also high on the list of qualities of good teachers and parents. However, equal status is not an accurate description of young people's relationships with adults in these settings. In CBYOs, adults act as facilitators, mentors, and coaches but not as leaders. Youths lead, make decisions, carry through on plans, and learn from their successes and failures. For adults, striking the right balance between guidance and freedom is challenging. A laissez-faire approach, leaving youths to their own devices, is irresponsible and ignores age differences in experience. But having adults in positions of leadership robs young people of the practice they need in negotiating group decisions and seeing projects through. When asked, youths say they do seek particular kinds of interaction and support from adults in CBYOs. They want adults to dialogue with and coach them. They are also aware that adults are better connected to sources of institutional, community, and political power (Camino & Zeldin, 2002). The organization itself will not survive if adults are nonresponsive to young people. After all, CBYOs, unlike schools and families, are voluntary associations. If they provide a poor fit for the competencies and needs of young people, the young people can simply leave.

Adults in CBYOs, similar to teachers in schools, also set norms of civic and moral behavior. Although equal status is a condition that fosters intergroup relations and tolerance, peer groups are riddled with inequities that can surface and undermine their democratic potential. Leaving young people to handle disputes themselves is irresponsible and typically results in the bullies winning. Instead, adults should be proactive. When they set a standard of tolerance and civility, they nurture the democratic character of young people. In our school-based studies, we have found a positive relationship between young people's commitment to public interest goals (e.g., their desire to contribute to their communities and to make their society a better place) and their perceptions that their teachers have equal expectations for all students and would actively intervene to stop acts of intolerance (Flanagan & Faison, 2001). As a group, adults who work in CBYOs also tend to be models of civic virtue. They either volunteer their time or are employed in the field of youth work, where compensation for their time is relatively low. In this sense, they are not motivated by self-interest but instead are dedicated to the welfare of others, namely young people.

As one of the formative settings where young people spend time, CBYOs, similar to schools, are mediating institutions. They are settings where the principles of the social contract, the ties that bind members of communities, nation-states, and citizens together, are interpreted and negotiated. To the extent that principles of tolerance, freedom, and equality—values that are arguably the bedrock of our American identity—guide the goals of CBYOs and are reinforced in their practices, these virtues become part of the character of younger generations. But CBYOs are voluntary associations, and in their policies and practices, they can also marginalize and exclude people. The policy of the Boy Scouts of America to exclude gay men and boys from membership is one prominent example.

At the same time, as mediating institutions, CBYOs can be spaces where conventions are challenged and new organizational forms take shape. For example, in response to young people who have been marginalized by mainstream institutions, a range of youth-led grassroots CBOs is evolving. These organizations provide a "free space" where young people can test new ideas. They are safe spaces, places with structure provided by a set of rules that are collectively generated by the group (Flanagan, 2004).

In these organizations, the good of the group (or the common good) takes precedence over self-interests. Dedication to the group is the principle to which leaders are held accountable by their peers. Ample opportunities exist to spread leadership roles across the membership of the organization. This emphasis on the collective minimizes the likelihood that individuals or small groups will take over. The dispersion of responsibilities also means that individuals across the organization learn new skills and ensures that the organization will be sustained. Responsibilities are graduated according to individuals' abilities and experiences, with older youths coaching their less experienced peers. In these organizations, youths are not merely staying off the streets and out of trouble; they are also typically providing tangible products, things of value for their communities. Perhaps the best example is the affordable housing units that the YouthBuild program provides to residents of their communities (see Stoneman, 2002, for more details on YouthBuild).

## Trust

Another way that CBOs nurture a civic ethic in young people is by developing their trust in others, not just in people they know well but also their trust in humanity. Whereas interpersonal trust is our level of confidence in people we know well, social trust is our belief about humanity in general. That is, do we believe that people are generally fair, helpful, and trustworthy, or do we suspect that most people are out for their own gain and would take advantage of us if we let down our guard?

Among adults, participation in CBOs and levels of social trust are positively related and mutually reinforcing. In fact, the relationship has been described as a "virtuous circle": People who trust others are more likely to join CBOs. In addition, their faith in human beings increases as a result of their participation. In our program of work, we have found that compared with their peers who are not involved in any organizations in the community or at school, adolescents who participate in at least one organization have more benevolent views about people who live in their communities (Flanagan, Gill, & Gallay, in press). Their opinions are that "most people care about making this a good place to live; generally, there are people I can go to for help; people who live here can be counted on to pull together and solve problems that we face."

What might explain this connection? Two complementary processes may be at work. The first concerns how youths use their time when they are alone (i.e., watching television) and the stereotypical views of humanity on TV. The second concerns the enriched view of humanity one gains by working with other people in CBOs and the generally benevolent views of others that emerge when people work together toward a "common good." Young people who are not involved in organized groups are likely to spend significant amounts of their time watching entertainment television. Studies of adults and young people have shown an inverse relationship between high levels of TV viewing and trust. Compared with what we might call "real life," portraits of humanity on entertainment TV tend to be stereotypical and mean spirited. Between contestants competing to become a millionaire and those ratting on one another on survivalist shows, one has to wonder whether anyone on "reality" TV can be trusted. Likewise, tuning into news programs hardly engenders a sense of trust in the leaders of the financial, political, or even the religious institutions of society.

By contrast, in CBOs, people have multiple face-to-face opportunities to get to know real others and to generalize this rich experience to what they believe about most people. In real life, youths get to know others on good days and bad and come to know their virtues and their faults. They see other people in different roles and develop a more nuanced view of humanity. At times, any one of us may be out for our own gain. But at other times, we have the good of the group in mind. Furthermore, although people have different motivations for joining CBOs, the goal of these organizations is to bring different members of the community together in common pursuits. The organizations themselves are a "public good" shared by members of the community. As already noted, people who join CBOs tend to have higher levels of trust than those who do not join. In the course of participating in an organization's activities, the reciprocal relationship between trust and trustworthiness becomes evident. By fulfilling responsibilities to the organization or group, members demonstrate that they are trustworthy and that others can rely on them to come through on behalf of the group. And by learning about these same virtues in other members of the group, members' faith in humanity is reinforced.

However, CBOs may also have downsides regarding nurturing morality. Strong ties and loyalty to a group can exist at the expense of letting others in. Exclusionary practices can be intentional, but they are more likely to result from unintentional (and unexamined) factors. For example, organizations with long lives in communities may not have adapted their practices to respond to the increasingly diverse populations moving into those communities.

## Bonding and Bridging Trust

In his book *Bowling Alone*, Putnam (2000) distinguishes between trust that exists in close relationships with people we know well (which he refers to as "bonding social capital") and trust of others outside these close networks of association (i.e., "bridging social capital"). By no means are the two mutually exclusive. The latter, however, is essential for the sustenance of a diverse democracy. It is not enough that adults and youths interact with and trust people they know well; democracies need people who are also ready to work toward common goals with fellow citizens who are *different* from themselves.

However, many of our experiences with others are with people who are similar to us. CBOs are not an exception to this rule insofar as they are typically based in geographical communities and are thus rather homogeneous. "Virtual" communities via the Internet may be a means of overcoming these geographical boundaries, but the verdict is still out on whether the Internet is being used either by adults or young people in ways that promote democracy. Of course, citywide organizations may pool from a more diverse population; these organizations should be cognizant in their programming of their potential for nurturing intergroup relations and democratic character. Youths' views about the polity or even what they might consider the common good depends on the breadth of their experiences with fellow members of their communities. Ultimately, when faced with political decisions, our perspectives and our notions about a fair distribution of resources depends on whether we have learned to see issues from more than our own narrow point of view.

## Community Service

Well before service learning was institutionalized in schools, service to the community was a common practice of many CBOs. For example, members of the 4-H Club have for many years pledged to dedicate their heads, hearts, hands, and health "to better living" for their club, community, country, and world. Performing community service is one of the few opportunities youths have to interact with others who are different from themselves. Although engaging in community service could result in reinforcing group stereotypes (and for this reason, it is important that groups engaged in service collectively reflect on their experience), some studies have found increases in tolerance and reductions in racial prejudice associated with service. Why? Youniss and Yates (1999) argue that direct service with people who lack basics such as food and shelter is an opportunity for youths to interact face to face with fellow human beings and to enlarge the circle of humanity for whom they feel responsible.

In our studies (Flanagan et al., in press), we have noted three changes that youths mention when asked what they learned in their service experience that we believe are associated with the development of social trust. First, by having face-to-face encounters with real individuals who are members of stereotypical groups (e.g., elderly or poor individuals), stereotypes break down. Service provides an opportunity to, as one teen said, to "meet new people and learn that not all people are bad." The notion that "not all people are bad" suggests a mechanism whereby social trust is built through such encounters. Rather than malevolent images of stereotypical others, young people have mental schemas based on concrete experiences with real elderly people or homeless people.

Second, participants in our studies pointed to ways that they accommodated and ways that their preconceptions changed. "I learned to be patient with little kids, to respect the elderly, not to be afraid of homeless people, to know and to trust old people," said one young person. These remarks imply not only changes in the youth's attitudes but also changes in her conception of what we have called the "social contract," or the obligations that bind members of a community together. As one young person summarized, "Always give help because it will probably be there when you need it back."

Finally, participation in community service adds to the collective stock of faith in humanity by exposing young people to adults in human service professions and in the volunteer sector. One respondent wrote, "I learned that there are a lot of people who are kind, who care, and are willing to help others." In the literature on community service, little attention is given to the fact that the staff members of human service agencies are, for the most part, people who are not out for their own gain but genuinely do care about others. Insofar as young people are still formulating ideas about the kind of adults they aspire to become, interactions with those in public service or in nongovernment voluntary organizations could be inspiring. Whether or not they choose to do similar work when they are older, their concepts of humanity should be informed by these interactions.

Community-based youth organizations incorporate younger generations into the polity. They stabilize democracies to the extent that their practices develop democratic dispositions in young people. But opportunities for youths to join these organizations are unevenly distributed. Compared with more privileged neighborhoods, poorer communities have fewer economic resources and a lower adult-to-child ratio; therefore, they have a smaller pool of potential adult volunteers from which to draw (Hart & Atkins, 2002). In the United States, more privileged persons are likely to participate in the political process. Better-educated, better-paid, and better-connected people are more likely to have a voice. Participation in faith-based community organizations is one of the few venues that offer less privileged individuals the chance to practice leadership and organizational skills that later pay off in their political participation (Verba et al., 1995). If CBYOs were widely available, they could play a similar role in redressing class inequities in political participation.

As an early observer of American mores, Alexis de Tocqueville (1848/1969) referred to groups such as CBOs as the "schools of democracy" where citizens from different backgrounds met to resolve issues of common concern. Besides being places where local issues are negotiated, the dispositions of citizens are shaped by the practices of these organizations. De Tocqueville contended that it was the commitments people feel to the common good that keep Americans' individualist tendencies from corroding into narrow self-interest. In this sense, CBOs do provide institutional support for morality. Instead of promoting a "free ride," they nurture in youths a belief that bearing the cost is part of the benefit.

# References

Bazemore, G., & Walgrave, L. (1999). *Restorative juvenile justice: Repairing the harm of youth crime.* New York: Criminal Justice Press.

Camino, L. A., & Zeldin, S. (2002). Everyday lives in communities: Discovering citizenship through youth-adult partnerships. *Applied Developmental Science, 6*(4), 213–220.

Flanagan, C. A. (2004). Volunteerism, leadership, political socialization, and civic engagement. In R. M. Lerner & L. Steinberg (Eds.), *Handbook of adolescent psychology.* (pp. 721–746). New York: Wiley.

Flanagan, C. A., & Faison, N. (2001). Youth civic development: Implications of research for social policy and programs. *Social Policy Report: Vol. XV.* Ann Arbor, MI: Society for Research in Child Development.

Flanagan, C. A., Gill, S., & Gallay, L. S. (in press). Social participation and social trust in adolescence: The importance of heterogeneous encounters. In A. Omoto (Ed.), *Social participation in processes of community change and social action (Claremont Symposium on Applied Social Psychology): Vol. 19.* Mahwah, NJ: Erlbaum.

Hart, D., & Atkins, R. (2002). Civic competence in urban youth. *Applied Developmental Science, 6*(4), 227–236.

Kahne, J., Nagaoka, J., Brown, A., O'Brien, J., Quinn, T., & Thiede, K. (2001). Assessing after-school programs as settings for youth development. *Youth and Society, 32*(4), 421–446.

Putnam, R. D. (2000). *Bowling alone: The collapse and revival of American community.* New York: Simon & Schuster.

Stoneman, D. (2002). The role of youth programming in the development of civic engagement. *Applied Developmental Science, 6*(4), 221–226.

Thompson, J. (2000). Calling all change agents. *Momentum: Positive Coaching Alliance Newsletter, Winter,* 2–3.

Tocqueville, A. de (1969). *Democracy in America.* (G. Lawrence, Trans.). Garden City, NY: Doubleday. (Original work published 1848).

Verba, S., Schlozman, K. L., & Brady, H. E. (1995). *Voice and equality: Civic voluntarism in American politics.* Cambridge, MA: Harvard University Press.

Youniss, J., & Yates, M. (1999). Youth service and moral-civic identity: A case for everyday morality. *Educational Psychology Review, 11*(4), 363–378.

# Considering the Common Good

Wisdom is not just about maximizing one's own or someone else's self-interests but about balancing various self-interests (intrapersonal) with the interests of others (interpersonal) and with various contextual aspects (extrapersonal) such as one's city, country, environment, or even God. These interests must also be balanced over both the short and long term. In wisdom, one seeks a common good, realizing that this common good may be better for some than for others.

—*Robert J. Sternberg and Steven E. Stemler*

This book is not about how bad things have gotten on the moral front, and it contains no whining. Rather, the book's strong themes are *pluralism* or *diversity, responsibility, exemplarity,* and *affectivity*. Readers who gravitate to titles designed to spell out *how to* or contribute to *feel-good* forms of spirituality may not know to look here for practical counsel and inspiration. But they will find it here.

—*Martin E. Marty*

# Chapter 11

# Wisdom As A Moral Virtue

## Robert J. Sternberg and Steven E. Stemler

Some years ago, RJS gave a graduate student really rotten advice. This graduate student had received two job offers, one from a very highly prestigious academic institution and the other from a less prestigious one. The second one was well known, but the first one was near the top of the academic pecking order. The graduate student asked RJS which job offer he thought she should take.

The answer might seem straightforward: Why not take the more prestigious offer? But it was not straightforward. The reason is that the kinds of interests the student had seemed to fit the somewhat less prestigious institution better than they fit the more prestigious one. In particular, she liked teaching quite a bit, and the second institution seemed to emphasize teaching more than the first one.

RJS was young and naïve at the time—barely out of his 20s—and foolishly told her to take the more prestigious offer. She did, and it proved to be a mistake. She did not fit in. She did not value what the school valued, and the school did not value what she valued. Several years later, she left, and she eventually ended up at a place that particularly values innovative teaching.

About the same time, RJS needed some advice. He was being considered for tenure at Yale, and it came to his attention that the university was receiving letters that questioned why it would want to give tenure to someone in such a marginal and unprestigious field as intelligence. RJS sought advice from a senior professor, Wendell Garner, telling him that perhaps he had made a mistake in labeling his work as being about intelligence. Indeed, RJS could have done essentially the same work but labeled it as being in the field of "thinking" or of "problem solving," fields with more prestige. Garner's advice was that RJS had come to Yale wanting to make a difference in the field of intelligence. RJS had made a difference, but now he was afraid it might cost him his job, and he was right. But Garner maintained that there was only one thing RJS could do—exactly what he was doing. If this field meant so much to RJS, then he needed to pursue it, just as he was doing, even if it meant losing his job. RJS is still at the university.

At the time of these events, RJS realized that Garner had in ample supply something he pretty much lacked. It was not age; it was not experience, exactly. It was wisdom. RJS was determined to understand the nature of wisdom, but it is not until recently that he has made any serious inroads.

When we speak of wisdom here, we are speaking of it as a moral virtue, but not in the narrow sense of morality that one learns when parents or other authorities tell one what to do. Rather, wisdom is a moral virtue in the sense of having a compass for making judgments, a set of guidelines that recognizes that moral principles, however useful, need a set of guidelines for their application. Wisdom supplies such a set of guidelines. In the absence of wisdom, morality can be severely distorted, as when terrorists and saboteurs describe their work in moral terms; however, terrorism is not moral, and it certainly is not wise.

## The Nature of Wisdom

Wisdom is defined here as the application of intelligence and creativity as mediated by values toward the achievement of a common good through a balance among intrapersonal, interpersonal, and extrapersonal interests over the short and long terms in order to achieve a balance among adaptation to existing environments, shaping of existing environments, and selection of new environments (Figure 11.1). Sternberg (1990, 1998) offers more detail.

Thus, wisdom does not simply concern maximizing one's own or someone else's self-interest; it also concerns balancing various self-interests (intrapersonal) with the interests of others (interpersonal) and with various contextual aspects (extrapersonal) such as one's city, country, environment, or even God. In wisdom, one seeks a common good, realizing that this common good may be better for some than for others.

Some may argue that the definition of common good is morally relative. We disagree. Although differences in values and beliefs may mediate alternative definitions of right and wrong, tremendous consensus exists across religions, cultures, and geographies with regard to some basic principles that may be used to define the common good. These fundamental

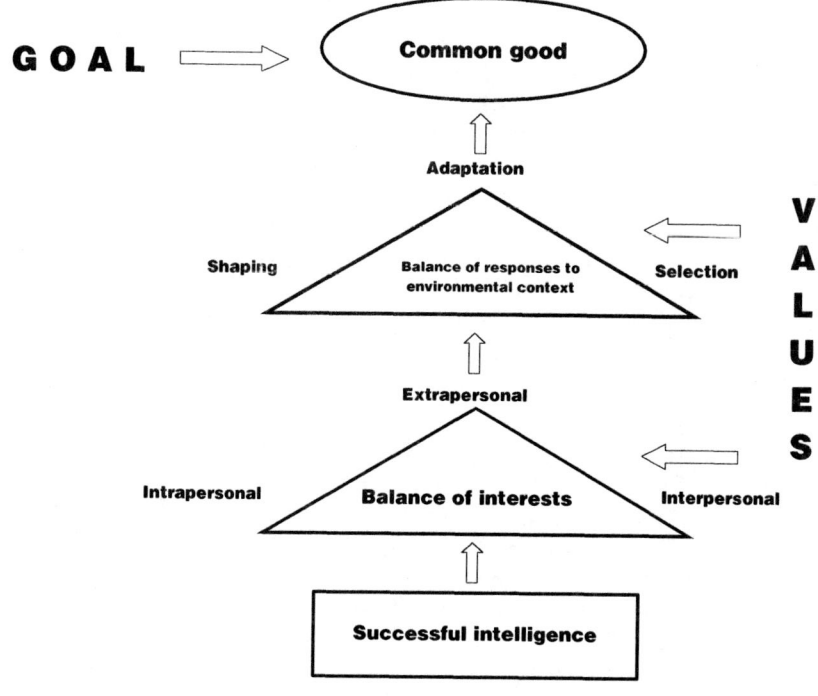

Figure 11.1. A model of wisdom.

principles include honesty, reciprocity, sincerity, integrity, and compassion. Although morality impacts the fine distinctions between right and wrong in particular circumstances, wisdom is broader in scope.

Clearly, however, the constructs of wisdom and morality overlap. The degree to which an individual is a wise decision maker is heavily influenced by his or her moral functioning. A person with a strong moral sense is more likely to adhere to most of the universal principles that define the common good within the framework of wisdom; however, morality in itself does not always lead to wise decision making. For example, people who bomb abortion clinics often justify their behavior on moral grounds, yet the decision may not be wise in the sense of balancing intrapersonal, interpersonal, and extrapersonal interests in a way that achieves the common good. (Chapter 4 provides some other examples of the ways that morality and caring can go awry and lead to decisions that may be moral but unwise.)

Problems that require wisdom always involve at least some element of each of intrapersonal, interpersonal, and extrapersonal interests. For example, a minister might decide that it is wise to take a new position in a different location, a decision that seemingly involves only one person. But many people are typically affected by an individual's decision to take a job, including parents, friends, and even the congregation. Not only will the minister and his friends be impacted, but the institution itself may also be impacted by the loss of a charismatic leader. Furthermore, wise decisions always have to be made in the context of the whole range of available options. Thus, people must be aware of the options and what they mean. To be wise, one must be cognizant of what one knows, what one does not know, what can be known, and what cannot be known at a given time or place.

What considerations might be included under each of the three kinds of interests? Intrapersonal interests include the desire to learn more, increase one's spiritual well-being, enhance one's popularity or prestige, make more money, increase one's power, and so forth. Interpersonal interests might be quite similar, except as they apply to other people rather than oneself. Extrapersonal interests include contributing to the welfare of one's school, helping one's community, contributing to the well-being of one's country, serving God, and so forth. Different people balance these interests in different ways. At one extreme, a power-hungry corporate executive might emphasize his own personal power and wealth; at the other extreme, a workaholic physician may emphasize only serving others while neglecting her own family and health.

Wisdom involves a balancing not only of the three kinds of interests but also of three possible courses of action in response to this balancing: adaptation of oneself or others to existing environments, shaping of environments in order to render them more compatible with oneself or others, and selection of new environments. In adaptation, the individual tries to find ways to conform to the existing environment that forms his or her context. Sometimes adaptation is the best course of action under the circumstances. But typically, one seeks a balance between adaptation and shaping, realizing that fit to an environment requires not only changing oneself but changing the environment as well. When an individual finds it impossible or at least implausible to attain such a fit, he or she may decide to select a new environment altogether, leaving, for example, a job, a community, or a marriage.

Suppose, for example, that a particular teacher is committed to the importance of moral education. The teacher is then hired for his first job in a school. As the year progresses, he begins to understand that the administration within his school is obsessed with test scores and the school primarily focuses on the development of children's cognitive abilities. The development of morality is not valued. The teacher has some choices about how to proceed. He can adapt to the situation by staying with the school and learning to appreciate the value that is placed on test scores within the school. Or he can attempt to shape the attitudes of the administrators and the community by attending school board meetings and trying to convince people of the importance of moral education. Or he can look for a job at a different school, one that emphasizes moral education. Most likely, however, the wisest solution will involve some kind of balance of the three approaches. A wise teacher might make some modifications to his instructional approach in order to accommodate the push for cognitive achievement while at the same time engaging the administration in conversations about the importance of moral education. In the meantime, perhaps the teacher could also choose to teach in another environment (e.g., an after-school program, Sunday school) that is more in line with his views of moral education while at the same time keeping his full-time teaching position.

Wisdom also involves a balance of short- and long-term thinking. For example, research has shown that punishing and rewarding children is effective in getting them to comply with requests in the short term, but it often tends to undermine children's levels of intrinsic motivation in the long run (Kohn, 1999). Consequently, although a particular solution may be good in the short term, it may not always lead to the desired consequences in the long term.

Wisdom manifests itself as a series of higher order processes that are typically cyclical and can occur in a variety of orders. These processes include recognizing the existence of a problem, defining the nature of the problem, representing information about the problem, formulating a strategy for solving the problem, allocating resources to the solution of the problem, monitoring the solution of the problem, and evaluating feedback regarding that solution. In deciding about a teaching job, for example, one first has to see both taking the position and not taking it as viable options (i.e., recognize the problem), then figure out exactly what taking or not taking the position would mean for oneself (i.e., define the problem), then consider the costs and benefits to oneself and others of taking the position (i.e., represent information about the problem; Sternberg, 1990, 1998, 2001).

## Wisdom-related Skills

Wisdom requires many distinct skills. First, wise judgments require knowledge regarding the topics about which one has to make judgments. This knowledge is of two kinds. Formal knowledge is the kind of knowledge one learns in school and through books. Informal knowledge is the kind of knowledge that is picked up through experience.

Second, wisdom requires analytical thinking. However, this is not the kind of analytical thinking that is typically emphasized in schools or measured on tests of academic abilities and achievements. Rather, it is the analysis of real-world dilemmas in which clean and neat abstractions often give way to messy and disorderly concrete interests. The kind of abstract analytical thinking that may lead to outstanding performance on a test such as the Raven Matrices, which presents figural reasoning items, is of some but not much use in complex real-world dilemmas such as how to defuse the conflict between Israelis and Palestinians.

Third, wise thinking must be creative to some extent because it generates a novel, problem-relevant, high-quality solution involving a balancing of interests. Novelty and appropriate quality are two hallmarks of creativity. However, a solution can be creative (e.g., solving a mathematical problem) but have no particular characteristics of wisdom. A mathematical proof involves no balancing of interests and no search for a common good; it is simply an intellectual problem that involves creative thinking.

Fourth, practical thinking is closer to wisdom than are analytical and creative thinking, but again, practical thinking is not the same as wisdom. Practical thinking enables one to solve everyday problems or apply knowledge in a useful context. However, applying one's knowledge of physics to fix a broken automobile does not necessarily exhibit any characteristics of wisdom, for example. Practical thinking may help one fix the car, but it will not help inform the decision about whether to go home to one's family or out with one's friends for the evening.

Fifth, wisdom also seems to be related to constructs such as social and emotional intelligence. However, differences also exist. Social intelligence can be applied to understanding and getting along with others, to any ends, for any purposes. Wisdom, on the other hand, seeks out a common good through a balancing of interests. Thus, a salesperson who figures out how to sell a worthless product to a customer might do so through using social intelligence to understand the customer's wants, but the salesperson has not applied wisdom in the process. Emotional intelligence involves understanding, judging, and regulating emotions. These skills are important components of wisdom. But making wise judgments requires going beyond the understanding, regulation, or judgment of emotions. Instead, making wise decisions requires processing the information to achieve a balance of interests and formulating judgments that make effective use of the information to achieve a common good.

Perhaps the most salient difference among constructs is that whereas wisdom is applied toward the achievement of ends that are perceived as yielding a common good, the various kinds of intelligences may be applied deliberately toward achieving either good ends or bad ones, at least for some of the parties involved. Furthermore, whereas the preceding constructs are not necessarily driven by an underlying moral framework or values system, wisdom is inextricably bound to, and mediated by, values.

Interestingly, the conception of wisdom proposed here is substantially closer to Chinese conceptions of intelligence than to American ones. Indeed, one of the words used in Chinese to characterize intelligence is the same as the word used to characterize wisdom.

## Foolishness

Foolishness is the absence of wisdom. Smart people can be foolish and, indeed, are sometimes especially susceptible to foolishness. This is especially true when they find themselves in positions of leadership. Power can be quite seductive. Those in positions to significantly influence policies and the lives of others must be especially vigilant to guard against four fallacies in thinking that most often entrap foolish people.

The *fallacy of egocentrism* occurs when an individual starts to think that the world centers on him or her. Other people come to be seen merely as tools in the attainment of one's goals. Why would smart people think egocentrically, when one would expect that egocentrism would be a stage out of which they would have passed many years ago? We believe that the reason is that conventionally smart people have been so highly rewarded for being smart that they lose sight of their limitations. However, wisdom requires one to know what one does and does not know. Smart people often lose sight of what they do not know, leading to the second fallacy.

The *fallacy of omniscience* results from having available essentially any knowledge one might want. With a phone call, a powerful leader can have almost any kind of knowledge made available to him or her. At the same time, people look up to the powerful leader as extremely knowledgeable or even close to all knowing. The leader may then come to believe that he or she really *is* all knowing. His or her staff may believe the same thing, as illustrated by Irving Janis (1972) in his analysis of victims of groupthink. In case after case, brilliant government officials made the most foolish of decisions, partly because they believed they knew much more than they did.

The *fallacy of omnipotence* results from extreme power. In certain domains, powerful leaders can do essentially almost whatever they want to do. The risk is that these individuals will start to overgeneralize and believe that this high level of power applies in all domains.

The *fallacy of invulnerability* comes from the illusion of complete protection, such as by a huge staff. Powerful people, especially leaders, seem to have many friends ready to protect them at a moment's notice. The leaders may shield themselves from individuals who are anything less than sycophantic. As soon as things turn bad, many of the individuals who once seemed to be friends prove to be anything but. Harry Truman said that high-powered leaders who want friends should buy themselves a dog.

In terms of the balance theory of wisdom, foolishness always involves interests going out of balance. Usually, the individual places self-interest way above other interests. An exception can be found in the example of Neville Chamberlain, who may truly have believed he was doing the best for Great Britain. But in ignoring the interests of all the other countries that were being crushed under Hitler's brutal rein, Chamberlain ignored the common good and the long-term good of his own country.

Similarly, people occasionally sacrifice everything for another individual, only to be crushed by their own foolishness. The "classic" case is that of the prolonged war between Greece and Troy. Was Helen of Troy worth the war? Many wars have started over slights or humiliations, and the interests of the slighted or humiliated have taken precedence over the interests of the thousands who have then been sacrificed to avenge the slight. For example, some believe that the war in Chechnya resulted in part from the humiliation suffered by the Russian army in the earlier war in Chechnya. Certainly, post–World War I events contributed to Germany's humiliation after that war, thus contributing to World War II.

Wisdom involves a balancing not only of the three kinds of interests but also of three possible courses of action in response to this balancing: adaptation of oneself or others to existing environments, shaping of environments in order to render them more compatible with oneself or others, and selection of new environments. Foolishness is reflected in action that represents poor use and balance of these processes.

Placing undue emphasis on shaping the environment can result in foolish decisions. For example, individuals elected to Congress are sometimes more concerned with garnering power for their political party than in seeking the common good. In an effort to increase their party's power, they may vote to revoke particular programs that have been shown to be effective, simply because the programs were initiated by the opposing party. By revoking the effective program, they are shaping the environment, but they are doing so in a way that does not necessarily demonstrate a balance of interests or possible courses of action (e.g., creating supplemental programs that can be credited to their own party, making their own mark with new programs).

Foolishness does not only derive from inappropriate shaping of the environment; one can also adapt to a tyrannical environment to save one's own skin, only to find oneself paying the ultimate price. An example of this principle is shown in the quotation by Pastor Martin Niemöller:

> In Germany first they came for the communists
> and I did not speak out—
> because I was not a communist.
>
> Then they came for the Jews
> and I did not speak out—
> because I was not a Jew.
>
> Then they came for the trade unionists
> and I did not speak out—
> because I was not a trade unionist.
>
> Then they came for the Catholics
> and I did not speak out—
> because I was a Protestant.
>
> Then they came for me—
> and there was no one left
> to speak out for me.

Finally, an overreliance on selecting new environments can also be foolish. For example, a person who leaves his or her work environment every time the going gets tough will soon acquire a reputation for being an unreliable vagabond. By constantly selecting new environments, the person may eventually have trouble finding a permanent position.

## Developing Wise Thinking in Children and Adults

The development of wisdom is critical to the healthy functioning of society. Wisdom is clearly required of leaders, but it is also advisable to plant the seeds of wisdom in students, who are future parents and leaders and are always part of a greater community. Similar to adults, children benefit from learning to judge rightly, soundly, and justly on behalf of their communities.

If the future is plagued with conflict and turmoil, this instability does not simply reside "out there somewhere"; rather, it resides and originates in us. For all these reasons, we endorse teaching students not only to recall facts and to think critically (and even creatively) about the content of the subjects they learn but also to think wisely about it.

It is impossible to speak of wisdom outside the context of a set of values, which combine to lead to moral stances or, in Kohlberg's (1984) view, stages of moral development. The stages are (a) the primary concern is obedience to authority in order to avoid punishment; (b) the primary concern is to conform to social norms in order to gain rewards; (c) the primary concern is with behaving appropriately in order to gain approval from others; (d) the primary concern is with acting in a way that is moral in order to avoid guilt or censure; (e) morality is seen as a social contract, decided arbitrarily by group consensus; and (f) decisions are made on the basis of universal moral imperatives or one's own guiding principles. Stage six is purely theoretical; for practical purposes, the theory consists of only five stages.

Practical intelligence is a function of what is valued in a societal or cultural context. Values mediate how one balances interests and responses, and values collectively contribute to how one defines a common good. The intersection of wisdom with the moral domain can be seen in the overlap in the notion of wisdom presented here and the notion of moral reasoning as it applies in the two highest stages (i.e., stages 5 and 6) of Kohlberg's (1984) theory. Wisdom also involves caring for others as well as oneself, along the lines suggested by Gilligan (1994). At the same time, wisdom is broader than moral reasoning. It applies to any human problem that involves a balance of intrapersonal, interpersonal, and extrapersonal interests, whether or not moral issues are at stake.

## Characteristics of Wise People

One of the most important characteristics of wise people is their capacity for dialogical thinking. Dialogical thinking involves the ability to take on the perspectives of others, to understand significant problems from multiple points of view, and to understand that others could legitimately conceive of things in different ways. Tannen (1998) has stated that we currently live in an "argument culture." We are constantly faced with tremendously complex issues (e.g., abortion, gun control, the death penalty) on which we are expected to take one side or the other. These issues are frequently presented to us in terms of a dichotomous argument. This kind of myopic approach to the exploration of ideas is the antithesis of dialogical thinking. Few issues can be discussed in either/or terms, yet this attitude prevails in the popular media today. Wise people are able to see beyond apparent dichotomies and look for new solutions. An example is the tale of a young Zen student in search of enlightenment. Along the path he is walking, he encounters a Zen master who says, "If you move, I will beat you with this stick. If you do not move, I will beat you with this stick." When faced with this seemingly perilous situation, the wise Zen student recognizes that there is another choice. He reaches out, grabs the stick, and breaks it. Everyone is faced with seemingly dichotomous choices on a daily basis. The characteristic feature of wise thinkers is that they learn to see beyond the dichotomy and explore a wider range of possible options than those that are presented to them.

A second important characteristic of wise thinkers is their capacity for dialectical thinking. This kind of thinking involves understanding that ideas and the paradigms under which they fall continually evolve, not only from the past to the present but also from the present to the future, as noted by Georg Hegel (1807/1931). Dialectical thinking entails an active attempt to integrate the key elements of what may seem, on the surface, to be disparate ideas. Wise people understand that few ideas are completely worthless; they know that most ideas have some elements that are worthwhile and that can at least be combined with other ideas to form new, more interesting ideas. Wise thinkers consistently pursue new ways of synthesizing the most useful portions of disparate ideas.

Third, wise people recognize that almost everything can be used for better or worse ends. Policy recommendations can be manipulated, words can be twisted, and intentions can be undermined. Wise people realize that the ends to which knowledge is put *do* matter, and they are vigilant in attempting to anticipate and clarify potential misinterpretations of their ideas.

## Conclusions

The importance of nurturing morality and wisdom is not merely academic musing. Wars and terror currently plague our world, as they have throughout human history. We urgently need wise strategies for resolving conflicts and for guiding our behaviors. To nurture wisdom and morality, we must begin with ourselves. Wise thinkers are role models in that they practice what they preach. They are open to new ideas and seek to actively synthesize disparate points of view. They look to balance their own interests, the interests of others, and the interests of larger institutions in both the short and long terms. They attempt to balance the extent to which they adapt to, shape, and select their environments. Our efforts to nurture morality and wisdom must be aimed at all people in all societies, not just a select few.

## Authors' Note

Preparation of this chapter was supported by grants from the W. T. Grant Foundation and the U.S. Office of Educational Research and Improvement (Grant R206R00001). The financial support does not imply their acceptance of the ideas in this manuscript.

## References

Gilligan, C. (1994). In a different voice: Women's conceptions of self and of morality. In B. Puka (Ed.), *Caring voices and women's moral frames: Gilligan's view: Vol. 6. Moral development: A compendium* (pp. 1–37). New York: Garland Publishing.

Hegel, G. W. F. (1931). *The phenomenology of the mind* (2nd ed.; J. D. Baillie, Trans.). London: Allen & Unwin. (Original work published 1807).

Janis, I. L. (1972). *Victims of groupthink*. Boston: Houghton Mifflin.

Kohlberg, L. (1984). *The philosophy of moral development*. New York: Harper & Row.

Kohn, A. (1999). *Punished by rewards: The case against gold stars, incentive plans, A's, praise, and other bribes*. Boston: Houghton Mifflin.

Sternberg, R. J. (Ed.), (1990). *Wisdom: Its nature, origins, and development*. New York: Cambridge University Press.

Sternberg, R. J. (1998). A balance theory of wisdom. *Review of General Psychology, 2,* 347–365.

Sternberg, R. J. (2001). Why schools should teach for wisdom: The balance theory of wisdom in educational settings. *Educational Psychologist, 36,* 227–245.

Tannen, D. (1998). *The argument culture: Moving from debate to dialogue*. New York: Random House.

# Chapter 12
# Response and Next Steps

## Martin E. Marty

This book is *not* about two things and *is* about five others.

First, it is *not* about how bad things have gotten on the moral front. The authors know a great deal about the moral condition of children today and the problems presented by their surrounding cultures. The authors simply take for granted the notion that morality in our time needs nurturing. Morality in every time has needed it. Shelves full of books about moral decline are rarely helpful to teachers, parents, and other adults who want to see improvement. The chapters in this book are designed to be helpful.

For that reason, this is not a book on "how to whine," and it contains no whining. Of course, it includes some critiques. For example, the book refers to the isolation of the self among children who vegetate in front of television and are subjected to bad programming. Happily, however, this book will not find its place among books by authors who self-righteously whine and whimper about everyone but themselves. Parents are aware of the ineffectiveness of whining, both by themselves and by their children.

Secondly, this is not a book of moral philosophy or theology. The moral outlook of the authors may very well have been shaped by texts, whether by Aristotle (his influence shows) or Plato, Moses or Jesus, but the authors are not here called to come up with precise definitions of the beautiful, the true, or the good—and, hence, the moral. They are respectful of theory and have to rely on debates by others on it. Their expertise, however, is in the practical zone, and they put it to good effect for people on the moral front lines.

Having read the chapters with care, consulted personally with some of the authors, and brought my own curiosities about these vital topics to the work, I notice four strong themes that course through the chapters. I hope that such mention will whet the appetites of those who want to be engaged with or are engaged with "nurturing morality."

The first of these can pass under code names such as "pluralism" or "diversity" in the moral quest. Fifty years ago, when the American citizenry included people in multiplicities of subgroups—racial, ethnic, religious, immigrant, and more—one set of people nevertheless set the terms for much of public education and discourse. Today "nurturing morality" goes on in classrooms, neighborhoods, and clubs, where more people and peoples have found their voices and use them. I do not find the authors here saying "anything goes" simply because people come from various cultures. They are saying, however, that everyone must listen well, be sensitive, and watch for "overlaps" and intersections of moral philosophies and systems.

The authors are also aware that pluralism can mean conflict, what Lawrence J. Walker calls "stridently competing worldviews" and a "clash of moral values." Susan Opotow speaks of "conflict" but shows how those responsible can help bring out positive features in conflict and nurture morality for the common good.

Even the most diverse societies, liberated by a polity that makes good use of pluralism, find that some sets of ideas and practices guide the population. For example, José Ortega y Gasset (discussed in Marias, 1967; Weintraub, 1966) discussed the *creencias* of society, ideas that are so deep we hardly know we hold them, not the beliefs that we "hold" but the beliefs that we "are." He also referred to *vigencias*, the "binding customs" of society. Creative societies such as Canada and the United States encourage constant reexamination of both of these. But they also know that certain approaches to honesty, fairness, justice, and compassion are widely shared and have to be—or get to be—kept in mind by those nurturing morality.

The second of the four grand themes that courses through these chapters is responsibility. The word shows up in the title of only Sandra Graham's chapter on "perceived responsibility," but few authors develop their themes unmindful of it.

In the moral sphere (as elsewhere), responsibility implies being responsive to someone or something. Many focus response on their God, who calls them to vocation, to a way of life, to a moral path. Others draw on the need to respond to parents, teachers, peers, classmates, fellow members, colleagues, and (of course) conscience.

One can be responsible to evil people or causes and can follow paths of responsibility that are destructive. To take a gross example, Nazi leaders such as Adolf Eichmann claimed to see themselves as responsible because they were obedient and did what they were told. In the present context, however, the authors assume that there are also positive signals and demands in the social setting.

The philosopher Eugen Rosenstock-Huessy, who came to the United States to put his three German doctorates to work teaching and developing work camps, set the concept of response and responsibility in a terse history of Western education (Rosenstock-Huessy, 1970). The original foundation was *credo ut intelligam*, or "I believe in order that I may understand." The modern university took its charter from the notion of *cogito ergo sum*, or "I think, therefore I am." Now Rosenstock-Huessy proposed *respondeo etsi mutabor*, or "I respond, although I will be changed." The first has a vertical dimension, a grounding in God at the highest or in the depths of philosophy. The second has a necessary critical, testing function: Truth emerges out of questioning. The third has a social dimension: Truth emerges in a context of responsibility with others who share a time and place.

Graham neatly juxtaposes issues relating to "aggression" as a mode of being irresponsible to others and "not trying" as a way of being incapable of being responsible to the self and, then, to the other who must deal with a creative self. In their chapter, Daniel Hart and Robert Atkins discuss "religious participation and development." They note the surprising vitality of religious communities and impulses in the culture. They cannot decide which is the best, most true, most moral religion or community. These authors may even adhere to different systems or affiliate with different communities themselves, and there are a couple hundred million other American adults who make countless decisions with respect to religious response.

Multiple definitions of responsibility do not deter these authors from contributing to nurturing morality. They note that observers, from visitors to the United States such as Alexis de Tocqueville long ago to present-day polltakers, find that moral development largely comes from the fact of participating, without reference to any agreed-upon dogma, truth, or community structure of religion. The act of congregating itself turns out to be one of the indicators of a moral quest and support.

The third theme that continually appears in this book is a response to complexity—everyone agrees that these are complex topics!—that take the shape of exemplarity. One of the most measurably effective ways to promote moral responsibility in a pluralist society is to observe people or institutions that serve as models, examples, or exemplars.

These chapters call to mind a work on this theme by a literary scholar, John D. Lyons (1990), as he developed it in a book he called *Exemplum*. That word came from another, *eximere*, which means to take out or to remove, and refers to "that which is taken out." Exemplary teachers and administrators are taken out from and stand out from ordinary people. Good schools and neighborhoods deserve study for the exemplary effects they have on those who are part of them.

A few lines in Lyons's book prompted me to develop a vivid image of what *exemplum* can be. He mentions that in medieval lexicons, *exemplum* might well be referred to as a "clearing in the woods." I see this having relevance in three ways. First, a clearing defines the woods. At the edge of the clearing where the woods ends, one can draw a line. Exemplary people are such definers of the moral good. Second, a clearing is a place where the light falls away from the dark woods. It is hard to picture us speaking of someone or something being exemplary without seeing how light falls on a situation in her or his or its presence. And in the clearing, unlike in the woods, there is human cultivation. Exemplars encourage mental and moral plowing and planting, cultivating and reaping.

The authors know that many factors can ruin the opportunities for benefiting from exemplars. For instance, as Jennifer Steele, Y. Susan Choi, and Nalini Ambady show, early in life, children begin stereotyping. Typing people, cataloguing them, and having images into which they are to be fit are inevitable. But these authors show that in human interaction, stereotyping usually leads to prejudice. The prejudiced-against cannot be my model, my teacher. So this trio of authors concentrates on ways that role models and others help those being nurtured, at any age, from being blinded by prejudice and confused by stereotyping.

Nancy Eisenberg, Theresa A. Thorkildsen, and Constance Flanagan develop the positive context, for instance, in their reference to the human "clearing in the woods" that we meet in fellow students, friends, and teachers. The settings—the clearing, in their work—include families, schools, and neighborhood organizations, each of which can contribute to nurturing. Note also how Walker develops the positive side with reference to moral exemplarity that can be evidenced in quite different ways: Just, brave, and caregiving (or "care-full") exemplars provide balance and holistic approaches when the nurturing of morality is at issue. These chapters discuss connectedness, "the virtuous circle," the need to come out of self-isolation (e.g., engrossment in isolation before the TV set), and affection.

Many readers will be moved by the chapter on exemplarity by Robert J. Sternberg and Steven E. Stemler. (It is also a chapter on complexity.) The title "Wisdom As A Moral Virtue" might suggest that the authors had taken out a license to whine, to bewail the fact that there is much "foolishness" around, that we live in a culture in which values are skewed and moral virtue is reduced to moralism or evaded through amorality. Instead, Sternberg and Stemler chart ways that the pursuit of wisdom can be a quality, an expression, and intention for people of any age group. Their emphatic point is reinforced in the conclusion: "Wise thinkers. . . are role models in that they practice what they preach." Here is a strong

Aristotelian note, submerged but worth pursuing. Truths have to be acted upon, enacted through agency. Wise people are not afraid of complexity or the need to balance interests.

A little side tour into Zen approaches enhances wise people's endeavor to see wisdom as a moral virtue that is more than a textbook theme. Perhaps the best result of a reading would occur if some of us rose from the chair in which we are reading Sternberg and Stemler's chapter and decided to experiment with making a difference, one hopes on the positive and, thus, "wise" side.

As I kept coming across the word "affection," it occurred to me to trace "affectivity" throughout these chapters. Nurturing morality does not depend only on reason—although these authors do not minimize the role of reason—but on emotion, on "the affections." Oakeshott and Fuller (1991) speak of a "disposition," a "habit of affection and conduct," which several of the authors here develop as a means of nurturing morality.

Garry Wills (2002) has shown how Thomas Jefferson used the concept of "the affections," both in his own personal quest for the moral life and in his definition of the birth of the republic. "Affection" here is not of the Valentine's Day sort. Instead, it has to do with the sharing of an affective experience by a group of people. Those who go through an economic depression, a war, an earthquake, or the crashing of two planes into two towers find bonds of affection developing. They do not have to send amorous greeting cards or emit gooey and sentimental professions of love, but they have a bond on the basis of which responsibility, citizenship, and nurtured morality can develop.

Of course, some may choose not to be "engaged"; Albert Bandura has studied "selective disengagement" and the problems it creates. It can lead to "dehumanization." Bandura begins to approach ways of "humanizing" and avers that "morality is socially grounded." And although some authors have spoken of the need for "exemplars of care," Karl H. Hennig shows how care can go awry. He then suggests ways (in a revised Aristotelian framework) that what he calls "rich" forms of caring can develop.

Nancy Eisenberg takes off from a study of the "rescuers" of Jews in the Nazi scene and points to the role of the affections in the forms of empathy, sympathy, and altruism in cycles in which people reinforce each other.

At a conference at Wingspread where these authors; their respondents; and exemplary scholars, teachers, and citizens conversed, some made mention of the fact that for this book to make its way, it has to be deemed "practical." It is that. The reason of which it speaks and on which it draws is what Aristotle called *phronesis*, or practical reason. That kind of reason is not, in his eyes—nor need it be, in ours—a lesser form than that that is devoted to pure ideas and theories. It is a particular form that has most to do with nurturing morality.

Those who pointed to its practical intentions were not describing or calling for anything like a *How to Nurture Morality in Ten Easy Lessons* or *Chicken Soup for the Soul of Those Who Would Nurture*. Readers who gravitate to titles designed to spell out "how to" or to contribute to "feel-good" forms of spirituality may not know to look here for practical counsel and inspiration. But I am convinced that they will find it here.

These authors are well informed in various social sciences. They draw on surveys, experiments, laboratory work, and testing. They do not by any means despise testing. What they do is invite readers in to the families and schools, voluntary organizations and religious communities, neighborhoods and clubs to observe and learn from those who are both isolating the obstacles to moral development (e.g., stereotyping, prejudice) and discovering ways to knock down the barriers. They have us depending very much on the circles and cycles, the communities and colleagueship of those attuned to the moral quest.

Note that this does not mean that a nation, society, culture, subcommunity, or person close by necessarily embodies and exemplifies nothing but the good. Peers in a pluralist society or even in something as homogeneous as a family are not necessarily responsible, capable of being exemplars of the best, or stimulators of moral affections. By stressing the social context of responsibility and moral development, note that these authors do not seek to downplay individual consciences or to avoid confronting amoral and immoral peers, associates, and leaders. Theory and conscience have their places. What the authors do here is simply—yet so complexly—suggest how theory and conscience get put to work in present-day culture and how we might do better nurturing the good in respect to morals. The authors assume that inquiry, discourse, reading, and confronting diverse philosophical, often religious, systems and approaches will reinforce the total outlook and equipment of the nurturers. Their bet is a safe one.

## References

Lyons, J. (1990). *Exemplum: The rhetoric of example in early modern France and Italy*. Princeton, NJ: Princeton University Press.

Marias, J. (1967). *Generations: A historical method*. Tuscaloosa, AL: University of Alabama Press.

Oakeshott, M. J., & Fuller, T. (1991). *Rationalism in politics and other essays* (pp. 467–472). Indianapolis, IN: Liberty Fund, Inc.

Rosenstock-Huessy, R. (1970). *I am an impure thinker*. Norwich, VT: Argo.

Weintraub, K. J. (1966). *Visions of culture*. Chicago: University of Chicago Press.

Wills, G. (2002). *Inventing America: Jefferson's Declaration of Independence* (pp. 190, 273–283, 312–314). Boston: Mariner Books.

# About the Editors

**Theresa A. Thorkildsen** is an associate professor of education and psychology. She completed her Ph.D. from Purdue University in 1988 and has been actively involved in the field of moral development since 1986. Thorkildsen has published research articles, book chapters, and articles intended for practitioners, and two books (one edited and one co-authored). Serving on the editorial boards of three major journals in her field, Thorkildsen has also been involved in editing the work of other scholars. She is a member of six international research associations and is a fellow of the American Psychological Association. Her research interests focus on how young people come to understand the fairness of institutional practices and how issues of morality and motivation are inextricably connected.

**Herbert J. Walberg** is University Scholar and emeritus professor of education and psychology at the University of Illinois at Chicago and is a principal investigator at the Laboratory for Student Success, the Mid-Atlantic Regional Educational Laboratory. Editor of more than 40 books and author of more than 300 papers for psychology and educational research journals, he has also written extensively for practicing professionals. He has lectured in a dozen countries; often testified to federal district courses and Congressional committees; and is a fellow of the American Association for the Advancement of Science, American Psychological Association, International Academy of Education, and Royal Statistical Society.

# About the Authors

**Nalini Ambady** is a professor and Neubauer Faculty Fellow at Tufts University. She received her Ph.D. in social psychology from Harvard University in 1991 and served there as the John and Ruth Hazel Associate Professor of the Social Sciences from 1994–2003. Her research interests include examining the accuracy of social, emotional, and perceptual judgments; how personal and social identities affect cognition and performance; and nonverbal communication across racial and ethnic groups. She has received several awards for her research and teaching, including the Behavioral Science Research Prize from the American Association for the Advancement of Science in 1993 and the residential Early Career Award for Scientists and Engineers in 1998.

**Robert Atkins** is an assistant professor of nursing at Temple University and a doctoral candidate in the department of Public Health at Temple University. His research interests focus on how the intersection of poverty and urbanicity affect the civic and moral development of youths.

**Albert Bandura** is David Starr Jordan Professor of Social Sciences in Psychology at Stanford University. Much of his current research is aimed at advancing knowledge on how to enable people to exercise some measure of control over their own functioning and life circumstances. Part of this work centers on the self-management of moral conduct, not only to refrain from behaving inhumanely but also to behave humanely. The findings of these studies provide knowledge on how to cultivate a prosocial morality. Many inhumanities are perpetrated by people who, in other areas of their lives, behave considerately. They selectively disengage moral self-sanctions from their inhumane conduct. Moral disengagement occurs at the level of social systems, not just individually. Some of the efforts to promote a humane society must be directed at institutional practices to make it difficult for people to remove humanity from their conduct.

**Y. Susan Choi** received her B.A. in psychology from Harvard College in 2000 and her M.A. from the social psychology program at Harvard University in 2002. She is currently a doctoral candidate in social psychology at Harvard University. Her research interests include the role of emotions in prejudice and perceptions of injustice.

**Nancy Eisenberg** is Regents' Professor of Psychology at Arizona State University. She has published numerous books, chapters, and papers on social, emotional, and moral development, including *The Caring Child* (1992), *The Roots of Prosocial Behavior in Children* (with Paul Mussen, 1989), and *How Children Develop* (with Robert Siegler and Judy DeLoach, 2003). She has been a recipient of Research Scientist Development Awards and a Research Scientist Award from the National Institutes of Health (NIH and National Institutes of Mental Health). She was president of the Western Psychological Association, associate editor of the *Merrill-Palmer Quarterly* and *Personality and Social Psychology Bulletin*, and editor of *Psychological Bulletin*. She has served on the governing board of the Society for Research in Child Development, the governing council of the American Psychological Association, and the U.S. National Committee for the International Union of Psychological Science (through the National Academy of Science). Eisenberg is currently a member of the board of directors of the American Psychological Society. Her research has been used to create school interventions designed to promote empathy, prosocial behavior, and emotional regulation.

**Constance A. Flanagan** completed her Ph.D. in developmental psychology at the University of Michigan and is currently a professor of youth civic development in the Department of Agricultural and Extension Education at Penn State University. Her program of work, "Adolescents and the Social Contract," concerns the factors in families, schools, and communities that promote civic values and competencies in young people. She and her colleagues have investigated this theme in studies within the United States and cross-nationally. Flanagan co-chairs the Society for Research in Child Development's Committee on Public Policy and Communication. She is a William T. Grant Scholar and a member of the MacArthur Foundation's Network on the Transition to Adulthood and Public Policy. She is on the advisory board of CIRCLE and the editorial boards of four journals, and she writes and speaks frequently on the programmic and policy implications of the scholarship on youth civic development.

**Sandra Graham** is a professor in the Department of Education at the University of California, Los Angeles. She received her B.A. from Barnard College, M.A. in history from Columbia University, and her Ph.D. in education from UCLA. Her major research interests include the study of academic motivation, peer aggression, and juvenile delinquency, particularly in African American children and adolescents. Graham has published widely in developmental, social, and educational psychology journals. She is currently principal investigator on grants from the National Science Foundation and the W.T. Grant Foundation. She is also the recipient of an Independent Science Award funded by the National Institute of Mental Health. She is a former recipient of the Early Contribution Award from Division 15 (Educational Psychology) of the American Psychological Association and a former fellow at the Center for Advanced Study in the Behavioral Sciences, Stanford, California. Among her professional activities, Graham is an associate editor of *Developmental Psychology* and a member of the MacArthur Foundation National Research Network on Adolescent Development and Juvenile Justice.

**Daniel Hart** is professor of psychology at Rutgers University in Camden, New Jersey. His research focuses on the development of personality and moral character across the life span. Hart's recent publications include *Personality Development in Childhood: A Person-Centered Approach* (Monographs of the Society for Research in Child Development) and the chapter "The Development of Moral Identity" (forthcoming in vol. 51, *Nebraska Symposium on Motivation*). With Robert Atkins, Hart directs the Camden STARR (Sports Teaching Adolescents Responsibility and Resiliency) Program, which provides youth development opportunities to urban youths. Hart and Atkins also founded the Healthy Futures for Camden Youth initiative, which expands access to healthcare for urban youths by enrolling families in subsidized health insurance.

**Karl H. Hennig**, Ph.D., is an assistant professor in psychology at the University of Guelph in Ontario, Canada, where he teaches developmental and child clinical psychology. His current research focuses on the role of attachment and early peer formation processes in predicting the escalation of problem behaviors during early adolescence. Conversely, although a dramatic increase in problem behaviors (e.g., substance use, antisocial behavior, dating violence) is virtually normative in early adolescence, little is known about the equally normative de-escalation of these same problems in late adolescence and early adulthood. Hennig posits (moral) identity formation in the domain of peer selection and affiliation as a major component of this de-escalation process. Youths come to appreciate the negative as well as positive role that friends have on their personal development and begin selecting friends based on this insight. Hennig's current Building Healthy Relationships Project is a classroom-based intervention program being delivered within high schools by trained youths.

**Martin E. Marty** is a Fairfax M. Cone Distinguished Service Professor Emeritus at the University of Chicago, where he taught for 35 years and where the Martin Marty Center has since been founded to promote "public religion" endeavors. He writes the "M.E.M.O" column for biweekly *Christian Century*, on whose staff he has served since 1956; editor of the biweekly *Context* since 1969; and authors the weekly E-mail column "Sightings" for the Marty Center at the University of Chicago. Author of more than 50 books, Marty has written the three-volume *Modern American Religion* and *Righteous Empire*, which won the National Book Award. Marty is past president of the American Academy of Religion, American Society of Church History, and American Catholic Historical Association. He has served on two U.S. Presidential Commissions and was director of both the Fundamentalism Project of the American Academy of Arts and Sciences and the Public Religion Project at the University of Chicago. He has served St. Olaf College in Northfield, Minnesota, since 1988 as regent, board chair, and interim president in late 2000, and is now senior regent. He was the founding president of the Park Ridge Center for the Study of Health, Faith, and Ethics and is now the George B. Caldwell Senior Scholar in Residence there. Honors include the National Humanities Medal, Medal of the American Academy of Arts and Sciences, University of Chicago Alumni Medal, Distinguished Service Medal of the Association of Theological Schools, and Order of Lincoln Medallion (Illinois' top honor). He is an elected member of the American Antiquarian Society and the Society of American Historians and an elected fellow of the American Philosophical Society and the American Academy of Political and Social Sciences. Marty has received 69 honorary doctorates.

**Susan Opotow**, associate professor in the Graduate Program in Dispute Resolution at the University of Massachusetts—Boston, was a teacher and guidance counselor in the New York City Public Schools. Her scholarly work on moral exclusion develops and tests theory on the social and psychological factors that allow people to see others as outside their scope of justice and therefore as eligible targets of harm and exploitation. Her research contexts include urban schooling; environmental conflict; affirmative action; and social reconstruction after deadly, widespread conflict. She is a recipient of the University of Massachusetts President's Public Service Award, is a fellow of the American Psychological Association, and has published widely. She is associate editor of *Peace and Conflict: Journal of Peace Psychology* and has edited several journal issues on themes related to social justice, including issues of *Journal of Social Issues* and *Social Justice Research*. An upcoming book, *Identity and the Natural World* (MIT Press, coedited with Susan Clayton), examines how people understand their relationship with the natural world and the implications of this understanding for environmental action and conservation.

**Jennifer Steele** received her B.A. in psychology from Queen's University in 1995 and subsequently trained as a middle school teacher at the same university, receiving her B.Ed. in 1996. She completed an Ed.M. in 1997 at the Harvard University Graduate School of Education and received her Ph.D. in social psychology from the Harvard University Graduate School of Arts and Science in June of 2003. Steele's research examines children's development of stereotypes as well as the impact that stereotype salience has on people's perceptions, interests, and performance. She is currently a postdoctoral fellow at the University of Waterloo in Ontario, Canada, where she continues to conduct research aimed at guiding and informing policy decisions in education and in the workplace.

**Steven E. Stemler**, Ph.D., is an associate research scientist in the Department of Psychology at Yale University and is the assistant director of the Yale Center for the Psychology of Abilities, Competencies, and Expertise (PACE Center). He attended graduate school at Boston College, where he received his master's degree in education and his doctoral degree in educational research, measurement, and evaluation. During graduate school, Stemler worked at the Center for the Study of Testing, Evaluation, and Educational Policy, and served as a consultant in policy and planning to the Massachusetts Board of Higher Education. His research has examined the purpose of schooling in American society, factors associated with school effectiveness, policy issues in high-stakes testing, racial and gender differences in achievement, and the influence of social identity on the development of wisdom.

**Robert J. Sternberg** is IBM Professor of Psychology and Education and director of the Center for the Psychology of Abilities, Competencies, and Expertise at Yale University. He is also the 2003 president of the American Psychological Association. Sternberg received his B.A. summa cum laude, Phi Beta Kappa, from Yale University in 1972 and his Ph.D. from Stanford University in 1975. He also holds honorary doctorates from four European universities. Sternberg is the author of more than 900 articles, chapters, and books and has received more than $15 million in grants and contracts for his research. The central focus of his research is intelligence, creativity, and wisdom, and he also has studied love and close relationships as well as hate. This research has been conducted in five different continents. He has won many awards for his work and is most well known for his theory of successful intelligence, investment theory of creativity (developed with Todd Lubart), theory of thinking styles as mental self-government, balance theory of wisdom, triangular theory of love, and theory of love as a story.

**Lawrence J. Walker** is professor of developmental psychology and coordinator of the graduate program in psychology at the University of British Columbia in Vancouver, where he has been since 1979. He earned his Ph.D. in developmental psychology at the University of Toronto. He is a past president of the Association for Moral Education, the major international scholarly organization in the fields of moral education and moral psychology. He currently is associate editor of the *Merrill-Palmer Quarterly* and serves on the editorial boards of several other journals. He is the recipient of awards for excellence in research, university teaching, and service to the profession. Walker's research focuses on issues relating to the psychology of moral development, including processes in the development of moral reasoning and the formation of moral personality.

# University Advisory Committee for
# The University of Illinois at Chicago Series on
# Issues in Children's and Families' Lives

# National Advisory Committee for
# The University of Illinois at Chicago Series on
# Issues in Children's and Families' Lives

# Index